T5-BCL-575

THE SHIPWRIGHT'S TRADE

H.M.S. *VICTORY*. STRUCTURE AS BUILT IN 1765
AND REBUILT IN 1798

THE
SHIPWRIGHT'S
TRADE

by

SIR WESTCOTT ABELL

I tell this tale, which is strictly true,
Just by way of convincing you
How very little since things was made
Things have altered in the shipwright's trade.

RUDYARD KIPLING

CONWAY MARITIME PRESS

First published 1948
This impression published in 1981 by
Conway Maritime Press Ltd,
2 Nelson Road Greenwich,
London SE10 9JB

© Conway Maritime Press Ltd 1981
ISBN 0 85177 237 4

Printed and bound in United Kingdom
by R J Acford, Chichester

PREFACE

I T was from an old wood shipwright, born more than 100 years ago, that I first learnt about ships, and for many years since then my pleasure has been to gather knowledge about them and their early history. When the Cambridge University Press asked me if I would write a book which should put on record the craft of the shipwright, it seemed to me to be a chance I ought to accept. In this book—the result of that request—I have tried to give an outline account of the way in which men learnt to build ships, first of wood, then of iron, and later of steel.

Mass-output of ships, brought about because of the urgent needs of two Great Wars, might seem to the lay mind to demand quite new methods of building. It might also be thought that the skill of shipwrights would decline as machines took the place of men, and that the personal touch on which the British workman still places proud value would be lacking. But since the shape of any ship is bound to conform to certain laws of nature, the basic technique, begun in Tudor times and 'brought to rule' under the Stuarts, must persist, even though the work itself be shared with less skilled workers.

And so, in spite of many changes, the manner of the building of ships remains with us in essence much as it was when it first took formal shape some 400 years ago.

W. A.

CONTENTS

PART I: EARLY DAYS

PART II: THE GROWTH OF THE TRADE
(1485–1837)

CONTENTS

PART III: IRON, STEAM, AND STEEL
(FROM 1837)

TEXT FIGURES

TEXT FIGURES

x

The drawings on pp. 2, 3, 5, 7, 14, 16 and 17, were made by Frank Humphris

PLATES

PLATES

PART I

EARLY DAYS

The Tribe, when snow crept o'er the wintry hill and spoilt the hunting, made trek to a sun-warmed plain, where herd of deer grazed in the shade of murmuring woods, beside a river's flood of brimming silver.... There first I braved the current on a log, and taught the Tribe to cross in safety.

§1. THE 'DUG-OUT'

MAN began to build boats of sorts long before the dawn of history. His first attempts were to take a tree-trunk and hollow it by the use of fire and crude stone tools. It would be guesswork to try to describe

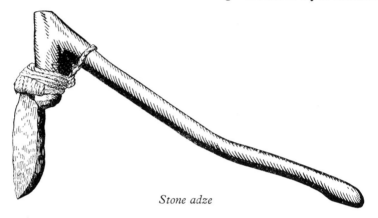

Stone adze

in detail how he set about his task, but a good idea of his methods after centuries of effort is shown by the manner in which the Maoris built 'dug-outs' when the early settlers came to New Zealand.

A bulletin of the Dominion Museum, written by Elsdon Best, contains records in detail of the methods used in the early part of the last century. It would seem that their practice had slowly grown up to suit the large pines of the North Island, where is found the Kauri pine from which the natives could get a log up to 70 ft. long and as much as 8 ft. across. For tools they had only hatchets and adzes of a hard stone said to be like marble. This stone was black

Maori using stone adze, showing tool-marks

and as mention is also made of quartz it may have been a volcanic rock such as whinstone.

First the experts chose their tree in the forest, their main concern

2

being the good nature of the timber. (It will be seen later in Stuart times that the master shipwright made a tour to select proper oak to build warships.) Distance from the sea does not seem to have caused much trouble, as hauls of many miles from forest to coast were known.

Natives felling trees, using stone ram-chisel

To fell the tree a notch was cut with axes and a second notch a short distance away was also made. The space between was removed with adzes working across the grain. In some cases a heavy stone chisel lashed to a spar and hung by a rope from the tree itself was worked as a ram by a gang of men. With great labour the trunk was felled and then topped by adzes and hatchets, helped sometimes with fire to char the wood. As an old native put it—'the adze used was a stone one, the other adze was fire'.

3

Before starting to shape the trunk, it was viewed to locate the lengthwise run of the shake or crack which most trees possess. That being done the log was turned to get the shake horizontal, care being taken to get enough wood to have the side of the future canoe well above water.

With the trunk in proper posture the top half was made level down to about the height of the gunwale, again with the use of adzes and fire. It should be said that the stone adze was not suited to cut across the grain of the timber and so scores were cut first across the grain and the wood between was hewn off sideways, the blade of the tool being kept in line with the grain. A steel adze is often used in the same way, the process being called 'dubbing'. The rough dressing was done with a heavy adze and a lighter tool used to finish off the surface.

At this stage a rough outline of the canoe was drawn on the upper side; the stern, being wider than the bow, was drawn at the butt end of the log. The workers began to hollow out the inside and used both adze and fire in the early stages of their work. When the inner lines of the hull were being neared further progress was made with light stone tools only, used by skilled men.

Meanwhile, others were getting on with the rough shape of the outside form, and when the work had gone far enough the hull was turned over to give better access to the bottom of the craft. The final shaping outside was left until the trunk had been hauled near to the sea in order to allow a margin for rough usage during transport.

There was great skill shown in the finish of the outer surface, often by small adze patterns such as may be seen on the timbers of old houses. There is mention that some of the canoes were smoothed off with lumps of sandstone. On the other hand the natives had the idea that there was merit in the wavy shape of the adze patterns. The object was said to be to break up the water through which the canoe was passing and to prevent it clinging to the surface, and so to give greater speed and to make paddling easier. 'Note the smooth surface of the racing craft. Does not the water cling to the sides and act as a brake from end to end?', is the remark quoted by Best.

To the dug-out log there was added a top strake to form a gunwale and also to give more freeboard or height of side above water. These extra planks were hewn out of a solid tree, some being as much as 60 ft. long and 15 in. deep. If more than one length were used, joints were made towards the ends and not at the middle of the canoe. The top strake rested direct on the hull as in a carvel-built boat; it was wider in the middle than at the ends. Holes were made with stone drills in both the hull and the plank, and rounded battens were placed fore and aft over the joint, both inside and outside. The plank was connected by a cord, rove through the holes, made taut by a special twisting tool. When this was done a workman inside drove a wooden peg into the hole with a mallet, thus keeping the cord tight and also plugging the hole.

Workers sewing on gunwale strake

Maori long canoe with paddlers

The thwarts for the rowers also served as cross-beams, being fixed to the bulwark strake with lashings; a floor-grating of small pieces tied together was fitted at the bottom of the canoe.

There were other troubles which had to be overcome. It might happen that the shake in the heart of the tree came to the surface of the boat when it was being shaped. If the weakness was serious and was towards the end, then the part would be cut off. A V-shaped notch would be left to form a kind of dovetail and on to this a new piece of proper shape would be fixed with lashings in the same manner as that used for the top strake.

5

At last the time came to launch the canoe, which was carried out with rites chanted by the priest. Then, fully loaded with men and with weights equal to the stores to be carried, the craft was put to the test. If the wake of the canoe followed it too much, it showed that the shape was not proper; in which case the canoe was put on shore and changes made until the form was deemed good enough.

The vessel was painted with two coats of red ochre mixed with shark-oil, which served for most of the canoe. Black was also used, the black being got from the soot of burnt wood.

This is not the place to tell of the complex carvings used for figure-heads and the stern-posts, which in themselves remain as marvels of craftsman's skill, a skill shown also in the ornate work on the gunwales of the Maori war-canoes: nor to tell of the precise ritual which was laid down for every step in the process of building these craft.

§2. SHIPS OF EGYPT

KNOWLEDGE of early efforts begins in Egypt, largely with pictures, one of which belongs to the fourth millennium. This ship had a mast and a single square sail. The form was high at each end, and suggests that

Workers shaping boat from short planks, c. 2000 B.C.

the early craft were in essence rafts, made up of bundles of buoyant reeds bound together. The sail and the rope may have been made of papyrus. By about 2000 B.C. models found in the tombs show crafts-men at work. The master is seen counting the cattle: the ox is shown being fed at the stable: the beeves are being killed: men are making blood puddings over braziers: the joints of beef are 'hung' to ripen. In the granary, the wheat is scooped into measures, placed in sacks and dumped into bins. The bakery and brewery are in the same building. Men crack the grain with pestles, women grind the flour: men mix the dough and make fancy loaves which others bake in ovens. In the brewing room women grind flour and men tread a mash in a barrel.

The rising mash stands in four tall crocks, while the yeast ferments. When it is 'worked' it is poured into a row of jugs with stoppers, placed along the wall. In the weaving shop women prepare flax and put it into buckets. Others spin, and when the spindles are full, stretch the thread on three pegs on the wall. Women weave the cloth on two looms stretched out on the floor.

The carpenter's shop is partly roofed over a furnace used to sharpen tools. A huge tool-chest contains saws, adzes, chisels and drills. In the open court gangs of men square great timbers with adzes and smooth the surface with blocks of sand-stone. A sawyer rip-saws a baulk of timber which is lashed upright to a post in the ground. A carpenter sitting astride a plank cuts mortise holes in the edge with mallet and chisel.

Sawyer rip-sawing plank of timber, c. 2000 B.C.

The tomb also held twelve model boats which are judged to be copies of the fleet of the dead Egyptian. The length of the models was about 4 ft. and the full size of the largest ship based on the number of men on board might be as much as 40 ft.

At this period, *c.* 2000 B.C., the people of Egypt had passed well away from stone tools and made full use of bronze which they may have known for perhaps 2000 years. Iron was rare until the Hittites began to make it about 1500 B.C. or a little later. Through its use for arms, Assyria rose to her grandeur about 700 B.C.: the arsenal of Sargon II was found to have some 200 tons of iron weapons.

Nearly 5000 years ago a fleet of Egypt brought overseas some

7

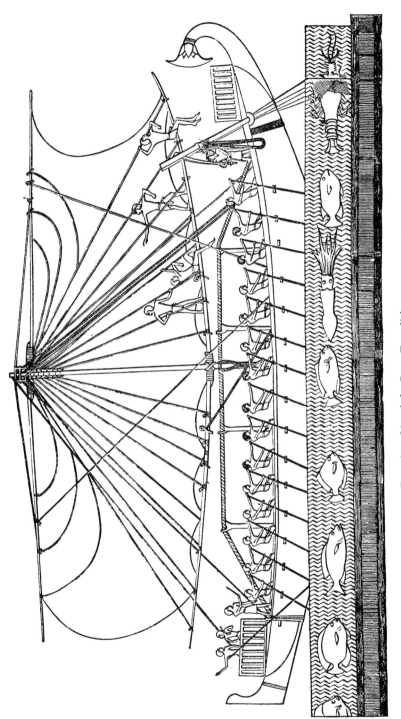

Egyptian ship of the Punt Expedition, c. 1500 B.C.

7000 prisoners of war, 200,000 head of cattle, and from Lebanon carried forty shiploads of cedar logs. Ships of this period seem to have been some 60 ft. long with a mast 30 ft. high. There were twenty-two rowers on each side and three steersmen with paddles. A Queen Pharaoh of about 1500 B.C. traded widely. Her fleet brought back from the Land of Punt, somewhere to the south of the Red Sea, oxen, giraffes, monkeys, ostrich feathers, skins, ebony, lapis lazuli, gold, silver and antimony. This Queen Hatshepsut built a temple in Thebes and on the walls there are limestone reliefs in colour which

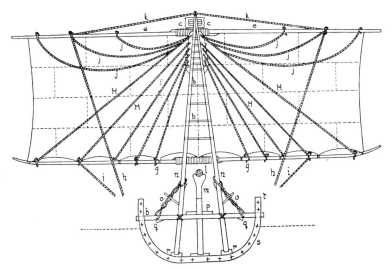

Midship section, showing mast and rig, c. 1500 B.C.

deal with these voyages. The ships were built with overhung bows and sterns, and to prevent 'hogging' (or dropping of the ends) a stout rope was carried on four struts for the greater part of the length. In effect this device gave depth to a shallow wood hull, the rope being perhaps 18 ft. above keel and 8 ft. higher than the cross-beam. These vessels seem to be about 100 ft. long and of 25 ft. beam, drawing some 5 ft. of water. At this draught they could carry perhaps 80 tons' weight of cargo.

The skin of the ship was formed of planks, about 4 in. thick, set edge to edge. The keel was flat, but of greater width and thickness than the other planks. The pieces of the keel were joined lengthwise by double dovetail pieces let into each part. Smaller dovetails joined the garboard strake (the strake next to the keel) to the keel, and in turn each plank was joined to the next in like fashion up to the gunwale (the uppermost strake or piece of plank). To prevent sliding, dowels (round wooden pins) were fitted into the edges of the planks. The butts of other planks did not have the lengthwise dovetails, those of the top strake or gunwale were laced through holes with strips of hide or copper wire. Through the strake below the gunwale, holes were made through which the ends of the cross-beams were passed: it does not appear that transverse ribs were used, the beams in some way holding the upper shape. There was no deck, but two planks were fitted

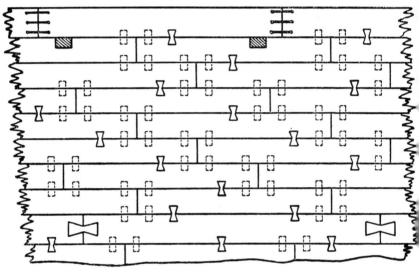

Plan showing fixing of skin planking, c. 1500 B.C.

lengthwise on top of the beams, one on either side of the four struts, thus adding to the fore and aft strength of the vessel.

These ships of Egypt were heavy river craft with weak rigging, not well suited for sea, and altogether different from the light fast craft of the Viking which could venture into stormy seas.

§3. SHIPS OF THE NEAR EAST

THERE is little mention of the ships of Crete although there are many signs that their trade with Egypt was great. Nor is anything known of the fleets of Tyre, which began to flourish about 1500 B.C. when Knossos was sacked for the fifth time, to become after the sixth assault in 1200 B.C. a legend of the past.

Two other legends of about the same date are well known—the Ark of Noah and the Voyage of the Argonauts. The biblical account of the Ark was probably written down *c*. 600 B.C. The extreme figures given for the size of the Ark—length 300 cubits, breadth 50 cubits, height 30 cubits—seem pure fancy. Such a length as 500 ft. which these measures imply, would mean that the Ark was only a huge raft. There is one point of interest to the shipwright, that the ratios of length to breadth and of breadth to depth were such as to give a seaworthy vessel. The second myth relates how Jason, *c*. 1250 B.C., built the *Argo* for a voyage from Greece to Colchis in Georgia, at the eastern end of the Black Sea. This vessel seems to have had thirty rowers on each side and might be as much as 150 ft. long.

Although little is known of ships of Crete, of Tyre or those of Greece and Rome, there was a large sea-trade in the Eastern Mediterranean, perhaps begun by the Cretans and then taken over by the Phoenicians. All these peoples went far afield, whereas the ships of Egypt kept mainly to local trade as they were not built for long voyages. Tyre also led the way in forming the pattern of building these vessels. By 700 B.C. she had fighting ships—biremes—with a beak for ramming and two banks of rowers, with a long fine form built for speed. The merchant ships used mainly sails and were short and bulgy. The Greeks when they came to power paid great heed to the fighting ship by adding to the numbers of rowers, by building triremes, having up to 170 oarsmen in three tiers. These ships were like those of Tyre in other respects and it is not at all easy to conceive how so many men could work the oars with any ease.

Greece needed many merchant ships to support her population of 350,000. For one thing she had to import two-thirds of her supply of corn and as she had little timber and other stuffs needed to build ships, these had to come from afar by sea. It is likely that she had ships built at Tyre, near at hand to the forests of Lebanon, and that the Romans in their turn made use of the shipwrights of that city, famous for the 'ships of Tarshish'.

The 'land' powers of Babylon, Assyria, the Hittites and to some extent Persia, played little part in building up a type of ship to suit these waters. These patterns served with some changes all Mediterranean needs right up to the days of Venice and Genoa when large galleys were built for war and the bulgy galleon used for sailing merchant ships.

§4. ROMAN SHIPS

THERE are a few traces of Roman ships, one of which is on record in the writings of Lucian the Greek, c. A.D. 150 to 200. In one of his dialogues, *The Ship; or, the Wishes*, he describes a visit to a vessel just come to the port of Piraeus. He says that one of his friends never spared himself if there was a sight to be seen. Timolaus retorts that he was told of this monster vessel of extraordinary proportions—one of the Egyptian corn ships, bound for Italy. He was taken round the vessel by the shipwright who said she was 120 ft. long and 30 ft. broad or thereabouts, and from the deck to the bottom of the hold where he measured it, in the deepest part, 29 ft.

We stood a long while by the mast looking up, counting the layers of hides and wondering at the sailors as they mounted by the ropes, and then with perfect safety ran along the yards holding on to the halliards.

What a mast she has! And how huge a yard she carries, and what a stay it requires to hold it up in its place!

Samippus adds:

With what a gentle curve her stern rises, finished with a 'goose-neck' all of gold! At the other end, in just proportion, the prow stands up, lengthening itself out as it gets forward and showing the ship's name—the 'Goddess Isis' on either side. . . .

The decorations and the flame-coloured fore-sail; and beyond these the anchor with the windlass and capstan; and I must not omit the stern cabins. Then the number of souls would make one think it was a camp.

We were told it carried enough corn to feed all the people of Athens for a year. And all we saw had so far been carried safe and sound by a little old man, using a slight tiller to turn that huge rudder. They showed him to me—a bald-pated fellow with a fringe of curly hair, Hero, I think, by name.[1]

There follows an account of a stormy voyage from Egypt taking 70 days to Piraeus. It is also said that the average return to the owner for such a venture was not less than twelve Attic talents. It would seem that the shipwrights, whether for Rome or Egypt, had learned to build well and truly.

Some slight knowledge of their skill comes from the remains of a vessel, c. A.D. 200, found in the River Thames in 1910. The portion left was some 35 ft. long with a breadth of ship of perhaps 14 ft. and

---

[1] *Six Dialogues of Lucian*, translated by S. T. Irwin. Methuen 1894.

a depth of 7 ft. The lightness of structure shows that she was a river craft rather than a deep-sea ship.

The vessel was built of oak, carvel fashion. The planks, placed edge to edge, are fixed with dowels and pins (draw-tongue joints). There are many ribs about 1 ft. apart but of small cross-section—6 × 4½ in. The planks are fixed to the ribs by treenails—round wood plugs —1½ in. in diameter. Small side-keelsons were fitted lengthwise inside the frames or ribs. There was also a 'wale'—a strong fore and aft

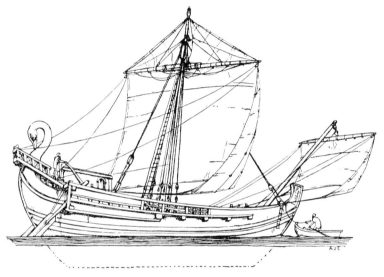

Roman merchant ship, c. A.D. 200

plank—outside the vessel at the level of the thwarts. The frames seemed to have been cut from grown timber in which the grain follows the curve of the rib.

Julius Caesar's description of the invasion of Britain in 55 B.C. shows that the British had fleets in those times. The hulls were flatter than those of the Romans, more suited to the shallows and the great rise and fall of the tides in the English Channel. The bow and stern were upright and the general shape of the vessel made it more seaworthy in the stormy seas. The vessels were built of oak; the beams were 1 ft. deep and fixed by iron nails, 1 in. thick. Iron was made in Sussex and was used for anchors and cables; sails were of skin or thin leather.

Perspective drawing of hull of the Gokstad ship, second half of the ninth century A.D.

§5. VIKING SHIPS

THE Jutes, under Hengist and Horsa, settled in Kent *c.* A.D. 450; they were one of the German tribes from the region of Jutland. The Sutton Hoo burial ship, found in 1938, dates from the close of the fourth century A.D. The remains of a ship built before that time (*c.* A.D. 200 or 300) were found at Nydam, in Schleswig-Holstein, in 1863. This vessel was of the Viking type—low amidships, 4 ft., and high, 10 ft., to the top of the prow and stern. There were fourteen rowers on each side, but no sign of a mast. She was clinker-built, that is, the planks lapped over each other and iron nails fixed the overlaps. There were five planks on each side of the keel. This practice differs from that of the Roman ships, where the side planks were placed edge to edge and the seams caulked between the edges.

The Nydam ship, some 75 ft. long and 11 ft. wide, had nineteen frames or transverse ribs, placed square to the keel. These were not nailed to the planks, but lashed to ridges worked on the plank for that purpose. It seems that the skin was first built and the frames fitted afterwards to stiffen the planking. Much the same is done to-day in small boats, the overlap itself giving stiffness to the plank edges.

Charlemagne pursued the Gospel of the Cross with fire and sword into Saxony and Bohemia, even to Hungary, and before his death in 814 held the west coast of Europe from the Baltic to Spain. The Vikings, or Creekmen, and the Northmen, driven from their homes on the coast, began to scour the seas and, being pagans, to destroy the Christian teaching. They landed in England and Normandy and between A.D. 500 and 900 had roved far and wide. They reached Greenland and later, about A.D. 1000, got to Vinland, perhaps the coast of Maine in the United States. The myth of the great rich city of the south which they termed 'Micklegarth' drew the Northmen by sea to the Mediterranean, even to Constantinople, and when the Empire of Charlemagne broke up they gained control of the old land trade routes from the Black Sea to the Baltic.

Their vessels, judged by the remains of the Gokstad ship, second half of the ninth century A.D., and of the Oseberg ship of *c.* A.D. 800, were not much longer but were deeper than the Nydam vessel. The Gokstad boat had sixteen planks on each side of the keel, and strong cross-beams. There was a single mast and sail, while the rudder with a tiller was fixed on a swivel to a knob on the right hand or 'steer-board' side. The length of this ship was 79 ft.; she was 16·8 ft. broad and 6·8 ft. deep at amidships. The gunwale, low amidships, rose or sheered greatly both fore and aft to end in a high prow and stern-post. She was built of oak with a heavy shaped keel reaching well below the skin of the ship. Transverse strength was given by a number of frames or ribs. The lower end was joined to the 'garboard' strake (strake is a plank and garboard means next to the keel), and the lower eight planks were fixed to the ribs by lashing to lugs, cut on the plank. Above the turn of the bilge the frames were fixed to the upper strakes by iron spikes. The ship was clinker-built, that is, each of the sixteen

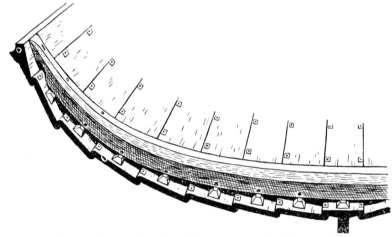

Perspective drawing of midship section of the Gokstad ship,
second half of the ninth century A.D.

strakes lapped over the one below, being bound through the edges by clinch-nails, and turned over inside on a rove (washer) just as boats are built to-day.

Some 2 ft. above the keel were cross-beams to provide sideways strength and to support the ribs. The single mast amidships had a massive step—housing—to allow it to be stowed with ease. There were 16 oars each side, about 18 ft. long; these were worked through small round oar-ports some 18 in. below the gunwale. These ports had covers to close the openings when sailing. On the right-hand side looking forward a quarter-rudder was placed towards the stern. It passed through a lashing under the gunwale and just about the water-line was held by a rope to a wooden boss fixed to the ship. This rudder was worked by a tiller, placed athwartship.

It would seem that the Norsemen rated their ships by the number of 'rums' they had. A 'rum' is the room taken by a pair of oars, one on either side; thus a normal war-vessel of 20 'rum' would have 40 oars. From A.D. 900 onwards 30 oars a side became more common, and Olaf Trygvason's *Long Serpent*, built at Trondhjem at that time, had 34 oars a side. The keel of the *Long Serpent* as it lay on the grass was some 75 ells long, or about 115 ft. If the same design was taken as for the Gokstad ship, the length overall would have been 140 ft. and the breadth some 28 ft. A vessel of this type and of such size would have been weak in the structure, and in fact, the *Long Serpent* was a failure.

Flagship of William the Conqueror, A.D. 1066

These later ships showed a great advance from the Nydam vessel some 500 or 600 years earlier. The fishing vessels of northern Norway up to this century were still of this type—double-ended with high bow and stern and with single mast and sail. One of the most useful for its seaworthy quality is the whale-boat still often used for ships' lifeboats.

The skill shown by these early craftsmen in building the Viking ships was in keeping with the daring spirit with which they pursued their foreign ventures. Yet there was skill also in England, for Alfred the Great, the first English ruler to see the value of sea-power to these islands, built larger vessels than the Danes, some of which had 30 oars a side. He changed their form to suit better the rough waters of the English Channel. His fleet fought the Danes with success and kept the seas clear of raiders. Although the Normans had landed in Normandy 200 years before the conquest of England, they had made little if any change in the design of the Viking ships.

From this time until *c.* A.D. 1400 there is little knowledge of the growth of ships except for the pictures given by the seals of some of the English towns.

There are records here and there of the use of the sea. In 1189 Richard I set sail from Dartmouth for the third Crusade with a fleet of 100 capital ships and 50 galleys. He added to his navy some 50 sailing-ships and 10 large store-ships which he hired from Venice. It is stated that Richard fought and sank a large Saracen ship with 1500 men on board.

In 1268 Louis IX of France caused to be built, both at Venice and Genoa, some two-deck vessels about 110 ft. long, which could carry 50 horses. Some time after, Venice built the *Santa Maria* of 123 ft. length with a crew of 110 seamen.

§6. THE TRAVELS OF MARCO POLO

The Travels written by Marco Polo, *c.* 1300, tell of the ships met with on the journeys which were made to China and on his return by sea to India. The three Venetians were given the task of bringing a princess by sea from China to Persia in 1292.

He writes of the vessels built at Ormuz that they were of the worst kind and exposed traders to great hazards. Their defects arose since, owing to the hard and brittle nature of the wood, nails were not used. 'When an attempt is made to drive a nail, it rebounds and is often broken.' The planks were bored near the ends with an iron auger and fixed to the stem and stern by wooden pins—treenails. After this they were bound, or rather sewn, with a kind of rope-yarn stripped from the husk of the coco-nut. From the threads they made twine to sew the planks. (This twine, known as 'coir', is still used for ropes for ships.) Pitch was not used to coat the bottom; instead fish oil was applied and the seams caulked with oakum. Such vessels had one mast, one helm and one deck. Their anchors were strong heavy wood with one arm or fluke, and were sunk by heavy stones tied to them.

For the homeward journey from China fourteen ships were fitted out, each having four masts and nine sails, and of these some four or

PLATE I

WORKERS BUILDING NORMAN VESSELS

(After the Bayeux Tapestry)

five had crews of 250 or 260 men. The ships were built of fir timber, which suggests that although they are called Indian ships they were not built in India.

There was a single deck below, on which were some sixty small cabins, each for one merchant. Of the four masts, two could be set up or taken down. Some of the large ships had thirteen transverse bulkheads or divisions in the hold, formed of thick planks let into each other by grooves with tongues. The purpose was to safeguard the vessel against leaks, should damage occur.

The ships were all double-planked; that is, sheathing boards were laid throughout, outside and over the inner planks. They were fixed with iron nails and caulked with oakum, both within and without.

Grose, writing *c.* 1770, says that at Surat on the coast north of Bombay, 'they excel in the art of building ships. The bottoms and sides are made up of planks let into each other with rabbet-work, so that the seams keep watertight'. He adds: 'There would be no exaggeration in averring that they—the natives—build incomparably the best ships in the world for duration and that of any size, even to 1000 tons and upwards....It is not uncommon for one of them to last a century.'

Marco Polo further says that 'ships of the largest size require a crew of 300 men; the vessels are likewise moved by oars or sweeps, each of which need four men to row. The large ships can carry about 6000 bags of pepper. Each has an escort of 2 or 3 large barks which are used to tow the bigger craft when needed. The ships carry as many as ten small boats, which are slung over the sides and lowered into the water.'

One more novel point was that, when a ship after a voyage of a year or more was in need of repair, it was the practice to apply a further layer of sheathing, which was caulked and payed to form a third course of planking. This practice was used up to as many as six layers, after which the vessel was deemed 'not seaworthy'.

It is well to note that at this time, before 1300, mention was made of the use of water-tight bulkheads to restrict the inflow of water after damage—a practice that only came back into use less than 100 years ago.

§7. EARLY ENGLISH SHIPS

IN 1300 Edward I made use of ships to help in the war against Scotland. He brought from Winchelsea to the Solway Firth some thirty large ships and nearly as many smaller ones. The term 'cog' seems to be used for the first time to refer to the big ships, some sixteen of which had crews of three officers and thirty-nine seamen.

Edward III in 1340 himself led a fleet of 200 ships against the French navy at Sluys. The English retook the *Great Christopher* which they had lost, and captured 200 French vessels and 30,000 men. Perhaps this was the first time it was proved that the Mediterranean galleys were not fit for ocean waters.

For nearly a century England made little use of the sea except under Henry V who became king in 1413. He mustered a fleet of 1500 vessels, mainly at Southampton, to provide transport to France for his army of 30,000, or perhaps 50,000. After his success at Agincourt he began to prepare for further warfare against France. About this time the king, having become aware of the large ships of Castile and Genoa, was moved to order the building of great ships at Southampton—'such as were never seen in the world before'. Three of these had the names of the *Trinity*, the *Grace de Dieu*, and the *Holy Ghost*. He also gave an order for a great ship to be built for him at Bayonne, which had a length overall of 186 ft. and a keel of 112 ft. The breadth was 46 ft., much in excess of the practice of Tudor times. The burthen was 1250 tons. This vessel was never finished, probably because of her large size.

The *Grace de Dieu* was built at Southampton in 1418 by Huggekyns, the master carpenter of the king's ships. She went later to Bursledon in the Hamble River where she was burnt in 1439. The record shows that she was clinker-built and caulked with moss and pitch. The tonnage was 1400, even a greater ship than the Bayonne vessel.

In 1933 the wreck—which the mud-bank on which it rested had kept in fair state—was studied closely by R. C. Anderson, Lieut. Prynne, R.E., and others. The most striking find was that the skin-planking was clinker-built. Each strake was made up of three planks with a greatest thickness of 2 in. The two outer planks were 12 in. deep and the third or inner plank only 8 in. deep. This kind of three-ply planking gave an overlap of 4 in. Bolts were driven at the laps through five thicknesses of plank. All three of the layers had tapers to give a mean thickness of 4½ in.; the total thickness through the bolts was nearly 8 in. More curious was the fact that the three layers themselves were worked only in short pieces some 6–7 ft. long.

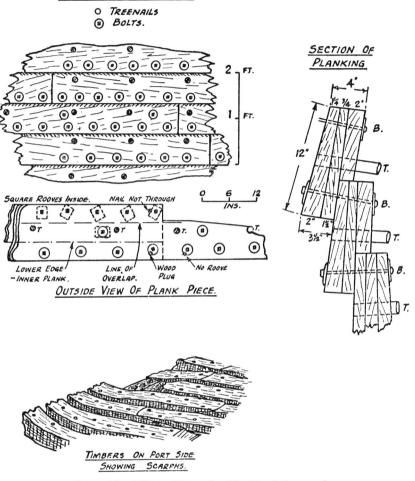

Great ship of Henry V, 1418—*The Bursledon wreck*

The iron nails used to fasten the planks were $\frac{5}{8}$ in. square with large round heads, over 2 in. across, and were hammered inside over flat washers about 3×2 in. Prynne says that the inside washers showed that the frames were put in after the ship was planked, and the scarph—the wedge-shaped overlap joints of the frames—confirms that this was the case.

The method of building such a structure of wood with a length of keel of 112 ft., and of putting the frames in place after the skin was complete, remains a mystery. And further, when the side planks were built up in three layers in pieces some 6 ft. long, it seems that 'moulds' of heavy nature, giving the shape at various parts, would have had to be set up at every 10 ft. of length. (Such a means is still used for the building of boats.) It is not known whether these moulds were kept until the frames were in place, or if they were built into the ship.

The frames themselves were heavy timbers, being 12 in. on the 'siding'—the width of bearing at the side of the ship. The depth—or 'moulding'—which is the size square to the siding, seems to have been 10 in. or more. It is not known how the frames were worked except that they were in short pieces, joined by tapering down the ends and lapping the two tapers. This simplest form of joint is called a 'scarph'. Between the frames there was a space of some 4 in. lengthwise. There was a further trouble, since the frames, in order to fit over the inside of the planking, would need to be notched to give better support or bearing surface. The skin and frames were joined by treenails—round tough wooden pegs of oak—driven from the outside through the middle of the plank, one to each frame or say 16 in. apart. The nails which fixed the planks through the laps were some 6–8 in. apart, whereas the treenails for the frames were some 16 in. from centre to centre. This again supports the view that the frames were fitted after the skin was complete.

It has been seen that the *Grace de Dieu* was larger than the Bayonne ship. She was thus two centuries before her time, since it was not until the reign of Charles II that ships were built of such great size.

As to the clinker-built ship, Anderson remarks that there is no record of such methods of building after the *Great Galley* of 1515. In 1523 this vessel was said to be 'the dangeroust ship under water that ever man sailed in', and Robert Brigandin, Clerk of the Ships to Henry VII, had to 'break her up and make her carvel'.

Although very few large ships were built in England in the fifteenth century, there is a mention that John Tavernor of Hull was given freedom from custom imports to build a large carrack, called the *Grace Dieu*. There were also the large ships of 400, 500 and 900 tons burthen, which the king took from Cannyngs of Bristol, which are thought to have been of foreign build. Again, in 1455, King Charles of Sweden asked leave for a vessel of nearly 1000 tons burthen to trade in English ports.

PLATE II

DUTCH HERRING BUSS, 1480

PLATE III

LARGE ENGLISH COG, 1485

Charnock, in the preface to his *History of Marine Architecture* (1801), makes these comments on the state of affairs after the fall of Calais in 1347:

With this expedition, the exertions of England in a maritime point of view might be said to have ceased for the space of an entire century....The victor at Agincourt was indebted for his success to the hand of Providence, the absurd measures of his enemy, and the gallantry of that miserable remnant of soldiers which disease had left him. The terror which he had carried even into the heart of France when his armies were in the most formidable state, by no means originated in the might of his fleet. Both the contending parties appeared actuated by the same opinion on this occasion. The navy of Henry was a mere collection of transports, destitute of any armed force specially equipped for the purpose of protecting them, that could deserve, in the most distorted sense of the word, the appellation of a fleet. The reason was obvious, and exactly similar to that which had contributed to the success of the expedition under William the Norman, whose vessels were of the same description. Philip of France had neglected to equip any armament capable of opposing the passage of his invaders.

With the defeat and death of the third Richard, who appears to have been destitute of a single ship calculated to prevent the free passage of his rival and antagonist Henry, the bloody dispute, as is perfectly well known, closed at once. Internal peace, added to the prudent policy of Henry VII, occasioned a revival of maritime pursuits. Commerce became considered one of the first supporters of the state, and the dreadful improvements which were rapidly made in the science of naval war, gave birth to that marine, which under succeeding monarchs, and in defiance of opposing difficulties, had attained its present power and consequence among nations.

The quest after the great ship dates at least from the time of Henry V with his *Grace de Dieu*. This idea was pursued all through the Tudor and Stuart times and remains to this day. History shows time and again that most of the real fighting work at sea has been done by the 'little ships'.

PART II

THE GROWTH OF THE TRADE (1485–1837)

§1. THE TUDORS

ALTHOUGH a few large vessels had been built before the end of the fifteenth century, it is worthy of note that the famous voyages of Vasco da Gama, Columbus and the Cabots were made in frail ships of small tonnage. An impulse arose to construct craft to better purpose and now that cannon began to be used for naval warfare the quest for the large ship took first place.

In 1506 there was built in Scotland the *Great Michael*, which, as Charnock quotes:

'was of so great stature and took so much timber, that she wasted all the woods in Fife which were oak wood, with all timber that was gotten out of Norway, for she was so strong and of so great length and breadth, all the wrights of Scotland, yea, and many other countries, were at her devise by the King's command, who wrought very busily in her, but it was a year and a day ere she was compleated. To wit: she was 12 score foot (240 ft.) of length, and 36 foot within the sides: she was 10 foot thick in the wall and boards, on every side so slack and so thick, that no cannon could go through her.'[1]

She was lost on her way to France in 1512.

Henry VII does not seem to have had more than six or seven ships in his Royal fleet. The largest, the *Grace de Dieu*, was unfit for service owing to age and decay. To replace her the *Henry Grace à Dieu* (called the 'Great Harry', and later named by Henry VIII the *Regent*) was laid down. Henry died before she was launched in 1509 when the fleet was said to have some 57 vessels, each carrying 21 men and a boy.

Henry VIII, in his early years, did much to build up a fleet and to see that measures were taken to obtain proper and better ships. In 1512 he gave a patent to Sir Edward Howard to take charge of the king's ships and all matters of crew and cost—the first step towards setting up a Board of Admiralty. The Navy then had fifteen vessels of which four were first- or second-rates. He set up the dockyards at Woolwich and Deptford and began to make Portsmouth more suited for naval work. He brought from abroad, chiefly from Italy, the best builders of ships of the day. He also made use of the British shipwrights to design and build the vessels he needed. He thus set up

---

[1] *History of Marine Architecture* (1801-2).

PLATE IV

ELIZABETHAN GALLEON, *c.* 1600

SPANISH CARRACKS AND GALLEONS, *c.* 1560

a technical corps with the result that 'the fame of Genoa and Venice, long the envy of Europe, passed quickly to the shores of Britain'.

In 1544 he sent James Baker, Peter Pett, and three others—men, as the order says, 'skilful in ships'—to Portsmouth to inquire into the state of the warships there. In 1514 he gave Trinity House its first charter 'for the relief, increase and augmentation of the Shipping of this Realm of England'. His purpose was to give to that body the charge of the well-being of the Merchant Navy. The copy of his statute of 1540 as printed in the Statutes of the Realm, sets out a policy for England. It is stated there how 'the Navy or multitude of Shippes of this realme' is needed for 'the intercourse and concurse of marchauntis transporting and conveying their wares and marchaundises'. This navy was to be a great defence and surety of this realm in time of war as well to offend and defend. The preface to the Statute goes on to detail the need to maintain many master mariners and seamen, and to make them expert and cunning in 'the arte and science of shippmen and sayling'. In the past this navy had been the chief maintenance and support of the cities, towns, villages, havens and creeks 'nere adjoyning unto the see costes'. The king's subjects, 'bakers bruers butchers smythes ropers shipwrittes taillours (showe makers) and other vitallers and handycraftis men', have had thereby a great part of their living.

And now 'the same Navy and multitude of Shippes' had been greatly impaired and decayed, so that a great multitude of the king's liege people were now diminished and impoverished and the towns, villages, and inhabitations near the sea-coast were utterly fallen in ruin and decay. From this it would seem that in spite of his many worries, and they were not a few, he made the time to concern himself with sea affairs.

Like his father, Henry VIII also built a big ship, the *Henry Grace à Dieu,* to replace the *Regent,* which was blown up in 1512 together with the French flagship *Cordelier,* which it was fighting. This vessel had a burden of 1000 tons and a crew of 700—soldiers, mariners and gunners. With all his efforts the Navy, at the time of his death in 1547, apart from the large ship, had 70 vessels of which 12 were between 250 and 700 tons, and 15 were galleys from 60 to 450 tons.

During the reigns of Edward VI and of Mary, the Navy declined, and when Elizabeth became Queen in 1558, the total tonnage of the fleet was little more than 7000 tons. Worse than that, the Merchant Navy had less than 50,000 tons of ships, in the service of lawful commerce, and in the whole of England there were barely 800 such ships, of which only some 135 were of upwards of 100 tons.

The glamour of the defeat of the Armada has thrown into deep shadow the solid work which Elizabeth put in to strengthen her fleet. During the first 20 years of her reign, her progress was slow. She had great trouble with finance owing to the base coinage brought in by Henry VII. Moreover, the money she could extract for the Navy was grossly ill-spent, for Cecil and the Privy Council lacked the technical knowledge needed to deal with the corrupt dockyards.

Well it was that in 1578 Elizabeth made Sir John Hawkins, Kt. Treasurer of the Queen's Majesty's Marine Cause, and the £250,000 which passed through his hands in the next 10 years was wisely spent. He, like Francis Drake, had wide knowledge from his trading voyages and his privateering to Africa and Spanish America, of what types of ships were needed. Now, in spite of the critics, he built the queen's ships low, long in respect of beam, easy to handle and well-gunned. Such a ship was the *Revenge* of 500 tons and 100 ft. length of keel and 50 guns, which carried Drake's flag as Vice-Admiral in the fight against the Armada.

Elizabeth owed much to her father's foresight in setting up a body of skilled shipwrights. It was his practice to reward good craftsmen by a life-pension, which was really a fee to engage the shipwright whenever he was needed. One of the earliest of these was James Baker, who, in 1537, was given the pension of 4*d*. a day. He won fame as a builder of warships, and the art of mounting heavy guns in ships was said to be owing to his skill. His son Matthew Baker, born in 1530, was the first to be called master shipwright in 1572, and his knowledge was a great help to Elizabeth and John Hawkins in the strenuous 10 years before the coming of the Armada.

In that famous battle the Queen's Navy proper had only 34 ships out of a total number of 197 which were used in the action. The Lord High Admiral, Lord Charles Howard, flew his flag in one of the new vessels, the *Ark Royal* of 800 tons. The Vice-Admiral, Sir Francis Drake, had as his flagship the new *Revenge*, while Sir John Hawkins, the Rear-Admiral, took the old *Victory* of 800 tons. The other new ships of the line were the *Elizabeth-Bonadventure* of 600 tons, and three sister vessels to the *Revenge*. There were of the older fleet the *Triumph* of 1100 tons, the *White Beare* of 1000 tons, the *Marie Rose* and the *Hope*, each of 600 tons, and the *Golden Lion*, and *Elizabeth Jonas* of 500 tons. In support there were 163 ships largely drawn from the Merchant Navy, some of which had been built as privateers. The largest of these was the galleon *Leicester* in the fleet of vessels under Sir Francis Drake. London sent 38 ships, the largest being the *Hercules* of 300 tons. The volunteers with the Lord Admiral were 18 in number, the biggest being the *Sampson* of 300 tons.

Fighting at sea lasted for a further 10 years after the defeat of the Armada, largely because Philip II of Spain still pursued his desires to conquer England. All he was able to do was to harass and cripple her sea trade.

Elizabeth kept in mind all these factors—the use of merchant ships for defence, the need to pursue foreign trade, and to arm the civil vessels which in their longer voyages the Royal Navy had not enough ships to protect. All this in its turn led to the building of larger merchant vessels.

The queen helped the City of London in many ways to found trading companies to deal with foreign markets. These bodies carried English goods to Russia, Prussia, the Baltic, Turkey, and the Levant. Of all these efforts, the greatest and the one most potent in changing the face of the world was the Charter given to the East India Company in 1600.

'The change over', as Trevelyan writes, 'was rendered possible by the adventurous spirit of the capitalist of the City of London, by the quality of the new school of sailors and sea-captains, and by the enterprise of English explorers by land as well as sea.'[1]

§2. THE MASTER SHIPWRIGHTS

THE actual drawing of the lines was kept a secret by the master shipwrights who passed on the art from father to son. Fuller remarks:

I am credibly informed that the Mystery of Shipwrights for some descents hath been preserved successfully in Families, of whom the Petts about Chatham are of singular regard. Good success have they with their skill and carefully keep so precious a pearl, lest otherwise amongst many friends, some foes attain unto it. It is no monopoly which concealeth that from common enemies, the concealing whereof is for the common good. May this mystery of ship-making in England never be lost till this floting world be arrived at its own haven, the end and dissolution thereof![2]

[1] *English Social History* (1944).
[2] *The History of the Worthies of England* (1662).

Sir Arthur Johns, late Director of Naval Construction, in his account of the master shipwrights of the sixteenth and seventeenth centuries details the growth of these offices, which had been begun by Henry VIII. It was on account of the work which they did for the Royal Navy and for the East India Company, that the basis for the future guidance of the shipwright's craft was laid down. The period from A.D. 1500 to 1700 saw the change from the craftsman who built largely by eye, by flair or by rule of thumb, to a skilled worker, who could draw out the form of the ship as well as settle the manner of her building.

The master shipwright became the head technical officer of the dockyard, and Matthew Baker, who in 1572 was the first to hold such title, built most of his vessels at Deptford or Woolwich. Sir Arthur gives in detail the duties of the office. The master had to design in all respects the ship to be built. He had to settle the shapes of the transverse sections at various parts of the length. From these moulds patterns of light battens were made which the master with a few shipwrights took to the woods, where he chose timber to suit the shapes and marked the trees to be felled which he needed. Transport to the shipyard was a matter for study. He had charge of rebuilding since in those days of trial and error changes had to be made after the ship was launched—a fairly easy matter, since the ships were built of wood and an extra thickness of planking might have to be fitted near the water-line where the vessel after building was found to be 'tender'; such a process was known as 'girdling'. Repairs and refits were part of the day's work and at times a question of salvage might require his help.

Apart from such duties he had to design and oversee the building and fitting up of wet and dry docks, wharves, storehouses and workshops; to see to the issue of naval stores, to house, feed and pay the shipwrights, and to police the dockyard. He alone up to 1608 settled whether a ship was fit for further service or needed to be rebuilt or scrapped.

His pay was small—about twice as much as a skilled shipwright. Thus in 1570 it was 1s. a day, raised to 2s. a day in 1605. In that year a further grant of 1s. a day, known as 'exchequer pay', was made. In 1695 the three master shipwrights at Woolwich, Chatham and Portsmouth each had £200 a year; the salary at Deptford, Sheerness and Devonport was fixed at £150. To add to their small income they took from the district as apprentices youths of promise, from whom they got a premium. From this class were chosen assistants to the master shipwright, of whom each master had two. They also built merchant ships in private yards which sometimes they owned.

Master shipwrights were chosen as a rule from the trained apprentices, although at times a private builder might be given such a post for some special service.

Of the early master shipwrights three names stand out, Matthew Baker, William Burrell and that of Phineas Pett who was born in 1570, built the *Prince Royal*, launched in 1610, and the *Sovereign of the Seas*, launched in 1637, and who died 10 years later. In Pepys's time, after the Restoration, there came forward a fourth, Anthony Deane, who took the first steps to apply the methods of science to the building of ships.

Although somewhat out of sequence, it may be well to relate here the story of William Burrell, who in 1600 was made General Surveyor of the first East India Company.

§3. WILLIAM BURRELL

PHINEAS PETT describes him in 1609 as 'principal Master Workman' to that body, a post which he held until 1626, when he fell out with the Company. He died in October 1630.

King James was present in 1610 at the floating out of dock at Deptford of the *Trade's Increase*, a vessel of some 1100 tons which had been built by Burrell to his own design. He bore witness in favour of Phineas Pett at the inquiry held by James I in 1608, into the building of the *Prince Royal*. Then Pett called him 'a worthy gentleman and good friend'. At a later inquiry in 1618, when he was the only commissioner of the Navy with technical knowledge, Pett said that he was his 'greatest enemy'—'tending to overthrow me and root my name out of the earth'.

In 1619 Burrell was asked by the Commissioners to contract to build the Royal ships at Deptford, where by 1623 he had turned out ten ships of large size. He still kept his post with the East India Company, but his salary with them of £200 was raised to £300. There were serious complaints about these ships, which were shown up in an inquiry in 1623. They were said to be 'tender' (not too stable) and needed to be 'girdled'—a term used to describe the fitting of extra planking on the outside of the ship in the way of the water-line. A writer of the time said that Burrell, 'a man friendless, but full of money', ought to pay for the repairs. However, he still kept his post and without loss.

In 1621 he made a scathing report on the state of the *Prince Royal*, mainly based on the poor nature of the timber used for her building. He stayed with the Navy, after he left the East India Company's service, until he died. He was made an Assistant Commissioner with Pett, whom he joined on a visit to the chief naval yard. On their return from Portsmouth in 1630 both Burrell and Pett were taken ill. Burrell died and Pett relates that he was kept in his room for eight weeks.

Although Burrell held these high offices he did not seem in 1605 to have been among the leading shipwrights of the country, since his name does not appear among the 21 members who made up the Court of the Shipwrights Company founded in that year. He made progress, however, for in the new charter of 1612 he had become First Warden.

Of the shipwrights who came after there was John Tippetts, master shipwright at Portsmouth, and later Commissioner there, who became surveyor of the Navy. From then until 1834 that office was held by one and sometimes two master shipwrights. Between 1834 and 1860 the post passed to two naval officers in succession. The sequence went on with a change of title to Chief Constructor of the Navy, Mr Isaac Watts being the first to occupy the post.

The present title of the office is Director of Naval Construction.

§4. THE SHAPE OF SHIPS

WHEN Henry VIII got shipwrights from Italy to come to England there is reason to believe that they brought with them their ideas for the best forms of ships, such as had grown up to meet the needs of the Mediterranean.

There the galleon was taking the place of the galley, a craft which was driven by many rowers. The lower part of the cross-section of the galley was almost round in shape. Above this was the deck which to find room for the rowers and the long oars on both sides of the ship had to be made about twice as broad as the hull below. Such a type was clearly not suited for anything more than fighting ships. Cannon, when first used, were fitted to galleys among the banks of rowers. It was seen very soon that changes in form were wanted because the port-holes for the guns had to be placed well above water and the sides built up around the cannon to provide shelter for the gunners.

Venice and Genoa had both built large carracks for their sea-trade, with much of their great bulk above the water-line. They were clumsy and awkward ships, not easy to handle, with the sails and the rig of those days. The upper parts 'tumbled home' to a marked extent, that is, curved inwards from the water to the upper deck. The Spaniards had found before the Armada that oared galleys were useless in Atlantic waters, and so when fighting at sea changed to cannon, the galleon type was taken as the pattern for the new warship.

It was thought proper to make the gun-decks, on which the cannon were carried, narrow, because of the length of the beams needed to support the decks and to connect the sides. It was hard to get long lengths of timber for the purpose, and when two lengths had to be used because of the breadth of the deck, the joints were a source of weakness and trouble. Rightly, there was a further fear that the heavy weights of the guns and the forces of their recoil would increase the strain on the beams which were the main ties to maintain the shape of the ship. So for a number of reasons, the breadth of the upper deck was very much less than it was at the water-level. In early types the width of deck was only a half, and even in 1635 was barely two-thirds, of the greatest breadth.

One of the main features of design was to settle the breadth and where the greatest breadth should be placed. The 'height of breadth', or the distance above the keel of the largest width, was as a rule a few feet *above* the water-line at which the loaded ship floated. This helped to keep the stiffness of the vessel when she heeled under sail. For a like reason, the height of the breadth-line was raised from midships towards the ends. This kept the buoyant support when the vessel 'trimmed' or shifted lengthwise to draw more water forward or aft as the case might be.

A further reason for raising the shape of the transverse form upwards towards the end was to reduce the forces acting against the motion of the vessel and to furnish an easier passage through the water. It also helped to make the ship more seaworthy in rough weather.

A further point to settle was the lengthwise place for the largest cross-section of the ship, which section is known as the 'midship section'. The usual practice was to put the midship nearer the bow than the stern with the result that the form is fuller forward than aft.

The idea in Tudor days was to make the shape below water conform to a 'cod's head and mackerel tail' which would give a full form forward and a fine form aft. It is curious that the same thought found favour right up to modern times—a thought that is shown in picture form by Matthew Baker before 1586.

Great care was taken to make the form, both transverse and lengthwise, 'smooth' in shape. The transverse section was built up by joining a number of 'sweeps' or arcs of circles. It began with a 'flat of floor', the lowest timber of the frame or rib, which crossed the keel on which it rested. The flat of floor was a term used for the width of the flat part at the bottom of the cross-section. (The term 'floor' might perhaps be taken from the idea that it was the floor on which the ship rested when she took the ground.) The width of floor was made less in gradual manner towards the end, and the height of the floor also rose towards the ends and was shown by what was termed the 'rise of floor-line'.

This manner of moving the form upwards is termed 'rising'. Thus the rise of the greatest breadth of each timber, from midships to the end, is shown by a curved line known as the 'height of breadth' line. Rising lines also ruled the shape of the sheer of the deck, and for most of such lines the curves used were arcs of circles of large radius.

The shapes of the transverse section are drawn to the outside of the frames or ribs, upon which, when they are set up into the form of a cradle, the planks are fixed later. The lowest plank—'garboard-strake'—butts on the main keel, in which a rabbet is cut to take the edge of the plank. The upper edge of this rabbet, or groove, is used as the lengthwise base-line from which distances are set up as well as other features such as the 'rise of floor' line and the 'height of breadth' line at various stations.

It may be well to mention here other base-lines. As a rule, when length was given the figure that was meant was the length of the flat part of the keel. This 'length on keel' was taken from the stern-post to where the lower part of the curved stem-post touches the keel. Sometimes the 'length on the gun-deck' is stated which, as the name implies, is a greater length; namely, that of the lower deck just above the water-line on which the first tier of guns is placed. This length is the one that is used when setting off the lines of the ship. From its ends, 'perpendiculars' are drawn down to the base-line—the top of the keel rabbet—and thus to complete a framework from which to mark off a lengthwise section through the middle of the ship.

Returning to the shape of the transverse section, which begins with a level-line showing the width of the flat floor, this width at midships is one-third of the breadth of the ship taken on each side of the keel since the floor which crosses the keel is made in one piece. The next part of the section is formed by a 'sweep', having its centre in the upright over the end of the flat of floor, the radius being about half of the half-breadth.

The 'height of breadth' is next set up and the breadth marked off. The shape in this region was thought to matter a great deal. The radius of the 'sweep' here was about the same as or a little less than that for the floor, and was carried downwards a little way towards the water-line.

These two arcs being drawn, they were joined by a 'sweep' of large radius, greater than the half-breadth, and the proper place for the centre of this 'sweep' called for much skill in drawing.

The upper part—'above the breadth'—began with an inward 'sweep' of medium radius which ran up to about half the height to the top of the deck or the topside of the ship. From thence upwards a 'reverse sweep', that is an arc swinging outwards, was used to end the form. Sometimes, because of the special nature of the upper parts, the draughtsmen might make use of a series of 'moulds' formed of 'arches' of various radii, made up of thin laths of wood shaped in proper fashion. In such case the ending of a form was a matter of 'eye' and judgement. This process, as will be seen later, was carried out for the shape of every frame of the ship.

After this length of time it cannot be settled whether the method for drawing the form was brought here from Italy, c. 1530, or grew up in England.

There is some support for the Italian theory, since much the same ideas are to be found in an amazing book printed in Florence under the title *Dell' Arcano del Mare* ('The Secrets of the Sea') with the date of 1646. The actual date of the drawings might have been as early as 1612, for it is on record that the plates of the book took 12 years to engrave, and after a second edition was printed in 1661 the plates were broken up to prevent further copies being made.

The author was Sir Robert Dudley—who was styled Duke of Northumberland and Earl of Warwick. He was filled with a great desire to put the English Navy on a proper footing, and put forward an idea for a new type of warship called 'Gallizabras'. He was born in 1573, being the son of Robert Dudley, Earl of Leicester, who became the favourite of Queen Elizabeth. Charnock mentions that he built a vessel at Southampton to accord with his views, and made a voyage to India in her with success in 1594.[1] He took part in the attack on Cadiz in 1596 when he was knighted by the Earl of Essex. In 1607 he settled at Florence and stayed in Italy for the rest of his life to avoid having to answer the charge of taking to himself the title of Earl of Warwick. The Holy Roman Empire in 1620 granted him the title of Earl of Warwick and Duke of Northumberland; he died at Villa Castello in 1649.

In the book itself there are designs and sections for seven types of vessels, one of which for the 'rambargo' is shown; the English built such vessels which were called 'ram-barges'. Here is seen the manner of forming the shape by a series of 'arches'. The centre, *A, B, C*, gives the floor 'sweep', the centre *E, F, G*, the 'sweep' at the greatest breadth, and *C, D, E* is the centre for the joining curve of large radius. Broadly, the scheme used is much the same as that found in English practice at the same time.

Again, the other drawings in the book show the 'rising line' and the 'width of floor' lines which were a marked feature of the methods of fixing the form in the later Tudor times. The broadside view, with a beak at the prow, is not unlike the ships built by Elizabeth just before the Armada.

Dudley had sound views as to the need for a strong hull, and it is well to note the use of oblique struts from the keel to the upper deck as well as the heavy angle pieces used to connect the ends of the beams to the sides of the ship.

§5. MATTHEW BAKER

MATTHEW's father, James Baker, was well known to Henry VIII, who in 1538 granted him a patent of 4*d*. a day—'wage and fee'. Once when Baker was in trouble for having certain books, contrary to the law, the king wrote to the law officers: 'His Majesty thynketh you will find him a very simple man and therefore would that without putting him in any great fear, you should search of him as much as you may.'

His renown as a builder of the king's ships was great, and he had the credit of being able to mount heavy guns on board a vessel. It was

---

[1] *History of Marine Architecture* (1810).

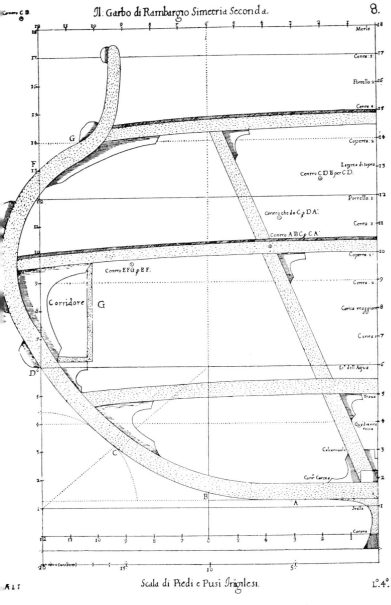

Il. Garbo di Rambargo Simetria Seconda.   **8.**

Scala di Piedi e Pusi Inglesi.   L°.4°.

Midship section of a 'rambargo' (or ram-barge)
Drawing, c. 1600

37

from his design and under his control that many of Henry's fleet were built between 1538 and his death in 1549.

His pension, as it was called, was raised to 8*d*. a day in 1544 when, with Peter Pett—the father of Phineas—and three others, he went to Portsmouth to inquire into the state of some warships lying there.

Matthew was born in 1530 and became an apprentice to his father. His Commonplace Book in the Pepysian Library, Magdalene College, Cambridge, contains a midship section of the first ship on which he worked. He seems to have stayed in the naval service for, in 1564, he joined with Bright in the building of the *White Bear* of 1000 tons, the second largest vessel of the Armada fleet.

When, in 1578, Elizabeth took stock of her Navy there were only 18 ships over 100 tons, and as a result a strenuous programme of the building of ships took place in the next ten years. This was more than likely under his control, for in the *Fragments of Ancient English Ship-wrightry*, again in the Pepysian Library, are plots—plans—for warships of various designs and sizes. All the evidence shows that these were the work of Baker with the date of about 1586.

In those ten years in question there were built some ten ships over 100 tons and eight lesser ones. The largest, the *Ark Royal*, was of 800 tons, the next the *Elizabeth Bonadventure* of 600 tons, and four vessels were of the *Revenge* class of 500 tons—the most useful for fighting the Spanish ships. Baker himself built the *Vanguard* of 500 tons.

Before this, in 1572, Baker was made master shipwright—the first to be given that title. Further, in 1588 he, with his brother Christopher, were members of an inquiry set up to settle the designs of three new vessels. The Lord High Admiral, Lord Charles Howard, Sir John Hawkins, Sir Francis Drake, as well as Sir William Wynter and Borough, Controller of the Navy, were the other members. As a result, the *Merhonour* of 800 tons was built by Baker and was rebuilt by him in 1613, the year of his death. The other two were the smaller vessels *Defiance* and *Guardland*.

Baker had a clear mind and was able to bring things to rule. Among his other work he laid down the methods of measuring the 'tonnage' of ships—the inside room or space in terms of the number of Bordeaux casks that could be stowed on board. These were the standard rules in his lifetime.

He also framed methods to fix the shape of the 'midship bend' or transverse section of the ship at the greatest breadth, and as his

PLATE V

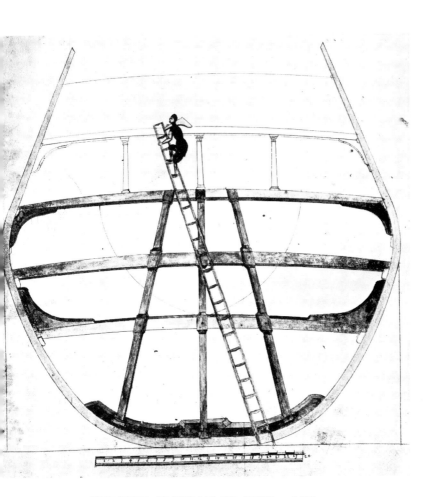

MIDSHIP SECTION OF SHIP *c.* 1586

PLATE VI

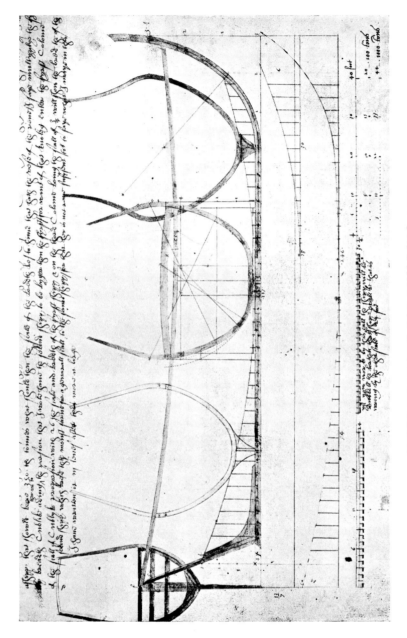

SHEER DRAUGHT FOR BUILDING, c. 1586

drawings show in 1586, to settle the form at the ends and the quarter lengths. There was broadly enough detail given to enable a ship to be built. He may be said to have been the first of the English shipwrights to set down on paper the 'lines' of a vessel.

He was held in high repute by his fellows. Phineas Pett, whose knowledge and fitness for the building of the *Prince Royal* in 1608 he strongly damned, wrote of him some time after his death as 'the most famous artist of our time'. Pett also refers to him: 'Mr Baker...from whose help I must acknowledge I received my greatest lights.' In a letter to Mr Baker in 1603 he wrote: '...for although I served no years in your service yet I must ever acknowledge what ever I have of any art (if I have any) it came only from you...whose ever memorable works I set before me as a notable precedent and pattern to direct me....'

The first Charter of the Shipwrights Company granted by King James I in 1605, which relates to the Art or Mystery of Shipwrights of England, names Matthew Baker, 'our servant and ancientist Master Shipwright to be the first Master'.

Pepys kept, among his treasures, a bound copy of *Fragments of Ancient English Shipwrightry*, a MS. of notes of many things done by the craftsmen of those days. It has neither date nor name of the owner. There is a note in a later writing in regard to a method for drawing the stern transom (the framing of the square stern) which says: 'the first wase made by this waye the *Vanguard*.' This suggests that the notes were written before that time, 1586, and that they were made by Matthew Baker himself.

These are the first known attempts to set down on paper the form of the ship. Plates VI and VIII show the lay-out of the keel, the stem, and the post or stern-post. There are cross-sections at amidships and at the quarter-length forward and aft: the framing at the stern or transom is shown in detail. Below is the half-breadth plan giving the greatest breadth of the sections throughout the length.

In the lengthwise section at the middle of the ship is drawn a curved shaded band to show the wale or thick timber in the way of the gun-deck. The 'height of breadth' would have a like shape, but some ft. or so higher. The lower curve gives the 'rise of floor' line, which can be seen to pass through the top of the floors at the three cross-sections given. There can also be seen the centres and the radii for drawing the various 'sweeps' to give the shape. The lower part below the flat of the floor is ended with a reverse 'sweep' because of the 'rise

of the floor' at the end. It is well to notice that the curve of the ster
is struck by a 'sweep' for which the centre is given, and the midshi
section is nearer the bow than the stern.

The picture of the midship section on a larger scale (Pl. V) agrees i
shape with the main plan, and gives some idea of the size and nature c
the frames, the beams, and the cross-struts. In modern eyes it woul
seem that Baker had proper regard to the transverse strength of th
structure. The work of the Tudor shipwright (Pl. VII) gives a goo
view of the Drawing Office and the large size of the 'sweeps' or com
passes which were used to give the shape of the lengthwise curves. Th
prentice lad is standing by to put down the figures as they are rea
off by the shipwright.

From other drawings by Baker, a model of an Elizabethan galleo
was made in the workshop of the Science Museum at South Kensing
ton for a ship of about 100 ft. length of keel and of 500 tons. This wa
such a vessel as Drake's *Revenge* in which he flew his flag at th
Armada and very likely one of the vessels which Sir John Hawkin
caused to be built. The clean shape of the form and the absence c
top-hamper contrasts in marked manner with the Spanish galleon
shown in the lower picture of Pl. IV. The simple manner of paintin
the top sides in chequer pattern with bright colours in contrast seem
more fitting than the complex and costly carving and gilding of th
Stuart ships, no doubt due to the vanity of the king and of Phineas Pet

The *Prince Royal*, built from 1608 to 1610, cost the country ove
£1300 for the carving and painting. Sebastian Vicars got £441. 0s. 4c
for the carvings, and the painters, Robert Beake and Paul Isaksor
were paid bills for £868. 6s. 8d. Of the latter sum £164 was spent 'fc
the Prince's lodging cabin, very curiously wrought and gilded, wit
divers histories, and very much other works in oil colours'. This is i
sharp contrast to the captain's cabin (the captain being the maste
mariner): 'For the Master's Cabin wrought and varnished, with h
mate's cabins, primed and laid in oil colours...110s.'

§6. PHINEAS PETT

THE first of the Phineas Petts—there were three of that name—wa
born at Deptford in 1570 where his father Peter was master shipwrigh
the second to hold such an office. The Petts came from a long line c
shipbuilders who had their own yard at Harwich. It was his fathe

Peter Pett, who was sent by Henry VIII in 1544 with James Baker, the father of Matthew, as men being skilful in ships, to survey the warships at Portsmouth. Peter was given a 'wage and fee' pension of 2d. a day in 1558 and was given his patent of master shipwright in 1582. When Phineas was nine he was at school at Rochester and later was sent to school at Greenwich, where, as he says, 'I so well profited that in three years I was made fit for Cambridge.' He joined Emmanuel College in 1586. After four years, during which his father died, and his mother married again, he left Cambridge at the age of twenty with an M.A. degree. It would seem that he had been meant for the Church or the Law. His studies at Cambridge had not made him a master of English and later he had cause to practise 'cyphering' in the evenings to acquire some knowledge of mathematics.

Under pressure from his mother he became apprenticed to Mr Richard Chapman, master shipwright at Deptford, until his death two years later, which time Phineas says he spent to very little purpose. In 1592, failing to obtain service with Mr Matthew Baker, which he wanted, he became a ship's carpenter for two years on board a privateer in the Levant seas, without any profit. When he came back to London in 1594, 'having neither money nor apparel', his brother Joseph 'out of his bounty lent me 40s. to apparel myself, which I bestowed as frugally as I could...contenting myself as well as I could with mean attire till such time as it should please God to provide better for me'.

This brother Joseph found him work, which he took in order to clothe himself 'in very good fashion, always endeavouring to keep company with men of good rank far better than myself'. Phineas made up his mind to get on in life, and was able to get to know the Lord High Admiral, Lord Howard of Effingham, afterwards Earl of Nottingham, an introduction which he described as 'the very first beginning of my rising'.

Around Christmas 1595 he spent a short time with Mr Baker who was 'some time forward to give me instruction, from whose help I must acknowledge I received my greatest lights'. During that winter he learnt to cypher and to draw, and thus to improve his knowledge. Through Lord Howard he became a surveyor of timber in 1599 and the next year the shipwright keeper of the plank yard, timber and stores at Chatham; which his Lordship urged him to take until a better offer was open. In 1602 he became an assistant to the master shipwright at that yard and built a small merchant vessel, the

Resistance, in a private yard at Gillingham nearby to Chatham. I
January 1604 there came an urgent message from Lord Howard t
build a little vessel for the young Prince Henry to disport himse
above London Bridge. Phineas worked day and night on this sma
ship, some 25 ft. long, garnished and carved to be like the *Ark Roya*
The coming of this craft to Lambeth on 18 March caused a great sti
and many visits were made that week which ended with the comin
of the young prince himself. As a result of this display Phineas wa
sworn His Grace's servant and presented to the prince. Through th
means Pett was given his patent as master shipwright in 1605 at th
early age of thirty-five, after his return from a trip which he made t
Lisbon with the fleet, making the voyage in his own vessel, the *Resistanc*

He rebuilt the *Victory* and the *Ark Royal* at Woolwich between th
years 1606 and 1608. He became Master of the Shipwrights Compan
in 1607 to follow Matthew Baker. In that year he made a 'curious
model for the prince, mostly with his own hands. Lord Howard tol
him to carry it to Richmond and then got the king to see the mode
The king was most pleased and asked Phineas whether he woul
'build the great ship in all points like to the same'. This idea of makin
a scale model of the design before starting to build the ship was th
first instance of what became the custom for large or novel vessels.

The order was given for Pett to build this new great ship, c
which the keel was laid about a year later in October 1608. Just befor
this King James was rightly driven to cause an inquiry to be made int
the corrupt manner in which the Navy Office was run. Queen Eliza
beth had dealt with this trouble by making Sir John Hawkins he
Treasurer for the Navy up to the time of the Armada. After tha
a great increase in abuse, deceit, and fraud was charged against th
officers and others 'working or labouring in or about our said Navy
Pett was among those blamed for his actions when he was keeper c
timber and stores at Chatham.

With such a searching inquest under way, it is not surprising tha
the question was raised as to the fitness of Phineas for the great task c
building the *Prince Royal*, as the new ship was to be named. Baker, th
senior master shipwright, had built the *Merhonour* with length of kee
110 ft., breadth 37 ft. and a depth of 17 ft. Pett's model had length c
keel 115 ft., breadth 43 ft. and a depth of 18 ft. Up to then Pett ha
built very little, nor, except to rebuild the *Ark Royal* just ready for se
had he been given charge of any large ship. Further, in the eyes c
the master shipwrights he had not learned the craft. Beyond all thi

PLATE VII

SHIPWRIGHTS DRAWING, c. 1586

PLATE VIII

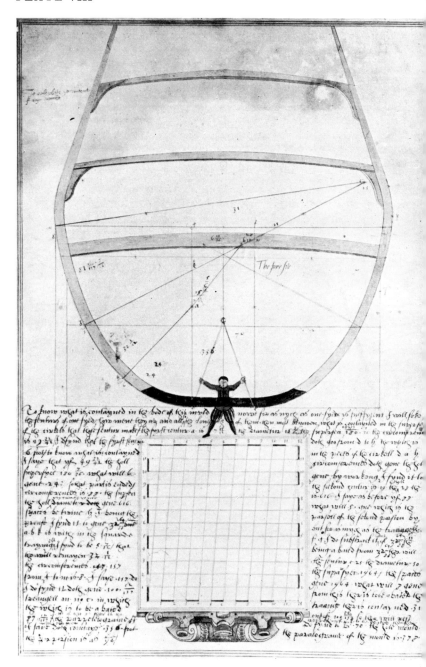

METHOD OF DRAWING THE MIDSHIP BEND, *c.* 1586

a man of thirty-eight who had risen to be master of the Shipwrights Company over the heads of his elders, by seeking favour at Court as an offset to his lack of knowledge, was not liked by his fellows.

The question dragged on and in May 1609 the king himself held an inquiry. The master shipwrights made a written report. They stated that 'her mould is altogether imperfect'. The mould is the complete shape of the widest cross-section which starts with a flat part at the keel—'the floor'—which they said was too wide. The rest of the shape was made up by using arcs of circles called 'sweeps'. Their comment was that the upper and lower sweeps were too long and the middle sweep too short. Her depth was too great and her side too upright, so that 'she must be tender sided and not able to bear sail'. Her draught was too much for the shoal seas and the shape of her bow would lead to danger at sea.

The more serious complaints were of the timber, which was called overgrown and cross-grained, and fault was found with the working of the wooden timbers or 'frame-bend' as the complete ribs were called. 'The futtocks have not scarph enough with the floor timbers.' (The floor timber and the futtocks make up a complete frame, and the pieces overlap each other to give more strength.) The 'treenails', or wooden pegs used to fasten the planking both inside and outside, and the frame were not worked in proper fashion.

This report by six of the chief builders of the time was a severe stricture. It ended by saying that Pett himself had made changes after their visit which seemed 'to show his weakness in art and the imperfection of the mould', mould being used as the name for the transverse shape.

On the whole, Pett had made little change in the usual rules for settling the 'mould', nor is there any record of the ship being 'crank'. But in regard to the timber used, and in the manner of cutting the curved frame out of straight wood instead of using 'grown timber', there were many complaints later. The *Prince Royal* never had any strenuous duties and in 1641 was rebuilt throughout at a cost of nearly £20,000.

A second inquiry in 1618 found the state of the Navy little changed from what is was in 1608. The fact that Burrell, a member of the Commission, was given direct contract to build two ships a year for the next five years was a distinct grievance with Pett, who, in effect, built very few ships after the *Prince Royal* until 1632 when Burrell had been dead some two years.

43

There must have been some great charm about Pett, because in spite of his many rebuffs he kept the trust of James I and Charles I as well as of the Lord High Admiral. So, when in his turn King Charles I wanted a great ship in 1634, he drew Pett aside on a visit to Woolwich to say: 'You have made many requests of me and now I will make it my request to you to build this great new ship.' The model was taken to Court for a vessel of 1500 tons in October and Pett was again subject to violent protests, among others from Trinity House. In April 1635 Pett with three others gave to the king a statement of the details of the ship which His Majesty approved with his own writing. Here for the first time on public records was given the 'sweeps' of the 'mould'—the radii of the main parts of the greatest cross-section. Pett went in haste to the north with all the moulds and workmen to obtain the frame and timber and plank and treenails. This was got from Chopwell Woods and loaded at Newcastle, as well as from Brancepeth Park, near Durham, which was shipped at Sunderland. The keel was laid in the dock just before Christmas 1635 and she was launched in October 1637, being then named the *Sovereign of the Seas*. She was loaded ready for sea in July 1638 and was tried out in the Channel in all respects and was found worthy. (Here Phineas Pett's Diary ends and there is no further mention of his name in the State papers.) When the Civil War began in 1642 he handed over the *Sovereign* to the agents of the Committee of Public Safety for which act he was made one of the commissioners of the Navy, which office he held at a salary of £200 a year until his death in 1647.

As to the *Sovereign*, Pett had learned his lesson of 30 years before, since she proved to be a pattern of durability, for she was rebuilt in 1660 and again in 1685, being burnt by mishap in 1696. She was the largest ship until the *Britannia* of 1730 tons was built in 1682. She had three complete decks unbroken throughout the length, unlike previous ships in which the decks were run in steps towards the ends.

As to Pett himself, Perrin, who edited his biography, remarks that regard must be paid to the age in which he lived. It was a time of great unrest in politics and religion. Violence of devotion went hand in hand with laxity in money matters. The servants of the Crown eked out their small salaries in what to-day would be termed devious ways. Phineas was a man of great ability and industry, kind to his friends, but short of temper and swayed by quick impulse. He made every use of his influence with the powers in office whether in the right or in the wrong. His fame in history hangs on the two large ships that he built. There is little to show that he added much to the knowledge of the shipwright's craft, unlike Matthew Baker before him and Anthony Deane after.

It is helpful to discuss more fully the form of the *Sovereign of the Seas* as set out in the proportion agreed to by the king in April 1635.

PROPORTION OF THE GREAT SHIP OF CHARLES I AS RESOLVED ON IN APRIL 1635

Items for the midship bend

	ft.	in.
Breadth, within the plank	46	6
Depth, in the hold from the breadth to the upper edge of the keel	20	0
Keel and dead rising	2	6
The swimming line—water line—from the bottom of the keel	19	6
Ports from the water	5	0
,, ,, deck	2	0
'Tweendeck heights (plank to plank)	7	6
The flat of the floor	14	0
Sweep, at the runghead	11	0
,, ,, right of the mould	31	0
,, between the water line and the breadth	10	0
,, above the breadth	14	0

Items otherwise

Length by the keel	126	0
Height of the tuck at the fashion piece	16	0
Height of the way forward	14	0
Breadth at the transome	28	0
,, ,, upper deck—not given but say from	15	6
to	19	6
Burden in tons and tonnage		
by the old rule		1522
,, new rule		1884

[The rung-head is the end or head of the floor timber. The tuck is the place where the square stern joins the form of the ship, and the transom is the square part of the stern.]

The report which Phineas Pett drew up and which was signed by the Lord High Admiral, J. Pennington, the Treasurer of the Navy, Sir Robert Mansell, and John Wells, Storekeeper at Deptford, was made to King Charles I for the design of the *Sovereign of the Seas*. It begins:

According to your Ma^{ts} command we have examined the particulars of the plot and the dimensions presented to your Ma^{ty} by Captain Pett and by comparing the rules of Art and experience together we have agreed to the Proportion underwritten, which we most humbly submit to your Ma^{ts} further pleasure.

And ends:

Your Ma^ty will be pleased to be informed that after mature debate we have likewise agreed upon the rules to be proportioned to each sweep of the midship bend, and where the bend is to be placed, and likewise of the rules to be held in her narrowing and rising lines, which we all pray may be only imparted to your Ma^ty.

This report is endorsed in the King's own writing: 'Dimensions resolved on for the Great Ship, 7 of April 1635.'

It may be said that John Wells seems to have had knowledge of design, for in 1627 with Pett, Gunter the mathematician and two others, he drew up new rules to measure the tonnage of ships.

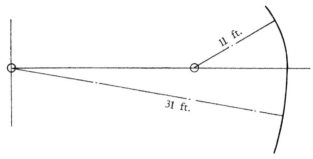

Joining two sweeps

In the last sentence of the report it is to be noted that the secrets of the trade were only for the knowledge of the king himself. The first of these secrets is 'the rules for each sweep of the midship bend'. The midship bend, as has been seen, is the shape of the biggest cross-section of the ship. The rules for the sweep are the radii of the arcs of circles from which the shape is drawn after the centres are fixed. The form of the shape had to be 'smooth' or free from abrupt changes in the curve. To effect this, the arcs of two parts where they met would have to have their centres on the same line. In that way two arcs, part of an 11 ft. circle and part of a 31 ft. circle, could be joined smoothly. The shape could thus be made by joining arcs so as to grow outwards and upwards as far as the greatest breadth, and then upwards and inwards to the line of the topmost deck.

These early craftsmen had a fairly sound idea that more could be done by the use of arcs of circles than by taking more complex curves, such as ellipses. They had not thought of, or rather viewed with dismay, such a section of a cone as the parabola, which in one form or other is the basis from which the lines of a modern ship are drawn.

It is well to try to construct the 'midship bend' of this ship of 1635 from the rules as given. The breadth was judged by the power of the ship to carry sail or to incline within reason with all sails set. Many, even famous masters, failed to give their ships enough beam, of which Pepys makes marked mention. To be just to Pett he did not fail as much as others in this respect.

The fault with the *Sovereign*, which Pett had meant to carry some 70–80 guns, was that King Charles wished her to have 100 guns, which added greatly to the weights above water. With a wooden ship there was a simple cure for this lack of stiffness. A 'girdling' of extra planks on each side was added in the way of the 'swimming line'—the water-line at which the loaded ship 'swam'.

The breadth being settled, the height of the greatest breadth was fixed to be some 3 ft. or so above the load water-line, so that when the ship heeled under sail the main breadth was held. Heights were set up from the upper edge of the keel or rather the point at which the inner surface of the plank forming the bottom of the ship meets the side of the keel. Likewise, the shape of the bend is drawn to the 'inside' of the plank which is the 'outside' of the frame timbers or ribs to which the plank is fixed.

To draw out the shape, take a level line, O, H, for the line of keel and an upright line, O, V, for the middle line of the ship. Set up the height of the main breadth, O, B, and draw B, M parallel to the base, being the half-breadth 23 ft. 3 in., some 3 ft. *above* the load-line. The curve starts from the keel with a flat piece, the 'flat of the floor' O, F, which is some 7 ft., about one-third of the half-breadth. From there an arc of small radius, 11 ft., starts from F with centre 1, 11 ft. above F. This is drawn in as shown, 1, for a distance not yet known. The next step is to draw the sweep of 10 ft. radius from the main breadth down to the water-line, L, 3 ft. below. The centre 2 is on the main breadth line, 10 ft. inside M.

Between these two arcs is a joining sweep of large radius—31 ft. In order to make a smooth join at L, the centre 3 must lie on the line L, 2 at a distance of 31 ft. from L. Join 3 to 1 and produce to meet the curve 1, at S and complete the sweep 3, 3. The shape below the breadth is now drawn.

The upper curve begins with a sweep 'above' the breadth, with its centre 4, at 14 ft. from M along the line M, B: its arc 4, is drawn upwards. The part above this is made with a reverse sweep to join the end of the top deck. This was done by using one of a set of moulds of large radius, the shape being chosen to please the eye. The height between decks was given as $7\frac{1}{2}$ ft. and the lower gun-deck is on the level of the main breadth, B, M. In the waist, the height above B, M to upper deck is 15 ft. The breadth is not given, but the

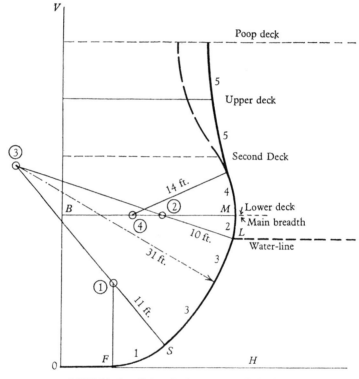

'*Midship bend*' *for the* Sovereign of the Seas

ending of the curve is shown for two breadths 20 ft., which is thought to be too great, and for about 15 ft., which is more likely to be the figure. A curve 5, 5, drawn to touch 4, completes the shape. It is carried higher to another deck, which exists at the end of the ship, so as to form a guide for the shape of the side at those parts.

With the form of the 'midship bend' as a key to the transverse shape, the lengthwise curves can now be drawn. Here comes in the 'second secret' to be settled, which is the correct place from the forward or after end of the largest section or the 'midship bend', a question for the master shipwright to decide.

For a number of reasons, put vaguely and based on crude ideas of forms of fishes and swimming birds, the fashion grew up to place the greatest cross-section some $37\frac{1}{2}$ to 40 per cent of the length on the gun-deck from the bow. This had the effect of making the forward part fuller than that at the stern.

The 'third secret' is 'the narrowing and the rising lines'. It is plain that the width of the floor must decrease towards each end of the ship to become zero forward and to have a certain width aft to allow for the square stern; this is the 'narrowing line'. At the ends where the transverse form becomes sharper, there would not be enough stuff in the floor to connect in proper fashion to the keel. So an elliptic line is drawn on the vertical plan showing the height of the floors throughout the length. This is one of the 'rising lines' on which the form of the hull depends.

The chief 'rising line' is the curve which shows how the 'height of breadth' rises from midships to the end. This curve is set off below a level line drawn through the ends of the lower gun-deck, a line which in the picture is drawn parallel to the keel. To complete the framework two vertical lines are set down at the bow and the stern from the ends of the gun-deck, called 'perpendiculars'. The 'rising line' for the half-breadth needs only a circle of small radius to derive the curve, or more simply the whole of the curved line is set off as an arc of a circle of large radius.

The third 'rising line' relates to the line of the topmost deck or the 'sheer line'. Here too, as the rise is small, arcs of circles were used.

There are thus three 'rising lines', one for the 'height of breadth', one for the 'sheer of deck', and one for the 'rise of floor'.

There is also the 'narrowing line' to show the decrease of the width of the flat floor towards the ends of the vessel.

It is perhaps well to explain in broad fashion the manner in which these lines were got from circles. Suppose a half-circle is drawn above a level diameter. Divide the radius into four equal parts and draw lines upwards to cut the circle, such lines being 1, 1, 2, 2, and so on. The line 4, 4 is half-way between 3 and 5 because the shape grows blunter quickly in that region. Now suppose the level radius is pulled out lengthwise to any length needed. This line is cut into the same fractions as the circle, and from it the same heights as given by the circle are set up. A curve drawn through the points 1, 2, 3, 4, 5 is an

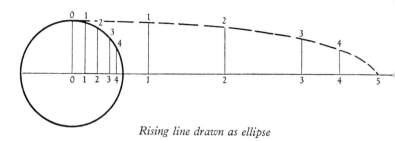

Rising line drawn as ellipse

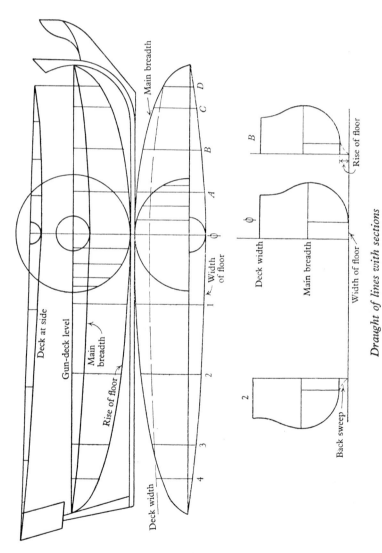

Draught of lines with sections

50

ellipse, and this was used to form the lengthwise shapes except that the portion from 4 to 5 was made less blunt. For the same reason arcs of circles of large radii were used when the curve of the lines was small in amount; such a shape would give lines with sharper ends.

The lengthwise form can now be drawn out. The place for the midship section φ is chosen. In this case it is taken five-eighths of the length from the after end of the lower gun-deck—the 'after perpendicular'. The 'rise of floor' line is drawn by striking a circle with its centre on the gun-deck level at amidships and with a radius reaching downwards to the top of the floor at its lowest point. This half-circle is used with four parts as in the method above, to describe the ellipse. The same process applies both to the forward and to the after parts, which it must be noted, are not the same lengths, one being three-eighths of the length and the other five-eighths.

Then the 'height of breadth' line, which gives the height above keel of the greatest breadth of any cross-section—is struck in like manner with a circle of small radius. This radius is about the same as the distance of the greatest breadth above the load water-line at midships. The ends of these two 'rising lines' meet the gun-deck level at the ends of the ship.

To complete the lengthwise section through the ship, the 'sheer line' of the topmost deck has to be drawn. The forward end of this deck stops short of the bow and the after end is some distance abaft the stern-post. The height above water is greater aft than forward. A straight line joins the ends of the deck and at midships is set down a small half-circle to the lowest point of the 'sheer', whence the 'sheer line' can be drawn in the same manner as for the other curves, or an arc of a circle of large radius may be drawn. The amount of 'sheer' is broadly two-thirds of that given to the 'heights of breadths' rising line.

The inner side of the stem-post is struck by a sweep with its centre at or about the gun-deck level; the forward part of the post is drawn with a straight line at a slope to the keel. The 'post', the name for the stern-post, is also drawn at a slope to the keel chosen by good practice; which slope is less than that given to the bow.

The plan of breadths in a lengthwise sense can now be drawn. It is not strictly on a level plane because of the 'sheer' of the deck and of the 'height of breadth' lines.

To construct this plan draw a centre line lengthwise, parallel to the top of the keel-line and far enough below to allow for the greatest breadths being clear of the bottom of the keel. Set out the places for the transverse sections as drawn for the upright plan. At midships ϕ describe a half-circle with radius equal to the greatest half-breadth. By the same process as before obtain the widths at the various 'stations'— the name for the transverse sections—and draw the curve to end forward and abaft at the same points as the 'rising line'. Two other curves are needed. The breadth of deck-line, which being only slightly curved, is drawn as an arc of a circle of large radius. The width of floor, or rather the half-width, is shown below the lengthwise base-line as an ellipse, using a half-circle of a radius equal to the 'flat of floor' at midships.

With these two plans drawn out, the transverse shape at any 'station' can be drawn. The figure shows how, by using a like process to that shown above in the case of Phineas Pett's design, the cross-sections at midships, at B forward and at 2 abaft can be got. It is well to notice the back sweeps at B and 2 to complete the shape into the keel. It should be said, as will be seen later, that it was the practice to draw out the shape of every frame timber in this way. The letters of the alphabet were used to give names to the forward sections while the after sections were known by numbers.

§7. ANTHONY DEANE, Kt.

DEANE was born in Harwich in 1638. Pepys first met him in 1660 when he was assistant to Christopher Pett, the master shipwright at Woolwich. It seems that Pepys had very little love for the Petts and was glad to find a young man, 'very able and able to do the King service...he would fain seem a honest man and yet will commend his work and skill and vie with others, especially the Petts'.

The clerk met Deane often in 1663 and on one visit Deane brought 'his draught of a ship and the bends (transverse sections) and the main lines in the body, very finely done, which do please me mightily and am resolved to study hard and learn of him to understand. I find him a very pretty fellow in it and rational but a little conceited, but thats no matter to me.' At that time Deane was just 25 years of age.

In 1664 he went to Harwich, which was now a king's yard, to build the *Rupert* and the *Resolution* of some 850 tons. In 1666 Pepys writes:

Mr Deane and I did discourse about his ship *Rupert* built by him which succeeds so well as he has got great honour by it and I some by recommending him: the King, Duke and everybody saying that it is the best ship that ever was built. And then he fell to explain to me his manner of casting —forecasting—the draughts of water which a ship will draw beforehand, which is a secret the King and all admire in him, and he is the first that hath come to any certainty beforehand of foretelling the draught of water of a ship before she is launched.

He seems to have known that the draught of water is given by finding the volume below water in say cubic feet, when the weight of such volume of water is equal to the weight of the ship when she floats at that water-line. This idea was first put forward by Archimedes of Syracuse who was born 287 B.C. Deane must also have been able to work out from the plan, and that very closely, the weight of hull. Records about this time give for a fourth-rate 125 ft. long on the gun-deck, a main breadth to the outside of plank of 35 ft., and a draught of water afore of 14 ft. 6 in. and abaft 15 ft. 10 in., adding that the cubic feet to the water-line is 29,814 equal to a weight of hull and guns and equipment, and four months' stores, of 851 tons 16 cwt. This is on the basis that 35 cu. ft. of sea-water weigh one ton avoirdupois—the same figure is used to-day.

Deane went to Portsmouth as master shipwright in 1668 where he built two large 100-gun ships, the *Charles Royal* and the *James Royal*. These were the greatest vessels built since the *Royal Sovereign* of Phineas Pett, some 30 years earlier. Pett had given a greater breadth to the ship than Deane did, and the *Charles Royal* had to be 'girdled' to increase the breadth of the water-line and make the ship less tender. Pepys comments in 1673 on this lack of breadth by saying 'the builders of England before that time having not well considered that breadth only would make a stiff ship'. It is curious to note that this liking for narrow ships stayed in men's minds until well into the present century. There seems perhaps an instinct that the narrow ship passed more easily through the water, whereas in the past 30 years it had been proved that breadth alone does not detract from easy travel because draught of water is also a factor.

A little later Deane asked Pepys for a book in which he might write his theory of shipping. This *Doctrine of Naval Architecture*, 1670, is in the Pepysian Library at Cambridge. It contains a series of plans for each of the six 'rates' of ships of the line. One set for a second-rate—a vessel to carry say 70 guns—is complete enough to define fully the shape of the ship, there being some eighteen transverse sections— one at every 7 ft. of length.

Some years later, in 1682, Pepys showed Evelyn:

a large folio containing the whole mechanic part of building royal ships and ships of war, made by Sir Antony Deane, being so accurate a piece from the very keel to the lead blocks, rigging, guns, victualling, manning, and even to every individual pin and nail in a method so astonishing and curious, with a draught both geometrical and in perspective and several sections that I do not think the world can show the like. I esteem this book an extraordinary jewel.

Deane became commissioner at Portsmouth in 1672. The king visited a French fleet there and being so pleased with the look of the French vessel, the *Superbe,* told Deane to build one as nearly like it as he could. This ship, the *Harwich,* of nearly 1000 tons and 70 guns, built at Harwich, proved to be the fastest vessel of the Fleet and was the first of ten sister-ships. Here it may be noted that Deane had added 31 in. to the breadth of the *Rupert,* which was of nearly the same length and depth.

Deane became Commissioner at Chatham in 1673 and was knighted the next year when he became Comptroller of Victualling. He had built three yachts, and at the request of the French king built two others which he himself brought to Havre. This French visit may have been one of the reasons for a curious charge of treason made in 1679 by a Colonel Scott, who said that Pepys and Deane had sent facts about the English navy to the French to help them to dethrone King Charles and to crush the Protestant religion. They were committed to the Tower, but let out on bail of £30,000 each. The charge was withdrawn in 1680, but it had caused Pepys to resign office.

When he came back as Secretary of the Navy in 1684 he found a grave state of affairs in the British Fleet. He urged the king to set up an inquiry and in 1686 wrote: 'the services of Sir Anthony Deane shall be secured at all costs, whose talents for this service seem to me (through every part of it) so much superior to all I ever yet met in the Navy.'

Deane had left the service in 1680, after the charge of treason, to become a private shipbuilder. He was loth to accept the post offered him, pointing out that his reward as a private builder was more than double the salary of £500 payed to a commissioner. He had a family of fifteen and was expecting more: he made an offer to attend the meetings in his spare time.

The king was not able to influence Deane. Pepys was told to submit names of proper master shipwrights as well as private builders.

His comment was that these were found a gouty, illiterate, intemperate, and ill-countenanced lot, and as a result Deane was made Commissioner on his own terms.

The Commission lasted for three years, built three fourth-rates, rebuilt 20 ships, and saw to the repair of 69 others, at a cost of $1\frac{1}{3}$ million pounds. Although there were nine members Pepys stated that 'the whole work conduct and care of it, had been upheld by two only, Sir A. Deane and Mr Hewer'—the latter looking after the accounts. Deane was made a Fellow of the Royal Society in 1681.

When James II fled the country at the end of 1688, both Pepys and Deane ended their Admiralty service. The new regime looked on them as suspect, for in 1689, and again in 1690, warrants were issued for their arrest with others. About this time Deane, who was just 50 years of age, wrote to Pepys: 'these are to let you know I am alive. I have nothing to do but read, walk and prepare for all chances attending this obliging world. I have the old soldier's request, a little space between business and the grave, which is very pleasant on many considerations.' Pepys replied in a cheerful letter, saying in his blythe way: 'the worst the world uses me, the better I am bound to use myself.'

Evelyn records in 1690: 'I dined with Mr Pepys where was that excellent Shipwright and seaman, Sir Anthony Deane. Amongst other discourse and deploring the sad condition of the Navy, as now governed by inexperienced men since this Revolution. He mentioned what exceeding advantage we of this country had by being the first who built frigats.' Deane said of the *Constant Warwick*, the first of these vessels, that she was so light and swift of sailing that in a short time she had taken as much money from privateers as would have laden her. He thought and seems to have been the first to put forward the idea that the building of capital ships was a mistake. His view was that the use of numbers of swift frigates and fire-ships would 'ruin the greatest force of such vast ships as could be sent to sea'.

From this time until he died in 1721, little is known of him beyond the gift of a mourning ring of 20s. from Pepys at his death in 1703.

Deane's work of 'finding the draught beforehand' may be taken as the first step to apply a knowledge of science to the shipwright's craft. The full title of his work is *Anthony Deane's Doctrine of Naval Architecture and Tables of Dimensions, Materials, Furniture and Equipment appertaining thereto. Written in the Yeare 1670 at the Instance of Samuel Pepys, Esq.* At the end is a set of engravings to which the title-page refers: 'With a Sett of Navall Prints engraved by R. Zeemen, publish'd by Art. Tooker and dedicated to Mr Pepys... Anno 1675.'

This treatise shows signs of being edited by Pepys himself. It is full of order and proceeds by proper steps to the logical end. Pepys seems to have tried to learn the art from Deane, the better to equip himself for his work for the Navy. Here are set forth the main details of vessels from first-rates to carry 100 guns down to sixth-rates of no more than 15 guns. Figures are given for the sizes of timbers for all classes and rules at some length for masts and rigging. In most respects this work set the pattern for the shipwright, up to 1800 and even later to the coming of the ironclad. True there were vessels of greater length than those of Deane's time; his 170 ft. became 205 ft. True also that the beam grew from 48 to 54 ft. in 1805: this was partly the result of the lack of stiffness rather common in Stuart times. There was little change in the depth of the structure at midships, and at the stern the upper works were rightly cut down.

It seems that this treatise also served as a pattern for the text-books on the shipwright's trade which began to appear from 1711 onwards, even to the manner in which the contents of these books were set out. Thus Deane starts with studies of arithmetic, mensuration and geometry—a practice to be found in some text-books even to-day.

Plates IX and X show a complete draught for a third-rate ship 153 ft. length between perpendiculars, 120 ft. on the keel with a beam of 36 ft. Details of the midship bend, with radii and centres for the sweeps, are given in a second drawing of the treatise where the whole process is set forth, step by step. The dimensions are much the same as those of the *Rupert*, the vessel which brought fame to Deane in 1666. There appears in the lengthwise section a level line at about half-depth at amidships, which gives the water-line, the draught for which is stated as 17 ft.

The cleanness of the form and its detail show the progress of nearly a century made between the first project of Matthew Baker and the later project of Anthony Deane.

The pages which follow contain details of the methods of drawing used by Deane.

ANTHONY DEANE MSS.
PEPYSIAN LIBRARY NO. 2910

Rules for Drawing the Bends

𝕹𝖔𝖜 all the lines are prepared for sweeping out the Midship Bend, I take from my scale one fourth part of my whole Breadth of my Shipp which is 9 foot and set one leg of my compasses in ye flower line at *K* and sweep it from *H* to *L*, this sweepe is called ye Flower Sweepe, haveing don with that I take 7/9 of the flower sweepe and stricke it under the Breadth line downeward from *E* to *N* and the center *M*....

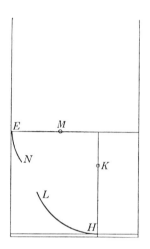

𝕳𝖆𝖛𝖊𝖎𝖓𝖌 prepared those two sweepes above mentioned I take of 20/36 of my breadth setting one leg of my compasses in *O* and strike the line. From *L* to *N* the sweepe is the sweepe with which maketh the upper and lower futtucke moulldes as you will peceave ere you have don....

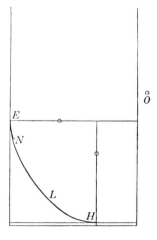

57

𝕳𝖆𝖛𝖊𝖎𝖓𝖌 don all my sweepes
under ye breadth I come unto
my top timber; for which I take
17/18 of the half breadth which is seaventene
foot setting one leg of my compasses in *P* and
stricke ye sweepe from *E* to *R*, haveing don that
I take the same sweepe and stricke a hollow for
the head of the top timber, by the same radious
the last was strucke by and sweepe out the
hollow sweepe from *S* to *R* which sweepe com-
pleates the bends of timber by which you are
to make the moulds for two gradiate all the rest
of the bends of timbers and for the whoulle
Frame....

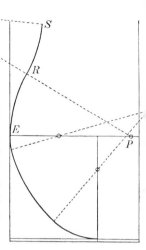

𝕺𝖓𝖊 the last place you were showne how ye
half bends of timbers were swept out by w^ch
you were to make your Moulds and being made
with a good scarfe for every timber you are to
proceed in ye sweeping out ye remaining parts
of the ship afte as you find out one within another where ye shipp is compleated, but for
feare raiseing them may be to dark for ye under-
standing I will show you one example more to
make you p-fit and shall suppose I were to raise
ye bend of timbers it is where I do thus. I look
at my draft and take ye riseing from ye pole to
ye line where it stands on ye draft wch I set of
from ye line *A*, *B* and is ye line *C*, *D*, haveing
done that, I take allso from my draft ye narrowing of my flower wch I set of ye line *D*, *E* and
is ye line *F*, *G* this is ye narrowing of flower,
haveing done that I take from my draft ye Height
of Breadth at 15 wch I set of from ye line *A*, *B*,
and is the line *H*, *I*, haveing done that I take
from my draft ye narrowing of greatest breadth
at 15 which I set of from *I* to *H* and ye like
narrowing and riseing for ye top timber head
which is ye line *K*, *L*, now haveing set of all ye
narrowings and hights in every place I proced
to swepe ye flower sweepe 9 foot as ye former

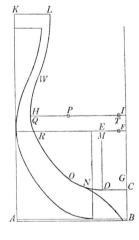

setting one leg of my compasses in *P* and
sweeping under breadth from *Q* to *R* haveing
don that I take the same 20 foot swepe of my
Midship Bend and set one leg in *S* and sweepe
from *R* to *O*, haveing don that I keep my center
all for ye top timbers as in ye Midships, setting
one leg at *T* and sweepe from *Q* to *W* and from
that ye follow sweepe as in ye other observing
to fetch out ye hollow at ye stearne, all ye
sweepes being thus struck you have ye ½ bends
of timbers compleated at 15 in like man^g and
all the other....

This latter is noe other than ye former for its
nature of workeing only as ye last was ye bend
of timbers aftward on marked 15 this shall be a
bend of timbers forward named *N* which is set
of by ye narrowings and riseings as ye other onely
as ye one is worked afte on the starboard side ye
other is wrought on ye larboard side that one
suite of moulds may serve your turne to build
by, as for example I look on ye drafte and take
ye true riseing from *N* where it stands on ye
keele to ye riseing line and set it of from ye line
A, B which is ye line *C, D*, this is ye riseing line,
then I take from my drafte ye narrowing and set
from ye line *A, E* which is the line *F, G* ye
riseing and narrowing or ye breadth is the same
as is often shewen, haveing thus done I proceed
to sweepe by the same sweepes as above sweepe-
ing out from *H* to *I* ye flower sweepe and from
K to *L* under ye breadth from *K* to *M* above
ye breadth and from *M* to *N* the top of the side,
which I hope by this you see perfect the riseing
of the whole ship's boddy in every part onely as
you have these single ye other be one within
an other as you will find in ye next place you
come at as appear to your better sattisfaction....

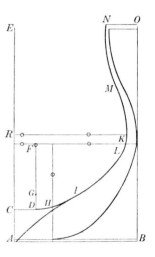

𝕳𝖊𝖗𝖊 [Pls. IX & X] you finde the whole body finished wth every line in its place, from wch is raised the severall bends of tymbers, being every third tymber from stem to sterne and doe stand just on the keele where you see the severall figures and letters marked, they are derived from six lines namely the Narrowing of Breadth, Height of Breadth, Narrowing of Flower, Riseing of Flower, Narrowing of the Topp Tymbers, Riseing of the Topp Tymbers, wch is the top of the side from all wth every bend of timber receing his part beeing guided by a square and all other works are truley performed and after they bee raised by these for breadth and height they are swept out by severall sweepes to make ye best bends and swiftest motion and soe full or leane as to cause the ship to carry all her weight wch is propper for her force, in fine these bends of tymber are ye greatest art wch belong to the Master Builder and have soe much of variety in them as you can have imaginations in ye thoughts as you will finde when you perceive the worde, and since ye variety is so greate on which depends ye good quality of the shipp, ye shall be showne a way to finde every part of Breadth, Depth and Sweepe which shall soe compleate your Shipps Bends, soe as to reconsile the way of ye Shipp to the Rother [Rudder] and alsoe a faire entrance into the water forward unto ye bildge and yet neither fuller nor leaner in no part under water than such as to cause her to cary her proportion stores and Gunnes and not to exceed the draught of watter spoken of nor want quality to any yet built. In short when you are fully senseable of this method you shall find the Boddy soe cleane under watter and her shapes so fine above watter as nothing more can bee added. And if so it must be concluded a good Essay to make a perfect Builder. And because this work now it is added together hath many lines I shall only name you these wch the severall bends are raised by and soe stands one with another those wth the figgures being the half breadth afte and those wth ye letters the halfe breadth of the severall bends forward, the raiseing of each bend is showed you more cleare in the last leafe you came from soe that my aime must bee here to show you them altogether and lett you see the Body in its true shape wch would be done could you but remove every one of those severall bends of tymbers and sett them on the keele according to their place as ye severall of bends aft wch is 3, 6, 9, 12, 15, 18, 21, 24, 27, and where sett thwart on the keele at the same figgures of 3, 6, 9, 12 and the like it would show you the shape of all ye shipp aft which now you see flatt, also those several bends you find marked with *A, D, G, K, N, Q* being removed from the flatt to their places one the keele where the like letters are of *A, D, K, N, Q*, it would make the whole body complete forward on, and then would you see the figgure of the shipp as they are a building which now appears flatt, and having now made and finished all ye Bends putt them to proofe whether they bee good or bad, by setting of soe many parallel lines beginning at the draught of

PLATE IX

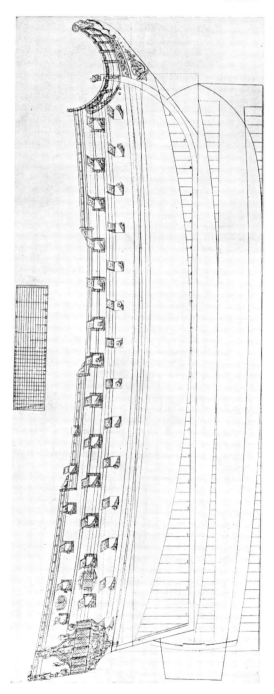

PLATE X

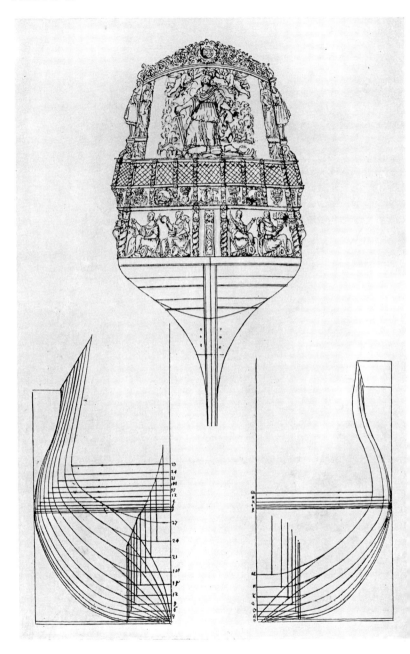

STERN VIEW AND TRANSVERSE SECTIONS OF THE *RUPERT*

Seventeene foot watter wch is don thus. Draw a line through all ye bends of timbers at the height as the pricked line crossing all ye Bends at *L, M* wch don take of the breadth at every Bend by his name and carry it to ye ½ breadth against each figgure where it doth belong setting one legg of ye compass in the line of the bottom of the keele and the other where that breadth will fall, haveing thus don to every bend throughout ye whole shipp you will find what line those points will make, this line I call the water line or seat of the shipp at her greatest depth of watter, having done wth that I proceed, to sett of one more at 15 feet water at lines *N, O*, and alsoe downwards untill I have seene how the body is shaped until I come next the keele haveing taken the paines and findeing all those lines to goe faire making neither swell nor cling I conclude my worke to be good aft agreeing wth the ould lesson where wee began every line beeing a part of the Circle and is reconsiled to every breadth of the shipp which is as great a truth as can be aforded for soe much sterne, bow and the like and untill you finde some better way I advise this to bee practized by Reason this beeing thus performed shall not miss one of the quallities afore mentioned and ye shall still see more clearer ere I leave you. And so proceed to the next place to show you the reason of swiming or stricking by the Hydrostaticall rule, it beeing worthy of yor paines and indeede no one cann bee a Good Shipwright who is not very perfect in this matter it beeing the dependency of our draught of watter which you shall clearely discover when you have perused it.

§8. THE STUARTS

JAMES VI of Scotland came to the throne of England in 1603 at the age of thirty-seven. It has been said that the place of the masculine Elizabeth Tudor was filled by the feminine James Stuart. Charnock wrote: 'Naturally of a pacific disposition which appeared to border on timidity, he was averse, not only to war but even to that inferior degree of spirit and love of enterprise, which was necessary to promote and protect the commerce of the people.'[1] The times were such that need drove him to appoint an inquiry into the cost of the Navy, which was asked to look into 'very great and intolerable abuses, deceits, frauds, corruptions, negligences, misdemeanours and offences' that were made by officers and others working for the Navy.

At the start of his reign he was able to make a peace with Spain which gave to England the freedom of the seas of Europe. Sir Walter Raleigh after 13 years in the Tower was let out to lead by king's orders

---

[1] *History of Marine Architecture* (1801–2).

a voyage to Guiana, from which great treasure was to result. He lacked good ships and was beaten by the Spaniards, so after that 'sea-whiff between dungeon and death' he lost his head to placate the Spaniards.

The king gave great help to the East India Company and lent his presence and his aid to help them to combine the various factions in 1613 to become the United East India Company. Their fleet for this venture had a warlike aspect with its well-armed ships, since at that time the Royal Navy could not protect them further than the Cape of Good Hope. It was well that they were armed since they were able to defeat a Portuguese attack when they reached India.

Phineas Pett, by the use of a model which he made for Prince Henry was the means whereby the king in 1608 made up his mind to build the great ship, the *Prince Royal*. The master shipwrights, almost to a man, made protest that such a project was beyond Pett's knowledge and skill. The question was set down for a hearing before the inquiry into the Navy, which was then under way. In the end the king himself had to take a part, which he did with skill and great judgement. It was found that Pett was correct as to the art of building, but that he had been careless in choosing timber and that his figure of costs, already high, was much more than the State could afford. Pett's Diary deals at length with the account of his success and he went on to build the *Prince Royal* which was launched in 1610. He relates that at the end of the hearing Prince Henry 'called with a high voice in these words: "where be now these perjured fellows that dare thus abuse his majesty with these false informations: do they not worthily deserve hanging?".'

The abuses brought up in 1608 were still rampant in 1618 when a Grand Commission of the Navy was set up. This body stayed in being until Charles I came to be king in 1625, and was granted a new warrant in 1628.

These same abuses led to the founding of the Shipwrights Company, to which body James gave a Charter in 1605 in a worthy attempt to ensure better skill in the craft. The terms of this Charter were added to in great detail in 1612 because it did not appear that much notice had been taken of the first attempt. There arose a struggle between an older City Company of the Free Shipwrights of London, which in the Charter of 1612 led to the newer Company's being known not as the Shipwrights of England but as the Shipwrights of Redrith (Rother-hithe). In short the control of the craft was driven without the City

The Free Shipwrights pursued their claim, bringing actions in the Admiralty Court throughout the seventeenth century. The struggle ended with a prayer to the House of Commons in 1705 to bring in a new Charter 'for the better breeding of Shipwrights and for the more firm and well building of ships and other vessels'. The House did not accept the motion to refer to a committee and this effort to improve the craft failed after a dispute lasting 100 years.

When Charles came to the throne in 1625 the increase in the Navy was well in hand, and Buckingham the favourite became Lord High Admiral. The restless spirit of the French under Richelieu, and the envy of the Dutch in regard to the freedom of the seas, began to rouse alarm. Charles, like his father, strove with Parliament. He raised money by forced loans, and by the ship-money tax, levied on inland towns as well as sea ports. He was able to display the flag in force, whereby the French and the Dutch were awed and the Spaniards driven to own that Britain had a natural right to the control of the narrow seas.

In spite of his troubles, Charles got the idea that he too must have a great ship—larger and more ornate than any vessel yet. In 1634 he told Phineas Pett of his wish and the scheme for her building was signed in the king's own handwriting on 7 April 1635, and slightly changed 10 days later.

The length of keel was set out as 126 ft., the breadth as 46 ft. 6 in., the draught of water as 18 ft. 9 in. The depth of the structure was about 40 ft. above the keel at amidships. Phineas Pett gave the building of the ship to his son young Peter Pett—'the most ingenious sonne of so much improved a father who before he was full five and twenty yeares of age, made the model. . . .' The *Sovereign of the Seas*, as she was called, was launched in October 1637, and in August of the next year was taken out for trial in the Channel as far as Shoreham on the South Coast.

When the clash with Parliament took active shape in 1642 that body was keenly aware of the need to control the Navy. On 20 August Colonel Sir John Seaton and Edwyn Sandis were sent on behalf of the Committee of Public Safety to Chatham Dockyard, which was surrendered to them by Captain Pett when he saw their warrant. They placed a guard on board the *Sovereign* and a little later Phineas Pett, because of his ready response to order, was made a commissioner of the Navy.

The Commonwealth paid urgent heed to the need for a strong Navy fearing that other States might take action against them because of the recent revolt. The tonnage of the fleet was raised $2\frac{1}{2}$ times in 11 years. This building of new ships was needed for the struggle with Holland and Spain, and the mere display of force at sea raised the prestige of England higher than ever before.

In 1660 Samuel Pepys, then 28 years old, began his service with the Admiralty of which he became the first secretary, an office which he kept until 1688, the year of the Revolution.

James II was having his portrait painted by Kneller as a gift to Pepys when the news was brought of the landing of William of Orange. The king told the painter to go on and finish the picture so that his good friend might not be let down. (Pepys during his naval service had been often in daily touch with James when as Duke of York he held the office of Lord High Admiral.)

Pepys withdrew to private life after the Revolution, but kept keenly in touch with human affairs until his death in 1703.

His service to his country deserves highest praise as does his service to all time. He made a collection of the manuscripts of his day which is now kept in the Pepysian Library at Magdalene College, Cambridge. Without his keen love of history the knowledge of the manner in which the shipwright's trade grew up would have been a matter only of surmise. Would that another such man had lived to record the story of the next century after him! At his death, it was written of him that he had been the greatest and the most useful of ministers. He laid down the main rules and establishments of the Admiralty, and brought up most of its officers. All his acts were subject to order and discipline. He saw to it that all to whom he gave his support were sober men, willing to work, fitted for the post, and such as could command respect. He did not swerve from these views for any influence, even of the highest. He feared no one, he courted no one, nor did he seek his own fortune. Throughout his life his concern for the arts and sciences was great; he became President of the Royal Society in 1684, an office which he held for two years.

James II carried on the Stuart concern for the fleet. He set up a new Commission which by 1688 had placed the Navy in such good order that it had nearly 100 fighting ships of some 90,000 tons, with some 30,000 men and 6400 guns.

Under William, 30 ships ranging in size from 1100 to 900 tons were begun in 1690; the largest carried 80 and the smallest 60 guns. When Anne came to the throne in 1702, England owned one-third of the whole naval power of Europe, equal to the fleets of both France and Holland. All through her short reign wars against France and Spain and throughout Europe raged up to the year before she died in 1714, after signing the Treaty of Utrecht. From this time began the hold which England had on Europe, and made her to a great extent the shaper of the future fate of the world.

§9. THE SHIPBUILDERS ASSISTANT

OR SOME ESSAYS TOWARDS COMPLEATING THE ART OF MARINE ARCHITECTURE

THE first text-book[1] for shipwrights was written by William Sutherland, who calls himself shipwright and mariner. Nothing is known of Sutherland but what he himself says in the preface:

'Tis the Product of 32 years Study and Experience; for 'tis very well known that I have been so long employ'd in Her Majesty's Service, and that of her Royal predecessors; so that I may say, I was in a manner born a Seaman, as most of my Ancestors were. My Grandfather was Foreman to the Shipwrights in Her Majesty's Yard at Deptford 30 years, my uncle Mr Bagwell died Master Builder of her Majesty's Yard at Portsmouth, my Father and several of my relations were Master Carpenters in the Royal Navy, and I myself have had the honour to act in the Quality of Master Carpenter of three of Her Majesty's Ships, and for fifteen years last past have served Her Majesty in the Inspection and Direction of the work done by part of the Shipwrights at Portsmouth and Deptford Yards. During which time I have made it my Study to forward Youth and make them expert in the Art of Shipbuilding.

The author proceeds to state the purpose of the book. From it the landowner can learn the kind of timber which is wanted for ships, and the shipwright is shown how to make the best use of timber for frames and planks. There is a section which shows how to measure 'tunnage' which should help owners to know what ships 'will safely bear'. The subject of masts and rigging is dealt with in much detail. The main features of the sail plan, the places for the masts and yards, were drawn out by the shipwright, from which the master riggers took over the work. In this they were guided by tables setting forth the sizes of the parts; the basis for these tables seems to have been the data given in the thesis of Anthony Deane.

[1] *The Shipbuilders Assistant* (1711).

65

The preface ends with these words:

I shall add no more, but heartily to desire it may answer the End I design'd by it, which is a general Good to these Kingdoms. If it proves so, it will be a Motive to a further Application of my Thoughts on this subject, which if duly prosecuted, I doubt not but in time it may be made appear, that Ship-building may be reduced to a certain Principles, and explained by a clear and demonstrable Rules, as any other Art whatever.

The first essay describes in quaint manner the outline of the science of those days. It refers to the great knowledge in 'Mathematics and most Parts of Philosophy'. Regular curves are such as the shapes got from plane sections of cones, whereas irregular curves have points of inflection where the curve is 'reverted'. Mention is made of the 'Solid of Least Resistance', as worked out by Sir Isaac Newton, which was thought to be very useful in building ships:

'Tis generated by the Rotation of a crooked (curved) Line about its axis, and is blunt and flat-headed. But being form'd by one Rotation, the Water equally effects it, and every Particle of Water passes direct, without being confused, or divided into irregular Shapes.

The essay goes on by showing the need to study nature, and how the forms of fish and birds, among others mackerels, dolphins and ducks, may give a guide to the best forms of ships. This idea of the dolphin-form for the shape below water was also studied by Matthew Baker. To quote Sutherland:

To see a Duck swim is not unpleasant, how nicely she makes her Stroke, and swiftly moves her large body, with only two Feet like Paddles in comparison with the Body so drove. And indeed the Bodies of such Creatures being Mathematically form'd according to their Length, Breadth and Depth, 'tis altogether impossible to mend their Shape, but they may be of service to us in laying down such Mathematical Rules, as are used in forming them.

The subjects of mechanics and hydrostatics call for comment. A knowledge of the lengthwise centre of gravity is needed to judge where the masts should be placed. It is pointed out that the weight of a floating body is equal to the room taken up by her under-water volume 'so that the whole Ship Equipping and what weighs or leans upon her, presses neither more not less upon the Bottom she swims over, than as much Water as is equal in Bulk to that part of the Ship which is beneath the Surface of the Water'.

From these ideas rules can be drawn up by which to equip, load and trim a ship, both for 'motion and conveniency'. The curves needed for the body of the ship are those formed by some line between a cone and a cylinder; solids got by turning around a lengthwise axis some shape lying between a rectangle and a triangle. The use of such methods will make the art perfect and help to avoid serious faults. Further, the use of proper plans will save waste of timber, on which subject the writer dwells at length, both as to the nature of the wood and its cost.

The third essay deals with 'Marine Architecture'—the mechanical part of the building of ships. A solid site is wanted on which to build the ship and the need to use sound material. Easy access to all parts of the ship is wanted, and order and method will secure a proper balance between the whole and its parts. Beauty and harmony are worthy of study; the whole fabric ought to conform to the rules of art to make it agreeable and to appear pleasing to the spectators. Lastly, the question of expense of timber and the transport to the building yard require thought.

Sutherland, in common with others of that time, showed much concern at the neglect and lack of esteem which was felt by the ship-wright's trade, so that men were put out of love with its study:

..tho' it so far exceeds several other Arts and Sciences that a proper and regular Ship cannot be composed or built, without making several other Sciences subservient to this; as Arithmetic, Geometry, with the Knowledge of the Laws of Motion, and the different Increase between Rest and the greatest Motion, as also how Bodies gravitate; and to order the Equipping, the Experience whereof is the noblest Part, without which all the rest would be but insignificant. But he that has acquir'd both the Theory and Practice makes an accomplish'd Shipwright!

One purpose of this essay was to expose those who pretend to lay down the rudiments and style themselves complete masters of ship-building, without having the least insight of what they pretend to:

..the proper business of a Shipwright is counted a very vulgar Imploy; and which a Man of very indifferent Qualifications may be Master of. Many have as mean an Opinion of it, as a certain Gentleman, who told one of our former Master Builders, that he had a Blockhead of a Son uncapable to attain any other Trade unless that of a Ship-carpenter, for which he design'd him.

Indeed the Business of Shipbuilding is of a large extent so that Men very meanly qualified may pass amongst a Crowd of good Artificers; but this is no Reflection upon it, that some unskilful Persons may be employ'd but an Argument of its general Use, since none can call themselves accomplish'd Shipwrights without several distinguishing Qualifications.

And certainly *England* may challenge the whole World for able Ship-wrights and Sea Discipline. I have a due Veneration for several Gentlemen in very good Posts for Management of Ship-building; notwithstanding I am well assured there are others well qualified, who have but very indifferent Encouragement. But I still hope that Truth may discover Itself in mean Language, as well as a wife and honest Man in mean Habit.

Under the title of 'Solidity' the author deals with the method of building a ship on a slipway and launching her into the water. He observes quaintly that the knowledge of Newton's Second Law of Motion should be in the mind of every master builder if he hopes to lower a vessel from the 'launch' into the water. Divers ships have stood fast on the very place they were first erected. Others, before the shores were cleared away, have without warning run away with such speed as to hurt workmen and the too curious spectators—'why such Variety in Launching has happened is yet a Paradox to most Men'.

To choose the place for the building slipway needs much thought. The ground must be made solid, the angle of launching chosen, the draught of water at the end of the 'ways' has to be taken into account, so that the ship may not plunge too much and strike the ground when she takes the water.

The site must be made strong enough to support the keel blocks which take the weight of the ship. The same remark applies to the laying of the 'bulge ways' which are lengthwise planks on which run the cradle to carry the ship when she is being launched into the water. Support is given by large pieces of timber called groundways, shown by *c*'s in Figs. *A* and *B*. On these are laid the keel blocks of hard knotty stuff. The topmost pieces—the splitting blocks—are of the freest timber that can be got so as to be split out with ease, when the launchways are put in place and wedged to take the weight of the ship. On these pieces, *a*'s, the keel is laid, trimmed, scarphed and rabbeted, set very straight and level. The keel is let into the splitting blocks $1\frac{1}{2}$ in., and the stops so formed confine and keep it right in its place.

The exact length is set off forward and aftward, from the 'touch' or place at the stem, where the keel's upper part 'ends to be streight. The stem is scarphed to the keel and the post at the stern is fixed by a 'tenant' or tenon. The stem and false stem or 'apron' are raised is one piece as are also the stern-post with 'transoms' and 'fashion pieces' all joined. If the ship is large, the stern-post is first set up and the other pieces added later.

The stem and stern-post are set 'out of winding' with and square to the keel—'out of winding' means getting the middle lines of the pieces into the same place and upright. The transoms, and chiefly the wing-transom, should be set level and well secured with 'shores' which ought to be placed on 'timber sholes all well nog'd or trig'd'. (A shore is a long pole to support the piece, a shole is a flat plank placed below the heel of the shore, and 'well nog'd and trig'd' means that a treenail is driven into the shole to trig the shore.)

Special mention is made of the 'crossing' of the timbers, by which is meant that since the curves of the ribs alter when going forward or aft, the moulds tend to lie across each other and thus care is needed to see that each frame is set in its proper place.

Every other floor timber is first put up and bolted through the keel. A ribbon, or ribband, is hung up at the 'floor sirmark' near the head or outer end of the floor. (A ribband is a piece of fir some 5 in. square; the floor sirmark is the mark on the moulds at which the level of the timber is shown.) If the shape is fair, the ribband is nailed and shored to take the weight. The floors must be put into correct place, for this 'is the first and principal seat which bears the ship', so the shores must be nogged to make them very secure. The floor timbers are filled in and the dead wood both forward and aft is built up. The half-timbers which do not cross the keel are put in place, and then the 'kelson' or keelson is run over the floors and scored where it crosses them. The keelson is scarphed and bolted through the floors to the keel.

When the frames reach the 'greatest breadth', a ribband is put on the proper level shown by the 'breadth sirmark', which is in such place that one 'wale' can be fitted later without taking it down. (As will be seen later, a band of three or four strakes of thick plank, known as 'thick stuff', is worked fore and aft in the way of the 'greatest breadth', along the line of the lower gun-deck. This band of planks known as the 'main wale'.)

The frames are now 'cross-pal'd', which means that light square planks are placed 'thwartship at about the deck-levels to keep the frames in place until the deck-beams are fitted. The ribbands are now scored and nogged, for the breadth sirmarks 'are the second seat of bearing...'tis certain if the Floor Sirmarks and the Breadth Sirmarks

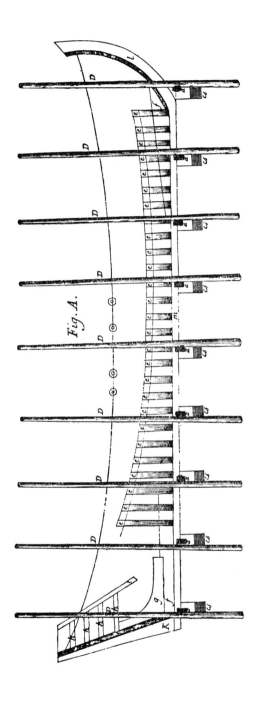

Fig. A.

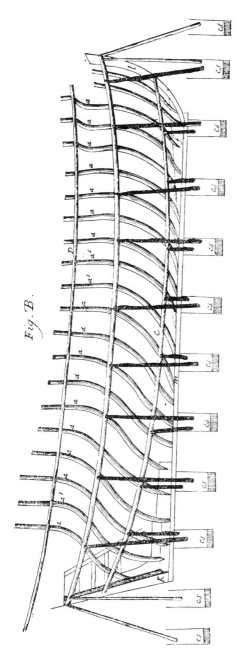

Fig. B.

Erecting the ship on the launchway

71

be not very well level'd you mar the whole work'. Without care a 'lapsided' ship may result and the vessel when built 'list' to one side.

The two Figs. *A* and *B*, with their captions, show very nearly the technique as given by Sutherland. There is only one point which he fails to explain and that is the ram-line. This line is a rope slung between the bow and the stern to show the middle line of the ship and from which plumb-bobs show the centre of the ship where needed.

Moulding Ships Timbers

The word 'mould' is used in two ways. First as a verb meaning 'to mould', that is to mark out any part of a ship by means of a pattern. It is also used as the name for a mould or pattern made out of slips of thin wood—'batting or batten'—and tacked to fix the shape of a timber or other piece.

When the length, breadth, depth and so forth are settled a 'draught' is made of 'her several shapes'. The draught—a drawing—is first set out on large paper and the scale for the purpose is mainly 1 to 48. 'So that 'tis to be understood that every $\frac{1}{4}$ of an inch on the Paper is a Foot or 12 Inches on a Platform fitted for that Purpose.' It is curious to remark that the common practice to-day, nearly 250 years later, is to make the first drawings on paper to this actual scale—$\frac{1}{48}$ full size. From the paper the figures are taken and 'laid off' or 'laid down' to the actual full size on the mould-loft floor, so as to get the true shape of each frame from which to make the moulds, and this too is modern practice. It is noted later that in 1677 Anthony Deane and Phineas Pett gave orders 'to lay 200 deals for the laying the mold for building the new ship'.

The Platform fitted for such a Design is call'd a Mould-loft; and in large Yards, where Great Ships are built, it is a spacious Floor with large and convenient Lights, disposed as much as possible for a direct Reception of the Light. The Floor is laid very smooth and even, and to render the Marks, which among Shipwrights are generally of Chalk, the more conspicuous, the Floor is wash'd over with black Size.

When the floor is laid, dry and seasoned deal is planed smooth to make the moulds, and to provide the 'Instruments which we term Sweeps to Mark out the Curves that compose the Body'. If the place is large enough a lengthwise section through the middle of the ship is set out to show the keel, the stem and the stern as well as the places for each frame. Here is also drawn the rising line and half-breadth lines or indeed all the lengthwise lines that form the ship's body, 'since it will be moulded much truer from Lines drawn at large, than from a Draught, which is but as 1 to 48, compared to the Ship's Body'.

Of Sutherland's Fig. *D*, here shown, the right-hand half gives the shape of every timber in the afterpart of the ship, and on the left-hand

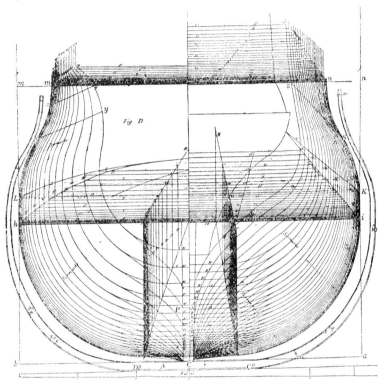

Lines of each frame as drawn on the mould-loft floor

are shown the curves of the bow frame. In the actual book the copper plate is drawn to the standard of $\frac{1}{4}$ in. to 1 ft. The actual width *a* to *b* is 38 one-quarter inches or 38 ft. for the breadth of this 1000-ton ship. The height of *m, m* and *n, n* above the base *a, b* is 30 ft. The lines shown are the actual shape of the *after* side of the frame timber for the *forward* half of the ship, and the *forward* side of the timber for the *after* body. It is from this edge of the frame that the 'bevels' are marked off. As the plank has to bed evenly on the frame it follows that since one face of the timber is kept square to the keel (or is kept in a transverse plane), the other face has to be trimmed away to slope inwards forward and aft from the shape shown by the mould itself. In the usual way timbers are cut square to the mould, and the 'bevels' or angles to follow the plank are shaped later by the shipwright.

To lay down this body as is shown in Fig. D the base-line a, b is drawn level through the line of the rabbet at the keel. Set up three lines square there to a and b to give the greatest half-breadth and a third line at C to mark the centre line of the ship.

The 'height of breadth' is given by levels through h and i for the midship section. There are also higher points L and K to show the upper 'height of breadth'. Sutherland puts in brackets: 'as regards upper Height of Breadth (if you approve of any)'. The purpose of this upper and lower height was to keep a vertical side for say 3 ft. at amidships falling off to nothing at the end as the figure suggests. With such a wedge the form kept its buoyant shape for a transverse heel up to some 10°. In Sutherland's own words 'from h to L and from i to K is streight, approved on to make a Ship stiff, or bear Sail, which is undeniably a good Faculty for that purpose'.

There are lines sloping upwards and inwards which are called 'sirmarks' which show on the mould where the 'bevels' of the frames are to be cut. The upper sirmarks show the breadth for the top of the structure or at the top timber where the frames end.

The flat of the floor is set off amidships as at P giving the 'rising' and the 'half-width'. From this point P there is a line sloping upwards and inwards which shows the 'narrowing' of the floor towards the end. For the forward body the width of floor comes to nothing at the end, but for the after-part the sloping line ends at 36 giving a fair width from the centre line—this in order to give greater width at the stern where it is wanted for the cabins and so forth.

From these two lower lines there is drawn a cage-work of upright lines with a further sloping line at the top running from r to M. This line r, M gives the centres from which sweeps are struck from the floor to the lower 'height of breadth' levels. These various heights of breadth are set off from the lengthwise plan and from the half-breadth plan, and thus the shape of every section may be struck both below and above.

In this more simple method, Sutherland says, for the midship bend draw a sweep with centre at r and with radius r, P in one piece from P to h 'which will describe a Midship Bend more agreeable and less perplexing than if you was to chalk out 100 Segments of Circles'. This is very true in a sense, but ignores the trouble caused by the 'reverse' sweeps which are needed to complete the shape down to the keel. These sweeps are very obvious on the Fig. D. He remarks rightly that he could well end the form without reverse sweeps and make something which he describes as a true 'conoid'. 'But such a shape being not approved on, 'tis thought proper to carry down every Timber to the Keel by reverting the Curve'. To get over this trouble he suggests the use of a 'rising streight line' to mark the tangent point where the reverse sweep meets the circular arcs.

To complete the upper works, sweeps are struck from the upper breadth line, such as K, S and L, S. These sweeps have the same radius throughout, that is both forward and aft. They are used in 'reverse' to end at the top timber height and thus complete the form of the frame timber. Broadly these two curves join along the lines $S-z$, $S-y$, about half the height to the top timber from the upper breadth line.

In Figs. E and F the hoop drawn around the main body shows how the midship timber is made out from a base line $Co-Do$. The floor timber crosses the keel and extends to some 9 ft. on each side, one end of which is shown I, a. From there the distance to the top of the frame is some 32 ft. which is much too long to be made in one piece of 'compass' timber, so it has to be run in two parts which meet at I, e. The lower half of this has a curious name—'second foot-hook' (now 'futtock')—and the upper-half is named the top timber. The question now comes how to join the ends to make a strong frame. The joints of the butts of timber must from their nature be very weak and a number of ways were tried with more or less success. The method which became common was to run a second rib nearby from keel to top, with its joints midway or so between the joints of the main frame. This twin member, when the planks were fixed to it, could be looked on as a 'compound' frame. This second rib is shown in Fig. F. It does not cross the keel but starts at $2a$, reaching to $2b$, which part is known as the 'first foot-hook'. It laps over the head of the floor timber and ends about the middle of the second futtock. Above this comes the third futtock which reaches to the middle of the top timber of the main frame. This part is ended by the fifth futtock which extends to the same height as the top timber. Even this complex structure did not prove sound in practice, and somewhere about 1800 all the joints of the timber were fitted with round dowels fitted into each timber to prevent sideways movement. Before this came about, and there was trouble in finding enough compass timber, the ends of the portions were connected by chocks of the shape of a triangle; this again, owing to trouble in fitting, was not found good practice.

This compound frame counts as one rib and the distance between two such frames taken lengthwise is known as 'room and space'—the 'room' being the part taken by the double frame, and the 'space', the gap between. The parts of the frame were of less thickness upwards, but the two faces of the frame and of the futtock frame were kept parallel. In such a ship as drawn the 'room and space' would be about 2 ft. 5 in. Two terms are used to describe the 'scantlings'—the measures of the timbers—the 'siding' or the width of the frame on the 'side' of the ship on which the plank bears. The other figure relates to the 'depth' which is called the 'moulding'. Thus in this case the 'siding' of the midship floor would be 1 ft. 2 in. and of the first futtock also 1 ft. 2 in. The 'moulding' at the head of the floor timber is some 12 in. Both 'siding' and 'moulding' get less as the frame grows upwards, to accord with a plan of taper which is shown below the shape of the 'mould' in Fig. G.

All other frame bends are set out in the same fashion, as the figure shows, except for the last frame aft where the square transom joins the curved hull. 'But you must observe first to pitch upon the Fashion of your foremost and aftermost Timber, which upwards chiefly depends on Fancy; for some chose to work more hollow, and some less, between the Breadth and the Top-timber Sirmark.'

Sutherland is careful to point out the need to check the 'smoothness' of the form. In his remarks occurs the first mention of horizontal parallels—which are really water-lines drawn parallel to the keel. The old shipwrights rightly saw that the test of smoothness of the shape is best shown by diagonal planes such as used for the 'sirmarks'.

It would also be very proper to try the Ribbon Lines, whether they are truly circular, according to the Shape of the Body where they are placed Which Custom would be much better than to prove the Horizontal Parallels, or what we call making fair Water-lines; since the Plank is placed upon a Ship according to the Direction of the Ribbons, which is nearly shew'd in the Figures by the Lines mark'd Sirmark, or those drawn at Right Angles from every Segment that composes the Ship's Timbers. It also shews you the true Course of the Water by the Ship, so that a great deal of Nicety ought to be used in adjusting those Lines, to make them truly circular.

Such material Cases being truly proved, and the Body adjusted in every respect, a Mould or Pattern may be made for every Segment sufficient to mark or mould out the Timbers. And the moulding the Timbers from such Patterns cannot be too well perform'd, but ought to be done by an able and throughly experienc'd Shipwright, both for the Preservation and Conversion of the Timber; so that no Errors may happen, but when the Timbers are put into their Places, they may be exact and fit, according to the design'd Shape. And no Piece should be moulded streighter than its Growth or natural Grain, but as circular as possible. Neither should any Piece be taken that will work longer or make a greater Length; but a Piece, or Chok, ought rather to be allow'd at each End within. Nor should large Pieces be applied to smaller Uses than what is requisite. Care ought likewise to be taken not to mould any Pieces that are rotten, or any way defective, both from the Consideration of the Charge of Workmens Wages, and spoiling such Pieces that might otherwise do Service for some Uses.

Of Planking Outboard

In Sutherland's words:

Planking...which is a Branch so very material, that unless it be carefully done, it will undeniably mar all the other good Properties belonging to any Ship. For Planking a Ship is like the Skin, Sinews and Ligaments to an Animal. But then the outside Planking is not barely meant, but all Clamps, Spirkit-risings, and thick Stuff, besides Wales, Channel-wales without board. This part of Planking ought to be well performed, by Joining, Fastening and Calking, and the Goodness of every Inch of those Materials carefully inspected.

The lower part from the keel upwards to the main wales is the first to be tackled, and planks are worked at the same time from the keel upwards and from the main wales downwards.

In Sutherland's time the main wales were planks of thick stuff worked above and below the line of the lower gun-deck beams, and also in the way of the main deck beams. They were really planks of thick stuff of large depth and about 8 in. thick. 'Plank' was the term used when the thickness was from 4 in. to $1\frac{1}{2}$ in. Below this size the word used was 'boards' and above this size 'thick stuff' was the name given. Between then and 1750 the wales had become a belt of timber worked in four layers of planks, thus in effect filling the space between the two wales with the same thickness of thick stuff—say four strakes of timber some 12 in. broad and 8 in. thick.

Wales were curved, just as ribbands were curved to follow the 'height of breadth' line, the deck-line, and the sheer-line. The main wale was the name given to the belting in the way of the lower gundeck which runs more or less along the 'height of breadth' line. Besides this there were other wales higher up in the ship of which the channel wales, in way of the deck above, were made of great strength because to these were fixed the preventer stays which came down from

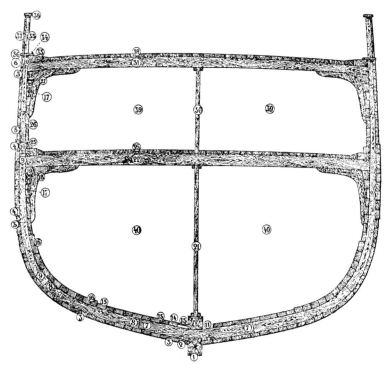

Midship section of wooden hull

the channel, which stuck out from the deck above, and to which the blocks that took the end of the main rigging were tied.

Thick stuff was also worked for two sheer strakes which were fitted abreast the top line of the timbers where the framing proper ends. In 1711 the garboard strakes, which are those near the keel, were made of the same thickness as the rest of the bottom planking. Perhaps 100 years later there grew up a practice of making two or three strakes from the keel of greater thickness. Below the main wales the thickness of the planks became less in gradual fashion until about the round of the bilge, where the usual thickness of bottom planking of some 4 in

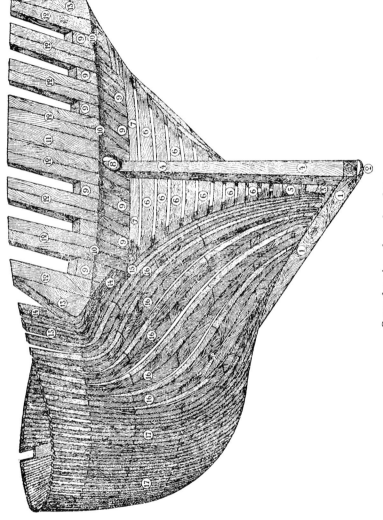

Stern framing of wooden ship

began and went down right to the keel. There was a special name given to these taper strakes—'diminishing strakes'. Above the main wales two more pieces of thick stuff, some 12 in. wide and 7 and 6 in. thick, went upwards to form the lower sill of the gun-ports. Above the first tier of ports and in way of the main deck, were worked in later days three strakes of thick stuff, 12 in. broad and 5 in. thick, to form the channel wales. Between these and the sheer strakes were planks some 4 and 3 in. thick below the sheer strakes proper, which were two in number, 12 in. broad and 4 in. thick.

It is very clear that while the framework was built up to form a smooth surface, there had to be applied thereto a skin of planks which varied in thickness at different heights. Further, this skin in later days was made to appear fair on the outside. It may be well to review the practice in detail. Starting with the keel, which may have thick garboards, comes the usual bottom planking, some 4 in. thick. Above the turn of the bilge the 'diminishing' strakes start and in these, say eight or nine planks, the thickness grows from 4 in. up to the thick stuff of 8 in. Then follow four planks of 8 in. to form the main wale, in way of the lower gun-deck. Above these are two more pieces of thick stuff some 12 in. wide and 7 and 6 in. thick. Above the first tier of ports are placed three strakes 12 in. wide and 5 in. thick to form the channel wale, then comes thinner planking ending in the two sheer strakes, 12 in. broad and 4 in. thick.

To lay the plank of such a complex pattern needed much skill and forethought. The practice was to fix first the garboard strakes, one of which was left off until the last to allow access to the hull. Perhaps at the same time the main wales were set up. Work went on with the 'diminishing' planks being put in place downwards and the bottom planking being put on working upwards. Somewhere these two layers would meet with a gap of one strake between. To close the gap a 'shutter-in' plank had to be fitted with great care to avoid any undue break in the run of the ship.

The laying out of the lines of the edges of the plank on the frame timbers is an art in itself:

All Plank ought as much as possible to lie on a direct Plane; for in any other Position 'twould be more dangerous (in bending or twisting of them to their Work) than if they rounded on a direct regular Plane, considerably more in proportion to such an irregular Twist.

Any twist of a plank into its place is to be shunned almost at all costs, and can be so done except perhaps towards the end. Plank is worked parallel. The edges are trimmed square to the timbers, but to allow for the caulk for the oakum a taper of $\frac{1}{16}$ in. for each inch of thickness has to be taken from the edge.

As in all timber structures the butts are sources of weakness, and so a rule is laid down for the spacing of the butts by saying that they are not to be nearer than, say, 6 ft. It follows that there should be three 'passing strakes' between two butts which lie in the same transverse section. This means the planks will have to be worked in lengths which are not less than 24 ft.; if planks can be had 30 ft. long, then there could be four 'passing' strakes between butts.

An attempt is made as far as can be done to work the planks parallel, but the girth of the ship is much greater amidships than at the end, so somewhere again towards the end the number of the parallel strakes has to be made less. To arrange this, 'it's therefore very customary in many Ships to drop or steal, as they term it, some strakes short of the Stern, and raise (increase) what you can regularly in the Bulge and Loof.' (Bulge is the turn of the bilge and loof is the afterpart of the bow between the stem and amidships.)

Again, when a strake of planking ends at the stem and at the stern, the end strakes are fitted first and the 'shutter-in' or closing plank is placed towards a part of the ship where the curves are not so sharp.

There is also trouble in getting planks to bend in an even manner at the end of the vessel. Here the edge may arch upwards in the middle, when it is said to have 'sny', or it may do the reverse, when the plank is said to 'hang'. Twist, when putting a plank into place, should only be done in extreme cases and then planks are 'steamed' to make the process more easy. Sutherland says that where thick channels or 'harpings' are worked at the bow, they should be cut out of the solid from compass timber, and shaped with great care. He goes on:

Snying is observed to make the working of Ships Bow very difficult, and the Planks to perform the same very chargeable to be purchased. Since all the Plank, which births up any Ship's Bow, must be converted from principal compass Timber. For altho' Plank may be easily bent flat-ways, yet take what Method you please, it cannot be near so well bent edge-ways, because of the great Disproportion between the Breadth and Thickness.

Planking Inboard—Beams and Knees—Riders

It is surprising to observe the amount of inside timber that was needed to build a strong hull for a wooden ship which was some 150 ft. long on the keel. Here it may be as well to deal with the middle

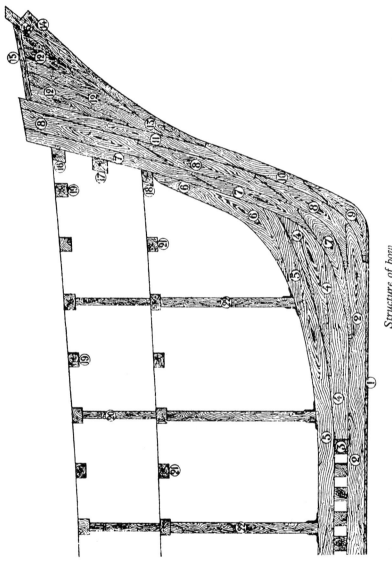

Structure of bow

82

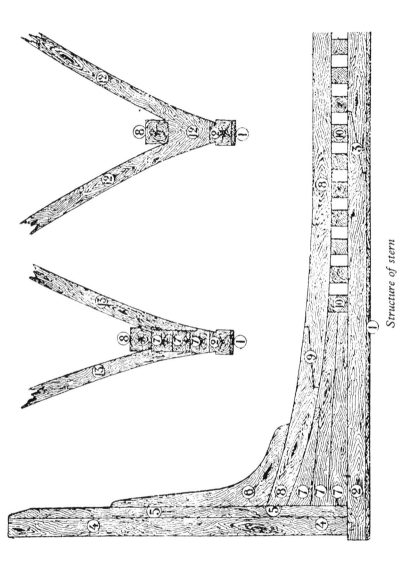

Structure of stern

eighteenth century and to have regard to the large ships then being built to get ready for Trafalgar. The *Victory* (see Frontispiece) rebuilt just before 1800, may be taken as a fair sample of the ship in question. It follows that some of the extra framing to be spoken of would have been added after Sutherland wrote his text-book.

It might have been thought that the main needs of the structure would have been met by the framework, whose main timbers were some 12 in. square, with little space between, and which further had an outer skin of planks ranging from 4 in. up to bands of belting of 8 in. thick. The fact that so much inner work was wanted shows the effect of the lack of strength in the various joints of the hull.

To start from the bottom and go upwards, there were two limber strakes on the edge of the limbers, which was the name given to the passage for water abreast the main keel. These helped to secure the end of the first futtock, which, unlike the floor timber, did not cross the keel. Then came a belt of five strakes of 'thick stuff' some 7 to 8 in. thick and each over 12 in. wide. These formed a lengthwise tie over the 'heads' or ends of the floors. A third belt of two strakes of less thickness was run at the first futtock head. Between these belts were laid, resting on top of the floors, planks of 4 in. and of 5 in., called the foot-waling. This thinner plank is now known as ceiling, the meaning of which is obscure, for it is strange to lay ceiling on the floors. It would seem that it may have meant 'sealing', that is to seal off the main framing on the inside. Anyway, the greater part of the structure is closed in with planks or 'thick stuff' worked lengthwise.

Below the orlop—lowest—deck beams are the clamps. These are formed by two deep strakes of 7 in. and 6 in. stuff to make a ledge on which the long deck beams rest, and also to form a base to which to attach the beam knees, which connect to the sides of the ship.

Above the orlop beams—some 15 in. square—is placed a water-way strake of 'thick stuff' 14 in. wide and 6 in. thick, the plank of the deck being only 2 in. Above this water-way for some four strakes are planks $4\frac{1}{2}$ in. thick.

Then follow the clamps for the lower gun-deck, which is placed very near the greatest breadth. These are the longest beams in the ship and are subject to heavy strain, so that their size of 16 in. square requires strong support. Here the clamps are formed by a belt of four strakes of 8 in. and 7 in. 'thick stuff'. It should be said that the spacing of these beams and of those of the other decks follows the lay-out of the gun-ports, which are some 8 ft. apart. The practice was to place one beam under a port—that is below a gun—and one beam between the ports. So two beams cover a space lengthwise of 8 ft., or a little less than the space taken up by four frame timbers. If there were 13 guns aside on this deck, then 27 main beams would be fitted.

To secure the beams two sets of 'knees' were used, the knees being crooked pieces of oak of 'grown' shape. 'Hanging' knees were timbers which fixed the side of the beam to the side of the ship in a transverse plane. The 'hanging' arm was some 6 ft. long downwards and the arm

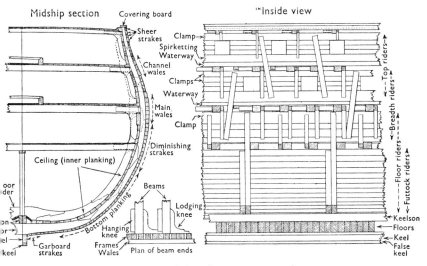

74-Gun vessel, inboard structure, c. 1760

on the beam about 4 ft. 6 in. Then there were 'lodging' knees fixed on a level with the top of the beam, but set parallel to the deck. The side-arm filled the space at the side of the ship between the beams and the arm on the beam was made some 5 ft. long.

On top of the beams was a water-way, 6 in. thick, which formed the edge of the deck-flat made of 4 in. planks. Above this, a further belt of two to three strakes, 7 in. and 6 in. thick, ran upwards to the lower sill of the gun-ports.

Above the ports come the 'clamps' for the upper deck formed by two strakes, the upper 7 in. and the lower 6 in. thick. The beams here are 13½ in. wide and 12 in. deep. These were fixed with both 'hanging' and 'lodging' knees slightly less in size than those of the gun-deck.

The water-ways are 11 in. broad and 5 in. thick; the flat of the deck is formed by 3-in. deal planks. 'Spirketting', which is the name given to the two strakes above the water-way and below the sill of the gun-port, was worked as for the gun-deck.

It must be added that the beams were shaped to have a 'round' or 'camber'—the middle being higher than the ends. The 'round' is less in the lower parts of the ship and ranges from 8 in. at the upper deck to 6 in. on the gun-deck, and 2½ in. for the orlop deck. The 'camber' curve is an arc of a circle.

Support was given to the deck between the beams by 'carlings' running lengthwise, there being some three of these in the breadth of the ship. Between these, but parallel to the beams, other joists—'ledges'—of smaller size were worked.

The complex is not yet ended, for 'riders'—heavy transverse frames —were fitted inside the limbers, the ceiling and the clamps to provide further strength. There are some six of these in the ship, that is, one on every fourth beam.

The floor 'riders' straddle the keelson, and are some 16 in. square. These are 'scarfed' to the lower futtock 'riders', again 16 in. square, and stop short of the keelson. Then with a 'scarf' comes the second futtock rider running up to the orlop-deck beams. The third futtock rider passes above the orlop deck and, still some 14 in. square, extends to below the gun-deck.

There are also the breadth 'riders' which cover the side of the ship at a slight slope to the upright, and extend between the ports to cover two decks only. And a still higher two-deck set—'top riders'—rises to the topmost deck. There are twelve of each of these classes of riders, made of timber some 12 in. square.

Joints and Fixings and Tools

The weakness of lengthwise joints of timber is clear, and many methods were tried to get over the trouble. The first of these methods was to trim the ends to a taper with a hook-shape so that one piece locked into the other. Such a process is termed 'scarphing' and the joint is called a 'scarph'. To increase the lock for such a heavy timber as the keel, which in a large ship might be some 15 in. square, the slope of the taper was 'tabled'. In each lip for about half the length of the joint, a tongue is shaped to fit into a groove formed in the other piece; the groove and the tongue take up some third part of the length of the joint and also of the width. The sketch shows a 'scarph' of a keel and the eight iron bolts through the joints, of which the two long ones pass

PLATE XI

THE BUILDING OF THE ARK OF NOAH
(*Bedford Book of Hours*, 1423)

PLATE XII

THE BUILDING OF THE ARK OF NOAH
(*The Nuremberg Chronicle*, 1493)

through both the floor timber and the keelson above. The ends of the bolts are clinched over on a washer.

Extra strength is also given to weak joints by running a second timber the same way, such as for the keelson in this case. The joints of the keelson are placed about midway between the 'scarphs' of the keel.

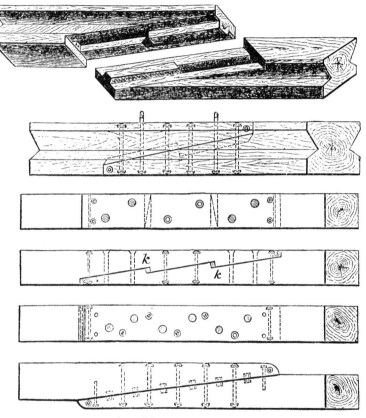

Scarphing of keels and beams

'Scarphs' are nearly always used for any heavy timbers, such as for the floor riders and for the deck-beams. In the latter case the 'scarph' was vertical and made with three steps in the lock instead of two. At the stem, which is built up of a number of heavy pieces, 'scarphs' were used for each of the main sets of parts, dowels or round pins were fitted across the line of the sideways joints, and the whole fixed by long through-bolts from outside to inside.

It is well to notice that both keel and keelson run right to the stem and to the stern-posts. In order to suit the rise of 'form' at the ends, the keelson is moved upwards and packing—'dead-wood'—fills the space between.

The build up of the double frame into floor and futtocks shows how, by lapping one set of timbers over the other, the end-joints were made stronger. The joints in the two sections were roughly midway apart. Partly because of timber shortage the ends between the parts were at one time joined by a wedge-piece—a 'shock'—shaped like a triangle and worked on the inside of the frame. This was rarely sound and was prone to decay, and so, somewhere about 1800, the ends were made square and fitted close with a dowel at the middle to prevent sideways movement. Extra strength was given to such joints by the wales, bands of strakes of 'thick stuff', the first of which were worked lengthwise inside the ship and over the joints of the frame floor.

To secure the ends of the beam—the 'members' which tied the two sides as well as carried the weight of guns or cargo above—called for much skill. In the first place the outer skin was planked with 'thick stuff' in some five strakes to form the 'main wales' abreast the lower gun-deck. Inside the ship were worked some three to five heavy strakes of lengthwise plank, called 'clamps', the topmost being the thickest, to form a 'shelf' on which the end of the beam rested. To secure the beams 'hanging' knees were used. The transverse downward arm was bolted to the side of the ship; the other arm lay along the side of the beam, its top flush with the upper surface and bolted through the beam. A second set of knees—'lodging'—was placed on the other side, one arm being fixed to the ship on a level with the top of the beam and the other arm fixed to the beam-end by bolts.

Further support was given above the beams by a thick 'water-way' which formed the outside of the deck-plank, fitted close. 'Spirketting', two strakes of 'thick stuff', was run above the 'water-way' up to the lower sill of the gun-port.

All such knees had to be shaped from 'grown' timber, which soon became very scarce and it was here, somewhere about 1800, that forged knees of iron bar were used with better results.

Outer plank was worked to provide a good 'shift of butts'. The distance between the ends of the planks near to each other was fixed at something like 6 ft.; while between two butt-ends in the same transverse section of the ship three strakes were run as a rule. The ends of these 'passing' strakes were not less than 6 ft. lengthwise from that section. For deck-plank, which was laid parallel to the middle line of the ship, a like practice was used.

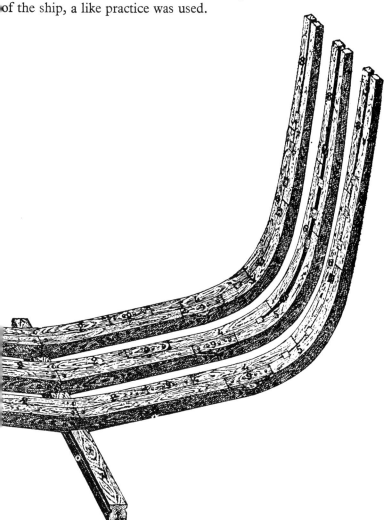

Frames and futtocks

To fasten the plank wood 'treenails'—trenels—were used. These were turned from oak and made up to 36 in. long and 2 in. diameter and as short as 12 in. and $1\frac{1}{4}$ in. across. Sutherland says that the value of the largest size was £12 per 1000, of which the wood cost £10. 10s. They were made of sound and seasoned timber, cut from the top part of the tree, so as to be free from knots and sap. Great skill was needed to drive them and the size of the 'auger' was a matter of concern. Sutherland remarks that 'an Augre of one inch and Half Diameter is suitable to drive a Trenel of one inch and $\frac{3}{4}$ Diameter, which is call'd a Broad-Arrow, and the Character is thus ↑'. He also says: 'The Augre is an Instrument of singular Use and Service in Ship-building and so very fitly adapted for composing the same, that if ever any Person was Deify'd for Inventing, I should highly recommend the Author of an Augre deserving of that Glory.' The shipwrights had the choice of some ten sizes ranging from 2 in. down to $\frac{1}{2}$ in. The length of the 'Ingineer Bitts' was 10 in. for the largest, 6 in. for the 1-in. bitt and $5\frac{1}{4}$ in. for the $\frac{1}{2}$-in. auger.

Saws were held by Sutherland in high regard: 'I cannot tell whether the Saw or the Augre is the most necessary Instrument.' There is the whip-saw used by the sawyers to divide timber length-wise. The cross-cut saws in daily use by the shipwright, in almost all their 'jobbs', are worked by two men. There is also the single hand-saw. He points out that good sawing saves the worker much labour with an axe or an 'addice'—his spelling of adze. Heavy axes for hewing and wood axes and hatchets are among the shipwright's tools.

For iron there were hack-saws to cut the bolts to length and cold chisels for the same purpose. Pitch-pots also appear in the list costing $2\frac{1}{2}d.$ a pound or 22s. 4d. per hundred—of cast-iron got 'by melting Iron Oar or Mineral Substances' in a furnace.

Nails were of all sorts and sizes. Spikes down to the smallest sort and 'weight nails', sold by weight; the next group is 'penny' nails from forty-penny nails, sold for 3s. 4d. for a hundred, up to two-penny nails. Nails were used to fasten all the deck-planks.

Calking—caulking—is the filling of the seams of the planks and the decks, with stranded 'oakham'—oakum—made by picking loose old hemp ropes. This was a special trade, that of the calkers. Their main tools were a wooden mallet and a calking-iron, a flat, wide-edged, blunt chisel. The calk was driven in loose strands, worked lengthwise into the seam until it was full and packed hard; below the water, strands of hair were first put in to protect the oakum from the inside. For a 1000-ton ship, some 16 cwt. of black and white oakum were used with 13 gallons of oil and four barrels of pitch with a little tar added. The seams were pitched to protect the calking on the outside.

The calkers also 'graved' the surface under water with a curious mixture which reads somewhat like Marco Polo's account of what he

PLATE XIII

THE BUILDING OF THE ARK OF NOAH
(M. de Vos, and graved by Sadelerus, c. 1580)

PLATE XIV

A SHIPYARD OF 1675

saw on his travels. (The word 'grave' means to smear with 'graves', a mixture of tallow and resin boiled together; 'graves' was the residue of melted tallow.) The amounts used for a 1000-ton ship were first 11 cwt. of tallow, then blacking made up of six barrels of pitch, three barrels of tar and three barrels of blacking. The graving was the term used for 19 cwt. of 'Rozam' (resin), $2\frac{1}{2}$ cwt. of brimstone and 25 gallons of oil. The tar, pitch and resin seem to have been got from fir trees. Under the accounts for graving is mention of 2500 sheaves of reed, or 2000 bavins (bundles) of broom if no reed can be got. The purpose of this fibrous stuff is not known.

This is not the place for a study in detail of the early tools of the shipwrights. It will suffice to present pictures of those days in which men are seen at work. Three out of the four deal with the building of the Ark, since the early gravers found much to inspire their art in the drama of the Old Testament.

The first picture (Pl. XI) shows that subject taken from the Bedford *Book of Hours*, which was made in France for John, Duke of Bedford, about A.D. 1423, a Missal now in the British Museum. The Ark is not shown, for what is seen is the building of a three-story wooden house. It would seem too that the workers are landsmen, since shipwrights' tools are absent. For instance, a carpenter is planing a large timber which shipwrights would saw to rough shape and finish with the axe and the adze. A curious point is that the plane seems to have two blades. There is shown a one-man cross-cut saw—the shipwrights use a two-man type. Here are augers, chisels, brace and bit, frame-saws, hatchets and hammers.

Some 70 years later, 1493, is the print of the same subject taken from the Nuremberg *Chronicle* (Pl. XII), which, though quaint, shows few tools—hatchets, augers, mallets and claw-hammers are the only ones.

The third print, drawn by M. de Vos about 1580, is one of a series of twelve (Pl. XIII) graved by Sadelerus to show the crafts of those days. Although the form is quaint, there is no doubt about the shipwrights being at work. The worker 'dubbing' the inside part of the ship with an adze, the vigour of the two men in the foreground using the cross-cut saw, the prentice lad driving a spike, the basket of tools with a mallet and chisel, the pitch-pot on the fire and the anvil to straighten the iron, make a fairly complete picture. There is a second adze below the log which is being cross-cut. The stern seems to have an iron forging at its centre line.

The last picture is taken from the set of 'Navall' prints which Pepys bound up with Anthony Deane's MS. The graver was R. Zeeman, the printer was Arthur Tooker, and the set was named after the most worthy Samuel Pepys. On the left is a ship on the stocks perhaps about to be launched, and to be made complete when afloat like the hulk by the wharf on the right. It will be seen that the ship is to be slid into the water bow first, whereas the practice to-day is to launch stern first. Perhaps this view was taken from one of the new shipyards begun by Anthony Deane with Phineas Pett during their tour in Norfolk and Suffolk about that time. On the left, workers—one of whom is smoking a pipe—are 'charring' timbers with a fire on one side and water placed on the back. The two sawyers, the top sawyer and the bottom sawyer, are sawing plank, and on the right a shipwright is trimming a heavy timber to shape with an adze (Pl. XIV).

§10. TIMBER AND IRON

THE question of the supply of timber for the building of ships was a serious one in Tudor times. Even in the first year of her reign, Elizabeth showed what was in her mind as to her naval policy, by a passage in an Act meant to restrict the use of timber as fuel for the smelting of iron and other metals. Further action was needed in 1585 and in support of her wish she gave Thomas Proctor of York a patent to make iron with coal. There is also mention of 'steel', though the meaning of that term is not clear. It appears that the value of steel was three times that of iron.

It was stated in 1580 that a beech tree, 1 ft. square at the butt end would make $1\frac{1}{2}$ loads of charcoal—a load being 50 cu. ft. About 1610 the 140 forges of Sussex alone used from two to four loads a day each. On this basis some 1700 trees were felled each week or say 80,000 trees a year.

In 1608 James I caused a survey of the royal forests to be made, and only some 500,000 loads or roughly 350,000 trees were found, and of these less than half were fit to build ships for the Navy. It would have been thought that sea-coal would have been used at an early date, but transport of coal by sea was too difficult.

The action of Elizabeth brought many changes, among others the many Tudor chimneys of the manor houses. By 1619 Dud Dudley of Worcester was able to smelt iron with the use of pit- or sea-coal

The Cradley forges turned out 'merchantable good bar iron' from an output of 7 tons of pig-iron a week. The ironmasters who used charcoal treated Dudley in scurvy fashion and tried without success to close down his works.

Just about this time, machines driven by water-power were used to cut bar iron into nail rods. Many girls and women were then at work in the blacksmiths' shops of England 'forging nails and wielding the hammer with all the grace of their sex'.

Before that, as early as the reign of Henry VIII, cast-iron cannon were made in Sussex. Mention is also made of hollow cast-iron shot stuffed with firework or wildfire, whereof the bigger sort had screws of iron to receive a match to carry fire kindled, that the work might .. break in pieces the hollow shot, whereof the smallest piece hitting any man would kill or spoil him'.

It is easy to gather the outlook of the ironfounders who wished to stick to charcoal when making cast-iron for such uses. Later though, by 1651, the English had learned to use coke got from coal instead of charcoal, paving the way for both the saving of timber and a greater output of iron.

When in 1677 Parliament passed the vote for building thirty new ships it took much labour and great search to get the timber needed. Henry Adams, who built the *Agamemnon* at Bucklershard in the Beaulieu River in 1781, records that the building of this ship of 1370 tons needed the felling of 2000 average oaks to supply 2000 loads of timber. Some 100 tons of wrought iron and 30 tons of copper were used. Such a ship with a length of 132 ft. on the keel, a breadth of $44\frac{1}{2}$ ft., and a depth in hold of 19 ft., took some 18 months building on the stocks. She carried 64 guns and a crew of 500 men.

In his Journal, Phineas Pett, the third of that name who was master shipwright at Chatham and later knighted, records a journey he made with Sir Antony Deane in May 1677 into the counties of Suffolk and Norfolk to get timber. Since most of the building of ships took place on the London river, and because of the demands of the ironworks of Sussex, the country around London and in the Home Counties was getting stripped of trees. Phineas Pett the first, who had been reprimanded because of the poor timber he had used in the *Prince Royal*, went far north to Durham and Northumberland to ensure that he got the right stuff for the *Sovereign of the Seas*.

Deane and Pett spent three weeks upon their quest. On the second day they reached Harwich, where they took the measure for a new 'launch' slipway. This meant making the yard larger, a question which had to be talked over with the mayor. Here there was now a naval dockyard and a depot for stores. They bought 200 dozen blocks for rigging the new ship, twenty loads of compass timber for the ribs, made a price for ironwork of £29 per 100 (weight), 'or as cheap as any in the River of Thames and gave directions to lay 200 deals for the laying the mould for building the new ship'. This last item refers to the mould-loft floor—a flat surface of wood on which the shapes of the frames were laid off to full size.

They went to Ipswich and then to Woodbridge, where they bought parcels of 4, 3, and 2 in. planks. Later they went to Aldeburgh to view the ground, and harbour to see if a ship might be built there which they found could be done.

They went to Yarmouth to lay up their timber and to inquire of the builders, and there Mr Stedman made an offer to build a third-rate to the 'wale'—about the lowest gun-deck—then to launch her and take her to pier's head to finish. He said he could deliver her afloat, within a year, for the cost of £10. 10s. 'per ton'.

On the way to Norwich they found that owners were holding out for higher prices and much of the timber was not bought on this account. 'There was one Haykins, who had £300 worth set out, but was not willing to sell it to the King and would not speak with us. They viewed 170 trees 'standing' in Redgrave Park. The owners would not sell them by the load, nor fell them, but standing they asked £500 for the 170 trees. 'We got them for £460, which is a very great pennyworth, being very fine timber and made by our estimate amount to 240 load....We felled a tree to see the nature of the timber, which proved very good. We agreed for 9d. per tree felling and 2d. a bough. The bark and lops we sold for £30.'

At Otley they 'found the Carters carrying away a stern-post for the new ship at Harwich, and the rest converting on the ground, as fast as could be'; the frames were being shaped in the woods.

They came back to Ipswich and agreed with an owner of a vessel to carry what timber he could stow at 2s. 6d. a load from Ipswich to Harwich—some 12 miles; also with a loader to place it on board at 1s. 6d. a load. Pett struck a price with Deane for his own timber at Otley of 55s. a load of 50 ft. square measure, the price to cover transport to Ipswich costing 8s. Here they ended their tour and came back to London through Colchester.

In spite of the pleadings of the diarist John Evelyn in Charles II's

me as to the need to conserve the forests, the demand for wood grew
t such a rate that 100 years later an inquiry was held by the House
f Commons, which failed to produce any results. Apart from the
reater needs for timber for shipping, more was being used for the
omestic arts. With the greater population more land was brought
nder tillage, since this gave more profit than from woodlands, which
ied up money for long periods. An oak tree took some 100 years to
each such full size as was needed for the building of warships. From
760 to 1805 the fleet of the Royal Navy grew from 320,000 tons to
ver 700,000 tons, with more than 900 vessels of which perhaps 180
ere ships of the line. By 1810 the tonnage rose another 100,000 tons.

A second survey of the royal forests in 1783 showed only some
0,000 loads of oak to compare with 500,000 loads in 1608; and in the
iter survey only 50,000 loads were found fit for the Navy as against
previous figure of 240,000. In that period the common annual
emand for oak for the naval yards was over 50,000 loads between the
ears 1760 and 1788.

This did not take into account merchant ships, which in 1790 needed
omething like 170,000 loads. In this total the needs of the East India
Company's ships, chiefly built on the Thames, were a large factor.
'or that year there exist the first figures of British merchant shipping—
ver 15,000 ships and nearly $1\frac{1}{2}$ million tons with some 115,000 seamen.

The prior claims of the Navy drove the East India Company to take
ction and Gabriel Snodgrass, their chief surveyor, did all in his power
) urge the country to deal with this matter. He began in 1771 with
ie House of Commons and was still at the question in 1796 when he
rrote to the Rt Hon. Henry Dundas: 'It is upwards of 24 years since
first introduced...it is now more than 17 years since I brought
ito use...about 27 years ago...I have made it a practice for many
ears.'

He was the first to use iron for 'knees'—the angle timbers used to
onnect the beams to the side of the ship—as the supply of 'grown'
r 'compass' timber was very short. The iron knees were cheaper and
ronger and took up less room in the holds—the lower parts of the
iip—and in the between decks or ''tween-decks'.

He claimed, against the naval view, that the side of the ship had too
uuch 'tumble-home', and should be made more nearly upright. In
iat way much more timber could be used for the frames. He remarks
iat the wastage of wood in the process of shaping was very great—
ie being made only of about one-half of the tree. It would help too

if the timbers were worked to shape in the forest, both on account of transport and to ensure better stuff.

It may help to set down in some detail the timber needed for a third rate ship of 74 guns launched in 1759. Out of the 182 line of battle ships in the fleet at the time of Trafalgar, some 90, about half, were of this type. The dimensions of this vessel were: length on the gun deck 166 ft., length of keel 136 ft., breadth 47 ft., depth in hold 20 ft —the burden was 1610 tons.

The timber detail was made up as follows:

Oak timber, strait	720	loads	
Oak timber, compass	1890	,,	
Elm timber	50	,,	
Fir timber	120	,,	2780 loads
Knees, square	70	,,	
Kness, raking	80	,,	150 loads
★Thick stuff, of 10 inches	20	,,	
of 9 ,,	60	,,	
of 8 ,,	80	,,	
of 7 ,,	30	,,	
of 6 ,,	150	,,	
of 5 ,,	70	,,	410 loads
Oak plank, English, 4 and 3 in.	200	,,	
,, ,, Danzig ,,	100	,,	
Plank, English elm	60	,,	360 loads
		Grand total:	3700 loads

★ Thick stuff is the name given to any plank over 4 in. thick and up to 12 in. width.

It would seem that for every ton of shipping, $1\frac{1}{2}$ loads of timber and more were needed for the building of warships and over one load for merchant vessels. The detailed account of the timber used for the ship quoted shows that more than two loads per ton were used.

On these figures the 700,000 tons of the Royal Navy in 1805 had used up over $1\frac{1}{2}$ million loads of timber. It is not then a matter of surprise that the known world was searched for timber. The oak which began to come from Canada in 1763 was found to be subject to early decay, a fault which was also shared by wood from the Baltic. The best oak came from the Adriatic—perhaps the *Ilex* evergreen oak which the Romans brought to England, where it still thrives on the South Coast. These trees, because of their curved branches, gave a good supply of compass timber used for the frames.

Then there came imports of larch, fir, pitch-pine, African oak, and somewhere about 100 years ago Burma teak from Moulmein, which was used by the East India Company in India. Honduras mahogany also began to be used about the same time. Some idea of the troubles of British builders is given by an account of a vessel of 400 tons which was built at Sunderland in 1835. The keel, 13 in. deep and 10 in. wide, was some 100 ft. long and made in three lengths of American elm. The 'main timbers', some 18 in. square, were of African oak, as was also the wood used for the bow and stern pieces. The outside planks were English elm for the bottom of the ship, above that the planks $3\frac{1}{2}$ in. thick were English, Baltic, African and American. Pitch-pine was used for the sides above the upper deck, which was planked with yellow pine. It is clear that most of this timber was brought from abroad.

One aspect of the timber shortage was that much thought was given to the rapid decay of the wooden hulls. From 1690 onwards, to 1719, the thick stuff and plank were charred. In this process the inner surface was slightly burned by placing it against fires of old timber, while the outside was kept wet. Then came the practice of 'stoving', where the planks were placed in wet sand and heated until supple enough to be bent to shape at the ship. This better practice lasted until 1736 when wooden trunks were used into which the timber was placed and suppled by steam. Such kilns are still used for the building of boats.

A little later, steps were taken to supply a current of air to the holds to reduce the moisture and to remove the bad fumes. Then in 1771 heed was being paid in detail to the need to season the timber. Large ships had to stand on the stocks in frame for at least a year so as to season before the plank and thick stuff were put on. Other timber was placed in stacks with access to a current of air for some six months.

Various ways were tried to protect the outside of the planks below water. Lead sheathing was used about 1670 but without much success. A mixture of light wood sheathing, 'graved' or coated with a compound of pitch, tar and brimstone, was found to be better. In 1761 the outer skin was coated with thin sheets of copper to prevent 'fouling'—growth of vegetable and animal nature—in the Tropics. A galvanic action between the copper and the iron bolts in the presence of sea-water caused great rusting of the iron. To get over this danger the bolts were made of mixed metal—an alloy of copper and tin. This practice of sheathing vessels liable to long service in the Tropics was in use until recent times, the steel hull being sheathed with wood planks to which copper sheets were nailed on the outside.

General Bentham, who had been a shipwright's apprentice at Wool wich, came back for a visit to England from service in Russia, where he got his army title. A little later he became a Commissioner of the Navy, being given charge of works. He set up saw-mills and metal shops. Through his influence the block-making machines of Brunel senior were at work by 1808, a device which saved the Navy some £20,000 a year. He set up metal-mills at Portsmouth, lead-mills at Chatham, supplied the smithies with machines, and put the dry dock into proper shape. To close the entrance to the docks he used a floating caisson of his own design, which was worked by the use of water-ballast.

This early use of machines at Portsmouth brought about large savings for the country, and paved the way for the shaping of iron which by about 1830 was starting to be used for the building of ships.

§11. THE EAST INDIA COMPANY

WHEN James I came to the throne in 1603 and made peace with Spain, there arose a great demand for shipping. The merchants hired ships from abroad once more instead of building them at home. It was said in 1615 that London had not more than ten ships of over 200 ton burden. Public concern was voiced by Trinity House, and there was talk of stopping exports in any but British ships. Charnock observes

The bubble, however, was on the point of bursting, and the mist, which had so long and so wonderfully obscured the sight of the British Commercial Community from its true interest, was on the verge of being dispelled. As in a thousand similar instances, the greatest events appear to have been occasionally brought about by the most trivial causes, so in the present, did accident affect that which neither the wise representations of honest and patriotic men, nor the very critical state both they themselves and the whole Nation were involved in, had ever awakened them to. The anecdote appears well authenticated and is a very forcible proof, among a myriad of others, of that strange, that sudden influence of whim, caprice and public opinion, which has in all countries and in all ages violently driven the human mind from wrong to right and from right to wrong.[1]

It appears that two Dutch ships, each of 300 tons burden, came into the Thames laden with coffee and cotton for their owners who lived in London. Some of the merchants who saw the vessels were spurred

[1] *History of Marine Architecture* (1801–2).

o follow likewise. The idea spread like wildfire and the traders gave more than support to the views that had been put forward by Trinity House. As a result, the nation with one accord sat down to construct a Merchant Marine. Ships were built for the Turkey and Levant trade, large enough to carry guns to cope with the pirates of the Barbary coast. As a result during the reign of James many ships were launched of 300, 400, or even 500 tons burden, whereas a ship of 100 tons was a large ship when he became king. In 1622 Newcastle alone owned nearly 100 sail of ships, each over 200 tons. In that year nearly 400,000 tons of coal were shipped on the Tyne, about half of which went to London.

Before 1613, the East India Company had gone through some troublesome times. Since their Charter some twelve voyages in all had been made in ships of small size, none larger than 300 tons. James helped in every way and in 1613 brought about a fusion of the rivals which became known as the United East India Company. A fleet of well-armed vessels was made up of the *New Year's Gift* of 650 tons, the *Hector* of 500, the *Merchant's Hope* of 300, and the *Solomon* of 200. When the ships got to India they fought and beat the Portuguese who claimed the Indian trade for themselves. This success led to further effort and a large ship of some 1200 tons was built. The king himself dined on board and gave her the name of *Trade's Increase*. He named a smaller vessel the *Pepper-corn*, as she was to be used in that trade.

Charles I, as a means of raising money outside of Parliament, granted patents of many kinds to those who had control of home markets. Among these he set up the Courteen Association as a rival to the East India Company, which action, by the time the Civil War broke out, had nearly ruined English trade in the Far East. Cromwell did much to put this right. He helped the Company to regain its place in the world, and Charles II backed its efforts against its rivals at home and abroad. The Company's agent carried on in those regions —a year's sail from London—with force and with a high hand, and strange events took place by sea and land between English rivals in high rage with each other.

Throughout the Stuart period there were great struggles for the profits of this wealthy trade. Between the years 1675 and 1680 some sixteen large ships were built with burdens up to 1300 tons. A further fusion came about in 1702 between the Old and the New Company. From that time onwards the East India Company ships became

smaller, down to as little as 350 or 400 tons, which by 1735 had risen
to some 490 tons. After 1750 a standard tonnage of 499 tons became
the rule. It was said that this figure was chosen, since by law vessels
of 500 tons had to carry a chaplain.

During the American War Indiamen were being built up to 800 tons
and by the time this was over, the normal tonnage had risen to about
750. Parliament at this time, for reasons not known, put a limit on the
total tonnage of their fleet of some 45,000 tons. This may have been
due to the great demands of the fighting Navy and the shortage of
timber. Bigger vessels were soon being built again because it had been
found that the Indian ships of France and Holland were much larger
than the British vessels. So in 1786 a number of ships of 1000–1200
tons were laid down and some sixteen such new vessels were afloat
by 1790.

A little later a plan was drawn up under which the normal fleet of
the Company was to be thirty-six large ships of around 1200 tons and
forty smaller ones of from 700 to 800 tons. In 1810 the Company had
some 90 vessels of which one-third were of 1200 tons, a third of 800
tons, and the rest between 500 and 600 tons. The largest ships were
used for the trade with China. These totals did not include vessels
which the Company built in India, chiefly at Bombay. It is well to
add that between 1800 and 1810 the annual number of vessels bringing
home cargoes was 100, the tonnage being some 90,000 and the number
of seamen engaged being 7000.

The prestige of the Company's service, which was as highly thought
of as that of the Royal Navy, left in shadow the other vessels of
the Merchant Marine, for in 1810 the common trader was only 200–
300 tons. A ship of 350 tons was thought to be of decent size and one
of 400 tons was deemed large. At that time the Merchant Navy
proper had nearly 24,000 vessels, with a total tonnage reaching nearly
$2\frac{1}{2}$ million, giving work to nearly 165,000 seamen. Out of all that
fleet, apart from the East Indiamen, there were only 20 vessels larger
than 600 tons and not a single one whose tonnage reached 1000. It
is helpful to compare the dimensions of a naval ship with one of the
Company ships:

	H.M.S. *Belliqueux* (64 guns)	H.C.S.
	A.D. 1780	A.D. 1804
Length of keel	132 ft.	134 ft.
Breadth outside	44 ft. 4 in.	42 ft. (note less beam
Depth in hold	19 ft.	17 ft.
Tons	1376	1257

The tons burden were much less than the actual weight of cargo that the ships could carry. The H.C.S. *Nottingham* of 1152 tons burden brought home from China on her first voyage 1570 tons weight of tea.

The cost of running a 1200-ton Company ship in about 1800 was pretty high, practically as great as building a warship. In 1802 the hull of one of these vessels cost nearly £29,000, of which sum £3000 was paid for the copper sheathing on the bottom of the ship. Masts, yards, sails and rigging came to some £8000 and the cost of the equipment and stores for a twelvemonth's voyage was another £11,000, making a total of £48,000 for the first year of work.

The repairs needed to maintain the vessel in service were not small, and something like £12,000 had to be spent at the end of each voyage. For the fourth year of service double this amount had to be found and after the sixth trip the vessel had to be partly rebuilt. To carry this out the copper and the wood sheathing were stripped off. The sides were 'doubled' by a layer of oak plank, 3 in. thick, from above the water-line down to 2 ft. below the heads of the floor-timbers. Extra iron-riders, pillars and knees were fitted to strengthen the structure, and all this had to be done to make the vessel fit for two more voyages.

False ideas were and are common as to the speed of the Company ships, and this is put down to their bluff bows. The fine lines of the clipper ship suggest speed, and yet for racing yachts the full bow still persists. There were many reasons for the length of the voyage; the Company were without rivals and time was not yet a matter of profit. The first thought was for safety and the second for comfort. Sails were taken in at the first sign of bad weather and all ships were made 'snug' for the night by taking in their topsails at dusk.

At the time of Waterloo the Company was faced with the fear of speedier rivals in the China Trade and they changed their sea practice. C. N. Parkinson, in his book on *Trade in the Eastern Seas* (1793–1813), relates that the China Fleet of thirteen heavily laden Indiamen reached the Channel only 109 days after leaving the Canton River. (In the clipper-ship days a voyage of 100 days from the Chinese port was thought to be good.) The newspapers of 1817 looked on this voyage somewhat as follows:

A triumph of Mercantile Navigation, a combination of nautical skill with good fortune, of which there is no record of an equal exertion; to cut through 15000 miles of ocean in that short time, is, with so many vessels, without example in Marine experience. With *similar* passages we ought to communicate with our Asiatic Presidency at Calcutta within *six* months, instead of *once* in 12 or 15 months, as is now the loitering and *dilatory* habit of that important intercourse. The Americans of New York and Washington will soon exchange letters and *products* with Bengal in 5 months! The only early account *we* had of the victory of Waterloo being heard of at Calcutta was from New York.

These were the same ships and the same men who were now in a hurry. They had risen to the call and showed that with all their failings the English were not very backward in the building of ships.

The East India Company was subject to many faults and its critics became more vocal. When in 1832, the period of great reform, the Navigation Acts of Charles II were repealed, the Charter of the Company was withdrawn. Most of the Indian ships had been sold by 1835, chiefly to the owners and builders who had chartered or built vessels for the Company.

§12. THE HANOVERS

THE century that began when Queen Anne came to the throne in 1702 saw a marked change from the outlook on sea ventures of the Tudor and Stuart kings. The main policy seemed to have been, like that of the Greeks, to build fighting vessels and, because of the need for timber, to withhold favour from the Merchant Marine.

It was no wonder that English thought and concern was to build more and yet more ships of war, nor that there grew up a myth that it was upon the Navy that the safety and welfare of these islands depended. There is little or no mention of merchant ships, unlike the direct thought and help which was given by the Tudors and Stuarts. That great trading venture, the East India Company, was subject to severe stricture, as shown by the trials of Clive and of Warren Hastings. In fact direct action was taken to reduce and restrain the tonnage of their fleet.

It does not surprise that there was little progress made in the ship-wright's trade. There was no time to devote to new designs. The demand for ships was so great that vessels were built to the patterns laid down under the Stuarts, right up to the death of George III, even to the start of Victoria's reign, if not to the end of the era of the wooden walls of England.

The Merchant Marine, which had only some 3300 vessels of 260,000 tons in 1701, by 1802 had grown to 20,600 ships and over 2,100,000 tons. The number of seamen had risen from just over 27,000 to some 155,000 in that period. The average size of ship, which was 80 tons in 1701, had reached only 104 tons a century later. Outside the East Indiamen, which about 1800 were of 1000 or even 1200 tons, the largest ships were only 500 tons, used for the trades of the West Indies. Paul Mantoux, in his standard work on the Industrial Revolution in the eighteenth century, gives the tonnage of ships 'cleared' from English ports. The figures which were 317,000 tons in 1700 rose slowly up to 574,000 tons in 1760; in the last 40 years of the century the total rose to nearly 2,000,000 tons by 1801—a more than sixfold increase, most of which took place after George III became king. The figures for exports and imports show a 'balance of trade' always in favour of England. The sudden rise in trade was so rapid as to be worthy of the name of Revolution.

It has been said above that apart from some changes in length and to some extent breadth, the patterns set up in Charles II's time stayed right up to Trafalgar. The sizes and details of ships of the line had been agreed in 1719 and changes had been made from time to time until 1745. After the war with Spain the English Navy was found to be in a bad way. The war had shown glaring defects. The builders had varied from the standards without control and with little success. Admiral Sir John Norris carried out a full inquiry into the whole state of affairs, but in spite of his efforts reform went on but slowly. Charnock writes:

...The British Navy was reduced to an inequality with respect to that of the different foreign powers, reckoning ship for ship, not only in the contracted dimensions, but the form or shape given to the vessels composing it, which neither the inconveniences experimentally and most seriously found to result from them, nor the example of those benefits found to be derived by other countries from the pursuit of the contrary system, were, for many years, capable of removing. This prejudice appears to have risen almost to a species of mania; so that nothing short of the most violent remedies and cohesive regulations seemed capable of effecting the return of reason.[1]

In the years leading to Trafalgar the medium-size 74-gun ship with two decks had been found to be the best type of fighting vessel for most uses. For a greater number of guns 'three-deckers' were needed. They were worse sailers with their great height of side above water and were less easy to handle.

[1] *History of Marine Architecture* (1801–2).

Records of speeds of ships are lacking. For instance, Nelson's cruise to the West Indies and back was made at about 4 knots. The greatest speed, which was that of the frigates, is given as 10 knots 'running free' and 8–8½ knots 'close-hauled'. Even in the light of modern knowledge, the form of the ships brought about by a lengthy and costly process of trial and error would be deemed good for their purpose.

The trend of naval thought is shown first by the vessels that fought at Trafalgar and in a second sense by the ships which were being built in 1805.

	At Trafalgar		Building
	Number	Average age	(number)
First-rate:			
120 guns	—	—	—
100/98 guns	7	20 years	2
Third-rate:			
74 guns	17	13 ,,	4
Fourth-rate:			
64 guns	3	24 ,,	—
Frigates:			
36 guns	4	8 ,,	19
Sloops:			
18 guns	—	—	52
	31	15 years	

The only modern ships at Trafalgar were third-rates and the four frigates. The two largest of the first-rates, the *Victory* and the *Britannia*, were over 40 years of age.

Of the ships building, those with 120 guns were a new type, one of which, the *Hibernia*, was on service in home waters in 1804. As these vessels were almost the largest warships to be built, their details will give some idea of the limits of size of wooden ships. Those for the 74-gun ships are very much the same as for the *Bellona* of 1768 (Pls. XV and XVI), of which pictures of the structure, taken from a model of that time, show the complex nature of the craft of the shipwright. This is also shown by the view of the *Victory* (Frontispiece) and of a ship in frame on the blocks dating about 1800 (Pl. XVII).

Ships of 1805

	120-gun ship	74-gun ship	36-gun ship
Length on gun-deck	205 ft.	176 ft.	149 ft.
Breadth, extreme	54 ft.	48 ft.	39 ft.
Draught of water (midships)	25½ ft.	22½ ft.	18½ ft.
Weight, loaded	4,700 tons	3,040 tons	1,450 tons
Total sail area	24,600 sq. ft.	22,300 sq. ft.	16,400 sq. ft.

It is helpful in thinking of the changes brought about by the use of iron in place of timber to see how the items of the total weight, for a 74-gun ship, compare with a battleship of a century later, the *Dreadnought* of 1905, the first of the modern type.

Percentage details of total weight

Item	(1805) 74-gun ship	(1905) Battleship
Hull	55	35
Armour	—	26
Ballast	6½	—
Masts, sails and rig	8½	—
Engines	—	10½
Coal	—	5½
Guns, powder, shot	10	19
Outfit, crew, stores	20	4
	100	100

It appears that the weight of hull and armour in the modern ship was more than the hull of the wooden vessel, of which the thick structure was perhaps as useful against the guns of that day as the armour of the modern Dreadnought. It might be said that hull and ballast was equal to hull and armour, the point being that all ships carried ballast, which in the 120-gun ship was as much as 375 tons. The weight of engines and coal was twice that of masts, sails and rig. The battleship was five times the size and had three times the speed of the old ship of the line.

Outfit, crew and stores at 20 per cent, or 600 tons for the 74-gun ship, seems a large figure, but the greater part of this was made up of provisions 215, fuel for cooking 52, and fresh water 260 tons.

The largest gun, the 42-pounder, weighed 67 cwt., fired a 42-pound shot, with a charge of 14 pounds of powder. The diameter of the shot was 6¾ in. and the range was just 2000 yards at 5° elevation.

There are records of the timber used to build a 74-gun ship about the year 1760. Broadly it needed some 3000 loads of timber, weighing perhaps 3000 tons, to build such a ship, whose hull weight came out to be about 1650 tons.

The account for timber was made up as follows:

Main timbers	Loads		Percentage	
Oak, compass	1350		45	
Oak strait	600		20	
Fir and elm	200	2150	7	72
Knees		140	under 5	
Thick stuff 10 in. to 5 in.		420	14	
Plank, oak 4 in. to 3 in.		300	10	
		3010		

The main timbers, with knees, took up some 75 per cent of the total, the thick stuff over 14 per cent, and the planking 10 per cent half of which came from Danzig. Very little fir and elm was used and oak formed nearly 95 per cent of the total figure.

Increase in length brought about heavier strains on the hull, and from about 1810 onwards changes in detail were tried to prevent the vessel 'breaking her sheer' by arching or bending. The spaces between the frames and the bottom were filled up solid to make the structure stronger in compression. The sides of the ship were fitted with 'trusses'—timbers which sloped at 45° inside the ship, leaning forward in the after part and leaning aft in the forward part. The lower end rested on a lengthwise timber running along the line of the heads of the floors. The upper ends were carried to the shelf below the lower gun-deck. These trusses took the place of the former heavy riders, which were placed in a transverse plane. The trusses were also kept in place by struts, sloping from their middle to the lengthwise timber.

Attempts were made to improve the fixing to the beams by stronger knees and thicker shelves and water-ways. Still the lengthwise strength of the decks fell far short of the needs of the structure.

Mr Snodgrass, the surveyor for the East India Company, did much to point out the use of iron to strengthen the inside of the frames and the beam-knees. His Company had been driven to such courses owing to the shortage of timber for knees, most or all of which was taken for the fighting ships. He further urged that diagonal braces of timber and iron should be used to cross-tie the keelson to the lower side of the gun-deck. This device, which was not liked in practice, gave great support to maintain the shape of the lower part.

Little more was heard for a long time of the use of iron, although the wood-knees of the fighting ships were made somewhat stronger by fitting brackets of flat strap-iron to their sides.

The wooden structure had reached about its limit, and was not to appear again in marked fashion until much later in the century. Then for a brief spell came the clipper-ships, vessels built with iron frames and with wooden skins and decks to amaze the world in the Swan Song of the Sailing Ship.

PLATE XV

PLATE XVI

H.M.S. *BELLONA* STERN FRAMING

PLATE XVII

FRAME TIMBERS OF A 100-GUN SHIP

PLATE XVIII

WOODEN MERCHANT STEAMER. 307 ft. LONG. 1918

PART III

IRON, STEAM, AND STEEL
(from 1837)

§1. THE COMING OF IRON

IF one could have been present at a village inn some hundred years ago, one might have heard a talk between Tom, the Shipwright, Dick the Smith, and Harry the Boilermaker, running somewhat as follows

THE SHIPWRIGHT. They tell me it won't be long before I shall be out of a job, as I don't hold with using such stuff as iron to build ships. It's flying against nature, that's what it is, since we all know that wood floats and iron sinks.

THE SMITH. Well, as I see it, you make a ship hollow and if you built it of iron, it would still be hollow. And I know that thin iron cans float because I have seen them.

THE SHIPWRIGHT. You think then that if I did the same thing with thin enough iron I could build a vessel that would float.

THE BOILERMAKER. Yes, that's what *I* believe. Look what we do when we make boilers. We cut iron plates and bend them to shape. We fasten the edges with iron rivets to make them tight, and we fix the ends with bars of angle shape—angle bars we call them. Surely you could do much the same.

THE SHIPWRIGHT. I think we might manage something like that if I knew how to handle such things, which I don't. It's one thing to take a nice bit of oak and trim it to shape—we can chip and dub till we get the right sweeps for the frames. I should not know really—nor do I feel I want to know—how to begin with that hard cold iron. It takes a power of strength to bend and it won't twist into place, like we work a plank.

THE SMITH. As it's my job to deal with iron, I feel I could do something if I knew where to begin. We should have to build it up in small pieces, like you do with the ribs and planks. These would not be too heavy to handle for a half-inch of iron would not weigh more than five inches of oak.

THE SHIPWRIGHT. That's all very fine, but I've got to put up the ship on to blocks on the slipway, and I am puzzled how to do that with this new stuff. With timber, I would lay the keel and the stem and the stern-post and set out a line by which to set the frame. Then I would put up the frame in as large pieces as I could manage. I should tie these with rib-bands and cross-spalls and make the cradle all ship-shape and Bristol fashion. That done makes a good start. Then if I have a good idea of the 'fling' of the form, I mark off the planking lines so that the planks slip into place with very little twist. To be honest I can't see myself doing this with iron.

THE BOILERMAKER. You could make the ribs of long angle bars which are not hard to bend and you could make it in one piece from keel to deck.

THE SHIPWRIGHT. But those bars, such as I've seen are very slight, and I doubt if they would hold up under their own weight. What sizes are they, by the way?

THE BOILERMAKER. They are three or four inches on each face and half an inch thick. I don't see why you could not strengthen them by working them double like you do with the wooden rib. And for the floor you could use a transverse plate with an angle on top. Make it flat on the top to form the bottom of a hold and shape it at the lower side to suit the sweeps.

THE SMITH. The top of the frames would get support from the knees that take the ends of the beams.

THE SHIPWRIGHT. But you forget that the frames must go up first before I can fit the beams. I can't think that these flimsy ribs will hold up strong enough to hang the heavy plates on to them. It would be a lot of trouble to see that they were kept to shape.

THE BOILERMAKER. If it were my job, and it is, in my own mind, I think I would make the keel of a wide flat plate. Above that I would run an upright strip lengthwise, joined to the keel with an angle on each side to make it stiff. For the same reason, I would put a pair of angles at the top of the upright—that ought to make a good start. Then to that I would fix the deep floors I spoke of which would reach to the turn of the bilge or so. Perhaps you could keep the floor ends right by bolting them for the time to a wood rib-band.

THE SHIPWRIGHT. I can see how that might help, since we could check the shape by the methods we use for the timber frames. But how to put up the thin ribs after that puzzles me. I could, of course, use more rib-bands and fix cross-spalls at the beam heights. I should expect though to find a lot of crazy work which would give much trouble to get right. Perhaps, Harry, you may have an idea to fix the lower end of the rib which you said might be all in one piece.

THE BOILERMAKER. Why couldn't you join this end to the floor-plate on the other side to its lower bar? This would act just the same as a beam-knee and ought to give a good hold. Yes, I think you might try something like that. It is no worse than building a boiler, except that in your case, as a rule, no two ribs have the same shape. Still a wood ship is just as bad, so apart from learning how to bend an angle bar you could make use of many of your old tricks.

THE SMITH. You can bend bars more easily if you heat them; we are doing that every day. You would want a flat bed to pin them down, to keep their shape when cooling. I think you could arrange that with slabs of cast iron, say six feet square and six inches thick, made level on top, and with holes to drive in the pins to hold the bar in place. All this could be done, but it needs skill to heat the proper places to get the right amount of bend. I could do this if you drew out for me the shapes for the bars.

THE SHIPWRIGHT. We are going too fast. I can see myself putting up a few of these ribs at a time; but I want to be able to work perhaps as much as a run of fifty frames. In that case I need much more in the way of cross-ties—something more solid.

THE BOILERMAKER. What about bulkheads? You will need some and they have to be stout if they are watertight. Could you put these up early and use them to help to tie up the frame?

THE SHIPWRIGHT. Let me see—A run of fifty frames would be about a hundred feet and we might have a bulkhead or bulk'shead, as they are called, every fifty feet or so. I see Harry's idea and I could have a strong frame or two or three in between. The way to build the cradle seems more easy to my mind. Shall I go over it to see how far we have got? It goes something like this. When the blocks are ready on the slipway, I lay first a broad flat keel plate in the proper line. The holes are punched as needed and over the ends inside is a flat strap joining the pieces lengthwise. These straps take the place of the scarphs we use for the wood keel, which take a lot of skill to shape and fit, as I think you know. On top of this I place the upright keel plate running lengthwise. Then I think it might be well to rivet up these parts for say a hundred feet. The next job would be to shape the floor plates, to build the bulkheads and the strong frames and set them up. Then we should bend the ribs, put them in place and tie with ribbands and cross-spalls as needed. Three or four ribbands should be enough, just about the ends of the floors and where the decks come. Yes I seem to see that far! But I would feel more happy to make up the frame in small pieces just as we do for wood. It would be easier to bend the angles in small pieces to suit the sweeps. (*The Smith and the Boilermaker nod their assent.*) We can't lay the plates edge to edge like the planks. There is nothing to hold the oakum to make the seam tight, and anyway with such hard stuff it would work loose and be useless.

THE BOILERMAKER. I don't see that should worry you, as the plates must lap over the edges at the seam to take the rivet.

THE SHIPWRIGHT. That's the way we build boats—what we call 'clinker-built', the lower edge of the plank outside the upper edge of the strake below. That gives me an idea that we should lay the plates this way. I would start with the garboard strake, and to go on in this fashion would not be so much trouble.

It was with some such talk as this in the background that the first iron ships were built, the new stuff being shaped as near the wooden pattern as it could be. All the old defects of putting much of the iron thwartship, and as little as might be lengthwise, stayed, except that the skin with its rivet joints was much stronger than the wooden planking could ever be.

Writing in 1862 Scott Russell said:

I consider the system of building iron ships with transverse frames in the common way as a mere tradition from the shipbuilders in wood to the shipbuilders in iron. Planks of wood would not hold together without other portions of wood laid across them to bind them in place, and keep them in shape. These cross-pieces curved to the shape of the ship, and scarphed to give them continuity, became the frame of the timber ship, and as such were a main element of her structure and strength. Thus frames of a ship became the tradition of the workers in wood. When iron plates were adopted for the skin of a ship, iron frames came in along with them by mere tradition. It was amusing to me to see how in early ships the copy of wood frames was carried so far that the frames were made in separate bits of angle iron, and scarphed and spliced just like frame timbers. Out of these ruts it is hard to rise. I believe the way out is by the adoption exclusively of the longitudinal system, which I believe by this time would have become universal but for the precedent of timber ships.

The real problem was to make the structure strong enough to stand straining in a heavy sea. A few trials soon showed that to build good iron ships needed much skill. Skill to know the nature of iron—skill to know the strains to which iron structures have to submit—skill to know the shapes which make iron more or less able to bear one kind of strain or other—skill to shape the parts so that they may best combine jointly to bear a strain—skill to know the ways to fasten pieces of iron to each other so that the joints shall give strength instead of being sources of weakness.

The kind of skill needed was new as well as rare; there was little knowledge of iron structure or of ocean ships. The shipwrights had to give guidance as to the parts, based upon wooden ships; they hated ironwork and their help was grudging. The smiths alone knew how to handle iron in simple fashion, but they had little in common with the shipwright. Iron was in most use for engines and boilers, and the class of workers had grown up who could cut, bend, shape and join sheets of iron with angles.

Thus it came about that the firms who built engines also began to build ships because the machines and plant needed to fashion iron served the common purpose. All the tools needed to deal with iron are quite unlike those which were used for wood. Treatment is quite changed. Heating, hammering, rolling, punching, shearing and welding were part of the craft of the workers—the smiths, the fitters and the boilermakers. Again, the plater and the riveter took over the work of the shipwright in regard to the skin of the ship. Later, as machines were more used to work the iron, there came about closer contact with the engine-builder.

Scott Russell gave the following idea of the training of the builders of iron ships. He said that for good training the builder-to-be should have served some time in an engine shop as well as in a shipyard. He should have a good knowledge of mathematics and of the theory of naval architecture, and should be a good mechanic. Next he should study the nature, the making, the qualities and costs of iron itself. He should learn to do with his own hands every process dealing with the fitting up and the building of an iron ship. And 'when he has done all this, he will still find that he has a great deal to learn'.

§2. I. K. BRUNEL

THERE are three men whose work and influence did more than any others to bring the iron ship to success and to replace sails by steam. They were all born in the first ten years of the nineteenth century and were all trained as engineers, both mechanical and civil. Thus they knew how to make use of the new metal to meet the strains of the structure, and both Brunel and Scott Russell strove hard to teach people the need to put more of the material lengthwise than was the practice with wooden ships. The third, William Froude, was keen on the study of the motion of ships, both as regards the power needed to drive them and in respect of the manner in which they rolled and pitched at sea. He was the first to show how to give ships a proper shape and the way to obtain, for a wide class of ship problems, a close idea of the power needed to drive them.

For most of their time the Navy stuck to the idea of wooden fighting ships. The modern gun had not yet been made—the first patent for the Armstrong gun being taken out in 1854. The need for armour and thick plating was soon seen, but it was not until after 1860 that the first ironclad—a ship of iron with iron armour—came to be built.

Isambard Kingdom Brunel, born in 1806, was the only son of Sir Marc Isambard Brunel of Norman descent. The father served in the French navy and fled to New York in 1793. He was a skilled mechanic and became engineer to the State of New York, where among other work he built a foundry for cannon. He came to England in 1799 to help General Bentham to convert the dockyards to the use of steam and machines. He built special machines to make the rigging blocks for the Navy. For this purpose he used a large number of machines with such effect that some ten men were able to make as many blocks as before that time were turned out by handwork of 110 people. This block machinery laid many of the patterns for machine-tool work. He used drilling, slotting, and shaping machines, and the details of the lathe were all found in his designs.

As a child Brunel showed a great talent for drawing, always neat and precise. In 1820, when at school at Hove near Brighton, he writes home: 'as to what I am doing, I have been making half a dozen boats lately, till I've worn my hands to pieces. I have also taken a plan of Hove, which is a very amusing job.' He studied mathematics and languages in Paris and paid visits to the engine works of that city. At the age of seventeen he began work in the office of his father in London, where various designs for bridges were under way, and the plans for the first Thames tunnel. On this project, where for the first time a 'shield' was used to bore the tunnel, he acted as engineer. Although begun in 1825 it was only completed in 1843, after many mishaps due to flooding, in the first of which Brunel nearly lost his life.

His success in winning the design for a suspension bridge at Clifton, at the age of twenty-four, brought him in contact with Bristol, then busy with the plans for a railway to London. His work for the Great Western Railway, which he planned and which ran to Land's End and Milford Haven, stands for all time. His bridges were land-marks, but his great idea of the 'Broadgauge' of 7 ft. between railway lines, which eased many problems of transport, had alas, to be given up some 50 years ago. The present gauge of 4 ft. $8\frac{1}{2}$ in. is the distance between the ruts made by the country carts in the north of England. Such is the effect of chance and the clinging to old ideas; whereas Brunel always had the great and the broad vision.

These contacts led him to devote much of his busy life to further his ideas on sea transport by steam. It began in a curious way at a meeting of the directors of the Great Western Railway in London in October 1835. Some one spoke of the 'enormous' length of the proposed railway from London to Bristol. On the spur of the moment Brunel replied: 'Why not make it longer and have a steam boat to go from Bristol to New York and call it the *Great Western*?' This was treated as a joke, since at that time only a small ship, partly under steam, had crossed the Atlantic. That same night Brunel, with T. R. Guppy, talked the question over, and later with three other members of the Board formed a committee to explore the project on which a report was made on 1 January 1836. The Great Western Steamship Company was formed and Patterson, shipbuilder of Bristol, began to construct the vessel launched in 1837.

The hull of wood was 205 ft. long on the keel and 212 ft. long on the water-line. At a draught of water of 16 ft. 8 in. the 'displacement' ready for sea was 2300 tons. (Displacement is the modern term meaning the weight of the volume of sea water displaced by the ship, given in tons avoirdupois.) The breadth of hull was only 35 ft. 4 in. but the width over the paddles and their shielding 'boxes' was nearly 60 ft.

Special pains were taken to give great strength lengthwise:

The ribs were of oak, of scantling (sizes) equal to that of line of battleship. They were placed close together and caulked within and without before the planking was put on. They were dowelled and bolted in pairs: and there were also four rows of $1\frac{1}{2}$ in. iron bolts, 24 ft. long and scarfing about 4 ft., which ran longitudinally through the whole length of the bottom frames of the ship. She was closely trussed with iron and wooden diagonals with shelf pieces, which with the whole of her upper works were fastened with bolts and nuts to a much greater extent than had hitherto been the practice.

Many adverse views were given as to the hazards of using steam engines, but Brunel was able to send the vessel away to New York in April 1838. She took 14 days on the voyage and made as quick a return journey. She ran the same service until 1846, when she was sold to the West India Mail Steam Packet Company, in which service she ran until 1857. She was broken up after a working life of 20 years, a tribute to the skill and courage of Brunel.

In 1838, the need for a second vessel of somewhat larger size being clear, the Company, on Brunel's advice, settled a design for a ship of iron, which was started in July 1839. Then, when the engines were being built, the *Archimedes*, fitted with a screw propeller of the design of Francis Pettitt Smith, came to Bristol early in 1840. After long trials Brunel was in favour of fitting a screw to the new ship, the *Great Britain*, and this was done.

The design of such a structure in the days before wrought iron bridges had begun to be built, and when little was known of the strains which floating structures had to meet, was a great venture. Brunel saw clearly the need to give lengthwise strength for a vessel 322 ft. long, 51 ft. broad, and which weighed some 3600 tons at 18 ft. draught of water. The skin was carried on transverse ribs of iron and fixed thereto by iron rivets. On top of these, at the bottom part of the ship, were laid ten deep lengthwise beams above which was an iron deck—not watertight—fixed by rivets to angle bars at the upper part

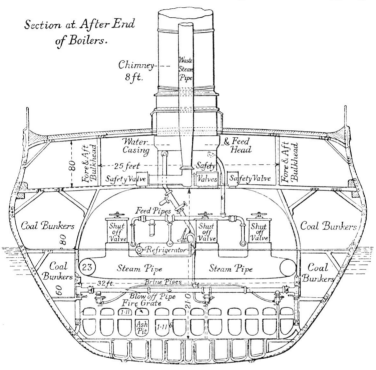

The Great Britain, *iron steamship*, 1840

of the beams. This in effect formed a 'double bottom'—a feature to be applied to most vessels years later. The transverse shape was queer, being very much like that for a wooden ship. The angle ribs, some 20–24 in. apart, were carried up above the upper deck. Two lengthwise bulkheads, running from the top to the bottom of the ship, one on each side, added to the lengthwise strength and formed the sides of the boiler room. The boilers were of a box type, built to fit the shape of the ship, which could be done with the low steam pressure of those days, some 8 lb. per sq.in.

The side spaces were used as coal-bunkers and were tied to the ribs by cross-beams to form a strong member for transverse strength and to support the thin iron skin. Brunel, instead of using beam knees, used angle struts to form a closed triangle fixing the beam ends. There were five main bulkheads across the ship which added to the transverse strength and, being watertight, gave a greater measure of safety after damage. There were two decks of wooden planks carried by iron beams to the ends of which were fixed heavy wooden water-ways scarphed and bolted to the frames and to the iron 'stringer' plates fitted at the side of the ship. The top or sheer strake of the side-plating was made stronger by an outer strap run lengthwise and 6 in. wide and an inner strap 7 in. wide—both 1 in. thick—which were fixed to the plating by rivets.

Progress on the ship was slowed down because of troubles with finance, since the profits of the *Great Western* fell with the growth of the Cunard Company, which by 1843 had three ships on the Atlantic service. So it was not until July of that year that she was floated and some two years more before her first voyage took place from Liverpool to New York. On her second return voyage she broke the screw propeller and reached England under canvas in stormy weather. Her troubles were not over, for in September 1846 she went ashore on the north-east coast of Ireland. She was got off and taken to Liverpool in 1847. These mishaps led to the ruin of the Company, and she was sold to Liverpool owners. After repair she was placed on the run to Australia in 1851. This was written of her in 1870 by Brunel's son: 'She is known as one of the fastest vessels on that line; and remains to testify to the ability and wisdom of those who more than 30 years ago were daring enough to build so large a ship of iron and to fit her with the screw propeller.'

It should be said too that after lying ashore for two winters, subject to storms and damage, the *Great Britain* did not suffer any change of form nor was her structure strained. These trials helped to convince people that iron was fit to be used for ships: wooden vessels, in such straits, would soon have gone to pieces.

One further point concerns the driving of the screw. The slow-turning engines could not give the propeller enough revolutions. Brunel built two drums, that for the engine being 18 ft. in diameter, from which chains drove one of 6 ft. on the screw-shaft. Here was a case of gearing up, whereas now the problem is to reduce the speed of the shaft very much below the revolutions of the steam turbine.

Brunel's thoughts on his work are shown by a letter he wrote to his friend Mr Guppy in August 1843:

I have been thinking a great deal of your plans for iron-shipbuilding, and have come to a conclusion which I believe agrees with your ideas; but I will state mine without reference to yours. At bottom and at top I would give *longitudinal* strength and stiffness, gaining the latter by the former, so that all the metal used should add to the *longitudinal tie*, while in the neutral axis and along the sides, and to resist swells from seas, I would have vertical strength by ribs and shelf-pieces, thus: the black lines being sections of longitudinal pieces, the dotted lines vertical and transverse diagonal plates, throwing the metal as much as possible into the outside bottom plates, and getting the strength inside by form, that is, depth of beams etc., the former being liable to injury from blows etc., the latter being protected.

And now for the screw of which I am constantly thinking, and in the success of which for the *Great Britain*, remember, I am even more deeply interested than you.

If all goes well we shall all gain credit, but 'quod scriptum est manet' if the result disappoint anybody, my written report will be remembered by everybody, and I shall have to bear the storm—and all that spite and revenge can do at the Admiralty will be done! The words 'better sailing qualities than could be given to the *Polyphemus*', which are used in my first report to the Admiralty, I believe have never been forgotten.

In 1851 Brunel became engineer to the Australian Mail Company and under his guidance two ships were built in 1852 by Scott Russell—the *Victoria* and the *Adelaide*. These ships were framed on the transverse system, perhaps because of the troubles to get a 'class' with Lloyds, a matter which was cleared up somewhat later. This work led him to look into the idea of 'a great ship' for the Indian and Australian service. In placing his views before the Eastern Steam Navigation Company in 1852 he says that the project was the same as when the *Great Western* was built. The *Great Eastern*, as the ship came to be called, should be made large enough to carry her own coal for her two engines, paddle and screw.

In April 1853 tenders were sought for both ship and engine. The length was 680 ft., the beam 83 ft. with a mean draught of water of 25 ft. At a draught of 30 ft. her displacement was just over 27,400 tons; the gross tonnage was over 18,900 tons. The screw-engines were of 4000 i.h.p. and ran at 45–55 r.p.m.; the paddle-engines gave an i.h.p. of 2600 at 10–12 r.p.m. The pressure of steam was to be

15–25 lb. per sq.in. The screw propeller had a diameter of 24 ft. and a pitch of 44 ft.; the paddle-wheels were 56 ft. in diameter, with 30 floats, each 13 ft. broad and 3 ft. deep.

There were troubles with finance, and the mishaps when launching the vessel caused a new company to be formed in 1858. Brunel's health began to feel the strain of all this work and he went to Egypt for the winter, to come back in May 1859. He saw the *Great Eastern* just before she left the Thames and died on 15 September, by which time the vessel had got as far as Weymouth.

She was started in the spring of 1854 and after many attempts was launched in February 1858. Her structure was a pattern in most respects, and from the mere point of view of size she was the largest ship to be built until 1899. In the details of the structure Brunel, who in his day built famous bridges, was to some extent guided by the design of the Britannia Bridge over the Menai Straits. The upper part of the girder in way of the topmost deck was built in cells. Two layers of plating laid lengthwise were joined by lengthwise girders which in their turn were held in place by transverse web frames, thus forming a strong upper member.

Brunel saw clearly the need to divide the vessel by bulkheads and other means, to restrict the flooding of the ship should damage occur below water. To this end he fitted an inner skin running up to the lower deck, some 35 ft. above the keel or 5 ft. beyond the deep load-line. This skin was joined to the outer bottom plating by lengthwise girders with transverse webs. The top and bottom parts of this main structure, some 83 ft. wide and 58 ft. broad, were thus formed in what is called 'cellular' fashion. Note the great lengthwise strength thus got by a strong upper and lower member. Perhaps Brunel was helped in this view by the small sizes of the iron plates and joining angles which were the largest to be got in 1854. In those days a plate 10 ft long, 33 in. wide and $\frac{3}{4}$ in. thick weighing 810 lb. was outsize. Whereas to-day plates of mild steel, say 30 ft. long, 6 ft. wide and weighing 3 tons, are not out of the way. The same comment applies to the joining angles: the largest size used for the *Great Eastern* had two equal flanges $4\frac{1}{2}$ in. wide. Extra strength was given by two lengthwise girders which ran from the bottom to the top of the structure throughout the engine and boiler spaces, which were some 350 ft. long, or about half the length of the ship, and 36 ft. wide.

To explain these ideas of structure: The weight of the ship and its contents does not vary, but when passing through waves the support given by the water changes much and quickly. Suppose the ship poised on the crest of a wave, the ends would tend to drop, whereas when across a wave hollow, the midship part tends to sag. These two effects are called 'hogging'—perhaps the shape of a hog's back, and 'sagging'—like the 'sag' of a rope. With 'hogging' the upper member is stretched and the lower part is compressed, whereas for 'sagging' the lower member is stretched and the upper compressed. The parts of the structure farthest from about the centre of depth are subject to the greatest strains, being 'pulled' and 'pushed' in turn as waves pass along the length of the ship.

Transverse strains are not easy to assess, but the pains that had to be taken with wooden ships show that they needed the use of much timber to prevent change of shape causing working of the structure. Such effects are termed 'racking' strains.

In the *Great Eastern* there were ten transverse bulkheads, eight of which ran from keel to upper deck. Brunel meant these to divide the ship into enough parts to restrict flooding after damage. This was the first serious attempt to divide the ship into 'watertight compartments'. This is now a legal question termed 'sub-division' which is applied to all vessels (except cargo ships) in more or less degree, to accord with the number of lives on board.

The bulkheads served to provide the main transverse strength. They are like the piers of a bridge which in this case were 50 ft. apart. The thin plating is made stiff by, and gets support from, lengthwise girders running between the piers. These girders enable the thin plating, here $\frac{3}{4}$ in. thick, to withstand water-pressure from without, loads of cargo above, and to resist 'buckling' or 'wrinkling' when the main structure is being compressed.

It must be agreed that Brunel's handling of the design of the *Great Eastern* before 1860 stands out as a milestone in the progress of building ships of iron and later steel. The vessel never carried out her purpose, but did serve in a marked manner in laying Atlantic and other deep-sea cables. Her troubles proved that paddle-wheels were not suited for ocean work and that screw propellers, in which subject Brunel did much for naval and other ships, could be made to function.

Brunel was greatly helped by J. Scott Russell who built the *Great Eastern* on the Thames. It was no mean task to construct the hull of such a ship weighing some 10,000 tons out of small pieces, the largest of which was less than 30 sq.ft. in area and weighed only one-third of a ton.

His work in the sea sense is shown by the table giving the details of the three 'great' ships which were only a part of his life-work. He built the first real wood steamer, to follow it in a short time with a much larger vessel of iron driven by a screw propeller. His *Great Eastern*, by her size some 40 years before her time, was a pattern of building for all that century, and as far as is known there was never a failure of the structure in any major sense.

Brunel's Ships

	1838 (wood)	1843 (iron)		1854–8 (iron)	
	Great Western	*Great Britain*		*Great Eastern*	
Length: Overall	236 ft.	322 ft.		693 ft.	
Perpendiculars	212 ft.	296 ft.		680 ft.	
Keel	205 ft.	289 ft.		—	
Breadth:	35 ft. 4 in.	51 ft.		83 ft.	
Over paddles	59 ft. 8 in.	—		—	
Depth: Hold	23 ft. 2 in.	32 ft. 6 in.		58 ft.	
Draught of Water	16 ft. 8 in.	16 ft. 0 in.	19 ft. 2 in.	30 ft. 0 in.	34 ft. 0
Displacement (tons)	2300	3000	3900	27,450	32,00

Power and Speed

Sea speed (knots)	8 to 10	12 to 14	13 to 14
Steam-pressure (lb. per sq.in.)	5	8	25 to 30
Coal per day (tons)	43 to 44	40?	350
Type of engines	Paddle	Screw	Screw and Paddle
Revolutions	—	—	Screw: 45–55
			Paddle: 10–12

Diameter 15 ft. 6 in.
Pitch   25 ft. 0 in.

Weight of Hull

900 tons wood	840 tons iron	10,000 tons iron
	160 tons wood	

§3. SCOTT RUSSELL

JOHN SCOTT RUSSELL was born in Glasgow in 1808 and died in 1882. He was meant for the Church, but he loved science and mechanics. He studied at the Universities of St Andrews, Edinburgh and later Glasgow where he got his science degree at the age of sixteen. A little later he went to Edinburgh, first to found a preparatory school and then to start classes in science at the University. These lectures drew many students because of 'the original method with which he treated scientific questions and his excessive force and clearness of exposition'.

He studied factory work at every chance, spending his holidays in he shops, learning from mechanics and millwrights. He also made xperiments at the University with steam engines and boilers. He was sked to allow his name to be put forward for the Chair of Natural 'hilosophy: he was only twenty-four and perhaps thought himself too 'oung, so did not apply.

In 1833 a Scotch Canal Company asked him to make experiments n the use of steam engines to drive canal boats. For this work he ▸uilt his first iron ship—a barge 30 ft. long and 4 ft. beam, drawing in. of water, in order to carry the observers and their instruments. ᴸ little later he built a shallow-draught steamer 120 ft. long in which ᴴe skin was carried by lengthwise girders and transverse web-frames nly, without the usual ribs. From then onwards he strove for what ᴸe called 'the longitudinal system' and used it as he found his chance. ᴸt was said above that Brunel at about the same time was also of the ᴸame mind, using lengthwise girders to a large extent for the *Great Britain* begun in 1839.

Scott Russell was struck by the curious waves that he saw were ᴸrmed in a canal by the motion of the barges. Here he found what ᴸe called the 'wave of translation', a wave-form with one crest only ᴸhich was formed in front of the boat. As a result the British Associa- ᴸon set up a committee to study wave-forms, and Russell read a paper ᴸefore the Royal Society of Edinburgh 'On the Laws by which Water ᴸpposes Resistance to the Motion of Floating Bodies' for which he ᴸas given the great Gold Medal.

Thinking rightly that the outward shape of the ship should be ᴸrmed to accord with the wave pattern it caused, he brought forward ᴸis wave-line system. When in 1836 he became shipyard manager to ᴸessrs Caird and Company of Greenock, he used these ideas for four ᴸhips of the Royal Mail Company, among others that he designed ᴸnd built.

In 1844 he went to live in London and there did much work on ᴸublic affairs. Among other things he became Secretary to the Society ᴸf Arts and Joint Secretary to the Great 1851 Exhibition. Of him in ᴸis work it was said by the Prince Consort: 'By dint of Mr Scott ᴸussell's tact, judgement, penetration, resource and courage, obstacles ᴸanished and intrigues were unmasked.'

He applied science and the study of structures to improve the ship- ᴸright's trade. He brought about a novel way of plating the skin of the ᴸssel. The early ships were built on the 'clincher' system which caused

much trouble because under that plan the plates were only in contac
with the ribs at the lap of the seams. This meant that the rivets joinin
the rest of the plate to the frame were without support along thei
length and had to depend solely on their forged head and their point
set up by the riveter with his hammer. To get over this defec
taper slips were made by the smith to fill the gap and, with mor
or less of a fit, were driven in by hand after the seams were fixe
to the ribs.

Scott Russell saw that it would be much easier to cut strips from
a plate itself of the actual width of the flange of the angle, and which
would ensure the proper bedding of the plate on to the rib. This mean
a new scheme for the skin plating. Each alternate strake was set ou
the thickness of the strip from the frame and lapped over both it
neighbours at the edges. This scheme was known as the 'alternat
system' and the strakes classed as 'raised' and 'sunken'. Thus, th
garboard strake, next to the keel plate, would bed on the flange of th
rib, becoming the first 'sunken' strake, and the next plate would res
on a slip, being the first 'raised' strake. In turn this process woul
repeat with 'in' and 'out' strakes in alternate order.

The fitting of the skin to the ribs was also made simpler since al
the 'inner' strakes, or every other strake, were first put up and fixe
and then the 'outer' plates fitted with ease.

From early days he sought various means to support the skin b
lengthwise girders as well as transverse frames. He thought very muc
on the same lines as Brunel with whom he worked on the building o
the Great Eastern. It is curious that he did not seem to see that to ge
his 'longitudinal' system into practice he had to provide the craftsme
with a simple method to erect a cradle to take the skin plating. It i
one thing to design the 'ideal' structure for a bridge, it is quit
another problem to devise a bridge which can be erected piece b
piece high in the air. Perhaps it was that the cost of building was lo
and workers were in plenty. Anyway, this neglect to study the problem
of erection put off the proper use of lengthwise structures until th
early years of the present century.

The first iron ship of the Royal Navy took up Scott Russell's view
on lengthwise girders, which were used for the Bellerophon, built i
1863 to the designs of the Chief Constructor of the Navy who late
became Sir Edward Reed. In the fighting ships, cost comes secon
to weight of hull since for a given weight the aim is to carry many gun
with proper armour at high speed. Thus the question of ease c

uilding does not enter into the picture so much as it does with the
merchant vessel.

In an early attempt Scott Russell put a lengthwise girder along each
trake of plating about at right angles to its surface. For the keel
which was flat he used a built-up section of a vertical plate with double
ngles at top and bottom. For other strakes the plate girders had
ingle angles only. These had the support of partial bulkheads at even
paces between the main bulkheads. He explains that if the skin is
nick enough and curved enough it can support itself between trans-
erse webs. In fact small ships have been built with cross-bulkheads
nly and without any other framing. The essence of his scheme was
ne manner of how to support the skin. Two plates at right angles can
e joined with two angle bars, one on each side of the line of contact.
he broad plate will not distort because the narrow plate above
revents it. The narrow piece will not bend since the broad plate
esists. The use of this right-angle couple forms the basis on which
 build up any member of such a structure as a ship.

In a paper read to the Institution of Naval Architects in 1862 Scott
.ussell explained his ideas and gave drawings of the *Annette*, an iron
.ipper of 700 tons with auxiliary screw. The vessel was 190 ft. long,
 ft. broad with a 'moulded depth' of 18 ft. This 'moulded depth'
as taken from the top of the flat keel plate to the underside of the
on deck at the side of the ship.

The structure, as he planned it, had at least 25 per cent more iron
aced lengthwise than if it had been built on the transverse system of
ose days. He concludes that the strength would be that amount
reater, the weights of structure being the same for the two ships.
is figures for weights are:

	Old system (tons)	New system (tons)
In the skin	110	110
In lengthwise framing	40	130
In transverse framing	130	40
Total	280	280
Transverse weight (%)	46½	14½
Lengthwise weight (%)	53½	85½

Scott Russell describes 'the *Longitudinal System*' as follows:

1. In dividing the ship by as many transverse water-tight iron bulk-
:ads as the practical use of the ship will admit. I like to have at least one
alkhead for every breadth of the ship in her length. In a ship eight
eadths to her length I wish to have at least eight transverse bulkheads.

2. I have between these bulkheads, what I call partial bulkheads, or the outer rim of a complete bulkhead, with the centre part omitted, so as to form a kind of continuous girder running transversely all round the ship and not interfering with stowage.

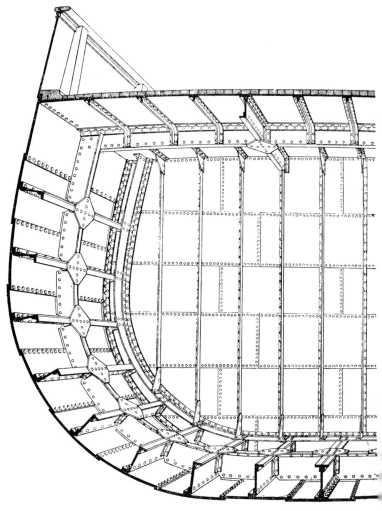

Lengthwise framed ship, Annette (1861)

3. I run from bulkhead to bulkhead longitudinal iron beams or stringers one along the centre of every plate of the skin, so giving each strake of plates the continuous strength of an iron beam, one portion placed at right angles to another. This longitudinal forms one continuous scarph across

ll the butt joints of the plates, hitherto their weakest part; and adds also
o the strength of the rivets of the joint the help of a line of rivets and angle
rons along the centre of the plate. These longitudinals and the skin are
herefore one.

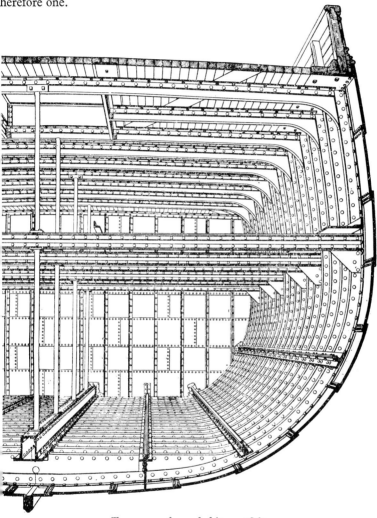

Transverse framed ship, c. 1860

4. What remains over after this is done, of the superfluous iron formerly
sed in ribs, I make into a continuous iron deck, mainly carried by the bulk-
eads, and by longitudinals under it; and I believe this iron is infinitely
etter applied in a deck than in ribs fastened to the skin.

He refers to the need for greater skill of the shipwright, but, as said above, he does not mention the troubles of erection nor does he speak about the natural dislike of the craftsmen to such a drastic change in the methods of building. He ends his paper with this statement:

It may be considered a disadvantage of the longitudinal system that somewhat greater skill is required in its design, greater intelligence in its construction, and greater accuracy and excellence in its workmanship; blunders made are less easily remedied, want of forethought in the beginning is less easily compensated by afterthought, and blundering execution will make a mess of it; but I trust that the growing intelligence among ship-builders, the growing science among naval architects, better information among shipowners, greater knowledge in ship captains and better training among workmen, of all of which this Institution is at once the index and the efficient means of promotion, will bring us to a point of design and execution in this country, such that we shall never be prevented from preferring the better to the worse for want of science, forethought, or skill.

A little later, in 1865, Scott Russell brought out his monumental work, *The Modern System of Naval Architecture*. It is one of the largest of printed books and has three volumes, one of text and two of plates. The size of the page is 27 × 20 in. and each page has 50 lines and some 1000 words. It contains much of the known knowledge of the time and were it more handy in size would be of greater value.

The text bears out the clearness of style and the power of analysis which were among the great gifts of Scott Russell.

One great debt owed to him was the action he took to found the Institution of Naval Architects—the first body of its kind and the parent of many others throughout the world—with the object of the study of the science of the shipwright's trade.

§4. EARLY IRONCLADS

NAVAL constructors, whose chief became Sir Edward Reed, were guided by the views of Scott Russell as to the use of lengthwise girders for the lower part of the structure. In the *Bellerophon*, begun in 1863 (Pl. XIX), a 'double bottom' like that of the *Great Eastern* ran for some two-thirds of the ship's length. To form this feature an inner watertight skin was fitted some 4 ft. above the keel plate and over 30 in. deep at the turn of the bilge. Such depths were needed to give access to the structure in order to paint and to inspect; such closed-in spaces are

PLATE XIX

The "Bellerophon"

THE EARLY IRONCLAD *BELLEROPHON*, BUILT ON THE
BRACKET FRAME SYSTEM. BEGUN IN 1863

prone to corrode in the presence of moisture. To connect the inner and outer skin, besides the upright or vertical keel, lengthwise girders were spaced about 6 ft. apart. These in their turn were fixed to 'bracket-plates', a novel type of transverse member at every 4 ft.

The upper part of a 'bracket-plate' was a single angle under the inner bottom, running in one piece right across the ship, through slots in the lengthwise girders (a sort of inner frame). There were two brackets, one on each side of the longitudinal at every 4 ft., reaching down to the frame angle forming the outer shape for the skin plating. These frame ribs were in short pieces between longitudinals and were carried by the lower ends of the 'bracket-plates'. The shape of these plates was also novel. They were made in one piece to be equal in extent to two single brackets (one at the top and one at the bottom). The free edge was curved, with its least widths at about mid-depth; it was wide enough at the bottom to take four rivets and at the top for three rivets. The brackets were fixed by upright angle bars to all lengthwise girders. In essence the double bottom was made up of cells some 6 ft. wide across ship and 4 ft. lengthwise. Every fifth transverse member was built solid, as was also the fourth longitudinal from the keel. They were made watertight by angles of staple shape forged by the smith. The 'cellular' bottom was thus formed of a series of watertight boxes some 29 ft. long and 24 ft. wide on each side of the vertical keel, which was also watertight.

Above the fourth longitudinal the inner skin ran upright reaching to the main deck, and forming side cells also split into watertight sections by transverse solid frames, just in the same way as the double bottom. The forged angles, making the solid transverse frames tight, were shaped in one piece like a staple, the lower part forming the rib frame and the two arms reaching half-way up the lengthwise plates. The making of these staple irons needed much skill and was costly. Each had to be of a shape to suit its special place and there were very few which were alike. To pass a lengthwise girder through a transverse bulkhead and to make it tight was not easy, because the compartments had to stand a water-pressure of some 25–30 ft. head. This pressure, about 15 lb. per sq. in., is that due to the draught of water of the ship and to a margin of head when the vessel after damage would float deeper.

Tightness was easier with salt water than it was later when oil came to be carried in 'bulk' in tanks which ran to the skin of the ship. With a water leak, rusting tends to make the joint tight, whereas oil keeps the joints clean. It must be kept in mind too, that iron is elastic and the ship 'works' as the support given by the waves changes and as the loads in the holds vary. So that a joint needs good rivets and good skill to maintain its tightness when the structure 'works', as it must do, to adjust the stretch of the iron to the strains brought on the structure.

This 'bracket-plate' system had as its objects to save weight, to make the detail simpler, to increase the strength and to improve the safety. It was not easy to erect on the slip and for that reason was costly to build, as indeed are the fighting ships of these days.

The flat keel was formed of two plates, an inner and an outer, the latter being the wider, and taking on its edge the lodgment of the next, or garboard strake. The other skin plates were laid 'out' and 'in' in turn, noting that the first 'in' strake was the garboard and that flat strips were fitted between the 'out' strakes and the angle ribs.

In the process of building, the first step was to lay the outer keel plate on the blocks with its edges 'flanged' as needed and the rivet-holes drilled. (Flanged means bending the edges as needed, since there was no keel in the usual sense; this applies towards the end of the ship.) The inner keel plate was got ready and laid above the outer keel, its end butts being about midway between those of the outer keel.

The vertical keel plate was planed to width and scores were cut at the top for the inner transverse angles to pass through. The scores were punched by machine to allow the complete angle to be set in, so that its top was flush with the upper edge of the vertical keel-plate.

To show the care that was taken, this account, given by Reed, may be quoted:

When a sufficient number of pieces had been prepared and fixed, a piece of the keel angle iron was fitted in place and the rivet holes having been marked, it was taken away and drilled, after which it was re-planed and riveted up.[1]

This practice of fitting a piece of the structure in place, taking it down and putting it up again, sometimes more than once, was kept up by shipwrights in the Royal dockyards until the start of the present century.

The keel members were then riveted and the bracket-plates fixed by bolts and nuts. These 'bracket-plates' seem to have been made in one piece before putting up, that is, a bracket at each end, with the

[1] Sir E. J. Reed, *Shipbuilding in Iron and Steel* (1869).

lower angle, which formed the outer part of the cradle which takes the skin plate. This same process went on as far as the next longitudinal, which was placed upon a ribband laid fore and aft to which it was screwed. These lengthwise girders had a continuous angle at the bottom, but at the top the double angles were in short pieces between the slots through which the inner transverse frame ran.

It seems curious that the rib proper, which supports the outer bottom plating, was not made in one piece from the keel outwards to, say, the fourth longitudinal. For in that way the proper shape of the ship could have been settled at the start. The lengthwise girders could have been dropped over these and the upper edge of the bracket-plate made of short pieces of angle. It would seem that an attempt to get the best out of both worlds was made—to allow both lengthwise and transverse parts to be continuous, and also to provide easy methods of building. Against this the amount of checking of the structure was great and the use of ribbands and shores called for much skill.

Plate XIX shows details of this 'cellular' bottom structure in which one lengthwise member is fixed to each outer strake. It will be seen that for the structure above the turn of the bilge the system of framing is transverse, as it is for the upright side and for the deck beams. The 'cellular' method used for the upper deck of the *Great Eastern* did not find favour for fighting ships, since it brought an increase in the depth of the structure.

The longitudinals, except where watertight, were made lighter by punching man-holes of oval shape about 2 × 1 ft. in the middle of the spaces between the transverse frames. These holes served another purpose, to give access to inspect the structure.

In the *Bellerophon* is seen the complex nature of the support needed for the thick armour plates at the side of the ship. A lower shelf formed the top of the 'cellular' bottom. An inner skin—really the outer skin of the ship—runs to the upper deck. Outside the skin are worked square logs of teak some 10 in. thick to form a bed on which to place the slabs of iron armour, which were some 6 in. thick.

The skin was worked with iron plates which ran to 10 ft. in length and 33 in. in width, such as were used for the *Great Eastern*. The Royal Navy used greater lengths, from 12 ft. up to even 16 ft., and wider plates, where these could be got. The 'in' and 'out' system was found to be handy, using parallel strips between the frame bar and the outer strakes. Special care was taken to get a proper 'shift of butts', so that there were two 'passing strakes' between butts which were in the same transverse plane. Further, the butt ends of adjacent strakes were not placed nearer than two 'frame spaces'. To achieve this, plates had to be six frame spaces long, which meant a length of some 12 ft. for merchant ships where the ribs were up to 24 in. apart.

In warships, owing to the wide spacing of the bracket-frames, 48 in., and the short length of the plates, 12 ft., this plan had to be changed. In such cases the butts of adjacent strakes were only one frame space apart lengthwise, giving the same distance as for the cargo vessel. With this change there was a gain, since the number of 'passing strakes' was three instead of two.

The purpose of this 'shift of butts' was to avoid any line of weakness in a transverse plane. Broadly, with proper planning the number of 'passing strakes' was one less than the number of frame spaces in the length of the plate. Thus for a frame space of 4 ft. a plate 12 ft. long would permit two 'passing strakes' and with a 20 ft. length there could be four such strakes.

The same idea was used for wooden planks and was thought to be needed when the skin was built of iron plates, although these were joined at the ends with inside straps, through which a double row of rivets passed through each plate. Taken as a whole, the iron skin had very nearly the same strength at the joint as elsewhere—a far stronger joint than in the wooden ship. The aim to provide equal strength in all ways was a proper one with an elastic structure, since it made the strain 'even' over the joints. Often at the ends of the lengthwise girders and of transverse members, there occur stiff areas which find it hard to yield under stress, and in such regions, rivets are prone to 'work' under strain.

Edges were joined through the overlaps by two rows of rivets. Many patterns, zigzag and three rows with every other left out in the line farthest from the joint, were tried. Somewhere about 1865 the 'double-chain' design was found to suit most needs. In this device the two rows each had the same distance between centres and were in the same line, square to the butt or edge. Holes were easier to punch and could be made to suit the angles joining the lengthwise and transverse members.

§5. METHODS OF WORKING

IT has become clear that the process of building a ship involves a high degree of order and method. Thanks to Sir Edward Reed there is on record an account of the various systems of work that were in vogue in the early sixties of last century. It may be well to describe the system used at that time on the Mersey by Messrs Laird, who were among the first builders of iron ships, and had built up a practice which was found to suit many needs. That firm, as early as 1837, had built for the coastwise trade from London the *Rainbow*, a vessel 185 ft. long, of 600 tons burden with engines of 180 h.p.

The form of the ship was laid off on the mould loft floor in the same fashion that was used for wooden ships, that is, to show the shape of every rib—ribs being spaced up to 24 in. apart.

While this was going on a block model of wood was made on a scale of $\frac{1}{2}$ in. to 1 ft. or $\frac{1}{24}$ full size on which could be drawn the whole of the outside skin plating. This was painted white and on it were drawn the frame lines, the edges and butts of the plating, the deck edges and the run of any lengthwise members. From this model the sizes to order the plates were taken. The strakes starting from the keel plate were given letters *A*, *B*, *C*, *D*, and so on, and numbers starting from aft were used to denote each plate of a strake. Plates were ordered 1 in. longer and $\frac{1}{2}$ in. broader than the model shown; larger amounts were added in cases where the surface was much curved or twisted. The length of frames was taken from the mould loft floor as well as the shape of floors and the floor plates. The model was also used to show the 'shift of butts' for all members such as keels and keelsons as well as plates, to ensure as far as could be done that there was a proper distance between the joints of the structure.

The frame lines when faired in the mould loft were copied on to 'scrive' or 'scrieve' boards near at hand to the slabs on which the frame angles were bent to shape. The 'board' of planks, planed to a smooth surface, is large enough to take at full size the lines of the forward body and of the after body which were each kept apart for ease of access. The upper surface is coated with a mixture of lamp-black and size, to make it easy to see fine lines and chalk marks. The scrieve gets its name from the practice of *scriving* the lines around a curved batten pinned in place with a special tool, a hook with a point like a gouge chisel, called a 'scrieve-hook'.

The screive, as well as giving the outside shape of the frames, shows
many other details. These include the plate edges, heights of floors,
beam-ends as well as the level (or water) lines, and the diagonals used
for fairing the form in the mould loft. These latter marks are useful to
measure the bevel or slope of the flange of the frame bar on the outside
of the ship; the other flange of the bar is always kept in a transverse
plane. The bevel is fixed by the inward slope between two adjacent

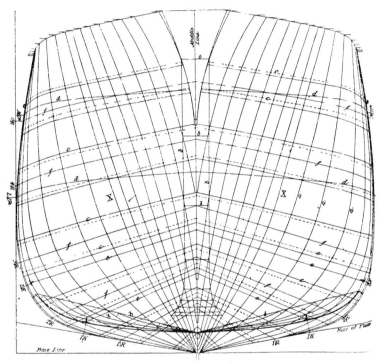

Scrive board for forward body of iron ship, c. 1880

frames, the distance apart of these two being known, and the flange is
so bent that the angle is 'open', or greater than a right angle.

The levelling blocks or 'bending slabs' were formed of cast-iron
blocks with a flush upper surface. These blocks were made up in
6 ft. squares and were 6 in. thick with holes 6 in. apart. A 'set iron'
or thin flat bar about 1 in. wide and $\frac{3}{8}$ in. thick is bent to the curve of
the frame as shown on the screive and has the spots needing notice
marked on it in chalk. This 'set iron' is laid on the 'bending slab' and
is fixed in place with iron pins and wedges and is made fast on top by

iron 'dogs', round bars bent nearly square and driven into the holes to give a wedge effect.

The angle is placed in a long furnace to be heated to a proper amount and is then drawn out and placed on the slab. One end is fixed by pins and with the help of levers, wedges and hammers, and working from the fixed end the frame bar is bent to the shape of the

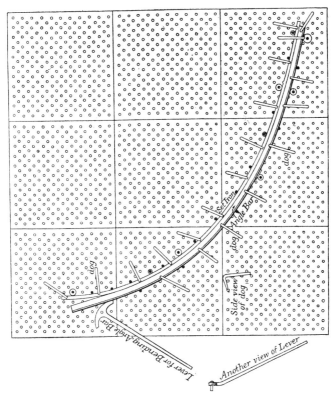

Bending slab, showing process of bending an angle bar

'set iron'. The flange is then worked to the bevel wanted, by the use of levers with slots which fit over the flange that has to be bent. As the bevel varies along the length of the bar, so skill is needed to get a gradual change between the places where the bevel is given. Care has to be taken to prevent the bottom of the flange from getting a hollow form near the corner, or else the plating will not be able to bed firmly. The angle frame is then 'dogged' in place, left to cool and then tried in place against the lines on the screive board. If correct, the plate edges are notched on the frames and the holes for the rivets to take the plates are marked off. If the frame is made up of two bars, the outer and the inner or 'reverse' bar, the rivet holes to connect the two bars are set off to avoid the holes that take the edges of the plates. The outer frame holes are punched from the outside, since holes made in this way are taper and the rivets should fill the holes when they are closed up. Holes in the frame flange for the plate edges are drilled in place after the ship is framed and the plating lines are marked off.

The keel is built up first on a line of blocks near to the slipway. It is then taken down and placed on the building blocks and riveted. The forward and after ends are fitted with scarphs to take the lower edge of the forgings which form the stem- and stern-posts.

Moulds for the beams showing the round up and the various lengths are got ready. The beams at this time were made of angle bulb plate—a flat plate with a bulb at the lower end. Double angles fixed on each side by rivets formed the top of the beam. Later bars were rolled in one piece, with a double flange at the top, which were known as T-bulbs. This double flange was needed to take the joints of the wooden deck planks. When it became the practice to fit iron decks this form of section bar was made simpler by using only one flange at the top, and to this the name of 'angle-bulb' was given, and known as L-bulb.

The 'camber' or 'round of beam' was small, some $\frac{1}{4}$ in. per ft. length. With such slight curve the beams, after being cut to length, were bent cold by the use of strong clamps with screws midway between the arms which straddled the beam. Such clamps are still used to bend tram and railway lines.

To do away with bracket-knees, the ends of the beam were heated and slit lengthwise along the middle of depth. The lower part was then bent to the proper shape for the inner side of a knee. The bar was again heated and a shaped plate welded into the gap so that the outer edge agreed with the frame line. The holes needed for the rivets to fix the beam-end to the frame bar were set off by the use of templates, which were marked off at the ship. The holes having been made in the arm, the beams were put in place, set fair to the beam-line and clamped so that the holes in the frame bar could be drilled with the beam in place.

After the keel is fixed the framing starts, working from amidships towards the bow and the stern. Before the frames are lifted staging is set up to support the ribbands which take the heads of the frames at the deck or gunwale level. The ribs are fixed with bolts to the ribband and to the keel and are shored and braced with cross-spalls. Other ribbands are now fixed and the fairing of the frames checked from the slipway. This account relates mainly to the building of a merchant ship without an inner skin and in which floors are used for the bottom structure. Hence, the next step is to prepare the floor-plates from the lines given on the scrieve board. These are put in place at the ship to mark the holes for the rivets which connect to the ribs. The plate is taken down, the holes for the reverse bar are set off and punched, while the reverse bars are being bent, bevelled, punched and faired. Floors are fixed in place with bolts to secure the frame, the plate and the reverse bar, and the whole riveted at the same time.

When enough ribs are set up a start is made with getting some of the beams in place. To ensure correct fit a strake of skin plating is worked near the beam-ends, fixed by bolts to the frames and shored. The notches on the frames show the plate edges. Ribbands and deck heights are faired by light wood battens held to the flanges by clips. The lines for the plating are marked off in chalk on the frames and the laying of the skin can now begin.

The lowest or garboard strake is an 'inner' plate and is the first to be put in place. There follow other inside strakes working upwards. These are fixed to the frames by rivets, and the ribbands which support the cradle as well as the shores are moved to bear on the inner strakes and to clear the way for fitting outer plates. The shape and holes are got by using a light batten template of thin wood built up of pieces wide enough to take the rivet holes at edges and butts and with cross-pieces along the frame flanges, again to fix these latter holes.

This template is taken from the ship and the holes are marked with a wooden plug with a hollow end dipped into a can of whitening giving a thick circle for guide. The lines for edges and butts are shown by a chalk line.

The template is laid on the plate and the various lines set out thereon. The edges are then sheared to shape and the butts are planed. These strakes being inside strakes, the edge rivet holes are marked off by a further template or set off by measure, the centres being struck with a hard steel centre punch. For the butts a special pattern is used and applied to the template, the hole centres are bored through and with a sharp pointed punch a 'pop mark' is made on the plate.

After the holes are punched the plate is curved to shape by passing through rolls. The machine consists of two rolls at the bottom geared to each other and driven by an engine. The third roll above is idle but can be raised or dropped as needed. The top roll can be tilted and the plates put through at an angle sideways to get the correct twist. To obtain the proper shape, section moulds are made of light batten at the end planes and at the middle. The back edge of each template is made straight so that the three moulds are kept in 'winding', that is to say the back edges can be sighted so as to lie in the same plane. The plate is now put up and held in place by cotters and pins.

For outside plates a template is also made at the ship, but in this case, where the inner strake is in place, the holes for the edge laps are marked through the plate. This brings about a slight change in the manner of setting out the holes for outside strakes.

The punching of holes in iron causes the hole to be taper on the side from which the 'wad' is forced out. The iron receives some damage in this process and so the cone shape is made smooth by a taper drill which takes away most of the stressed part; this work is known as 'countersinking'. Since, where two plates lap, the two holes should be parallel to suit the driving of the rivet, it follows that holes have to be punched from the plane of contact—or the 'faying [bearing] surface'. Thus *inner* strakes are punched from the *outside* and *outer* strakes from the *inside*.

This involves a device to mark off the holes for the edges of outer strakes, since the template is made for the outside surface and the holes have to be marked on the inside of the plate. A special 'marker' or 'reverser' is used. Two flat strips of wood are kept apart by a block at one end. At the other end the upper piece has a hole the same size as the rivet and the lower piece straight below has a wooden marking plug. The template is placed on blocks at a proper height above the inner surface of the strake on which the template rests. The hole is sighted through the template when the lower piece is pressed down to leave the round mark for the rivet hole. After the same routine as for inner strakes, the outer plating is put in place and made fast by cotters and pins.

The flat liners are marked by templates at the ship, curved and punched and driven in place between the frame flanges and the plates. Twisted and very curved plates were heated and brought to shape with hammers. In such cases iron rods were bent to the curve of the frames and of the edges. The corners of the four bars were welded. Rods were also bent to get the shape of each frame. A 'bed' of angle irons was made, kept in place with iron blocks below and the heated plate shaped to fit. For such cases a special grade of good iron was needed, and it was the duty of the shipwright to use as few as he could of these shaped plates, within reason.

Even at this time (1865) the ironwork in the merchant shipyards had passed from the shipwright to a special class of workman known as 'platers'. In the Royal dockyards, even 50 years later, the shipwright still carried out the main details of the work with the help of unskilled labour. Each 'plater' had a gang of some four to six men to assist him who were called 'platers' helpers'. There was also a group of iron-workers whose special task was 'frame turning'.

With the framing fixed, and a large part of the skin strakes shaped and hung up, the riveting squad gets to work on the outside plating. A riveting squad consists of two riveters who hammer up the rivet points on the outside, a 'holder-up' who places the heated rivet in the hole from the inside and holds up the head with a heavy hammer on a long handle which is carried by a hook slung through a nearby hole, to form a pivot about which the handle acts as a lever. There are two rivet boys to work the small forge by which the rivets are heated.

The first task is to get the 'faying' surface in close contact. This is done by 'screwing-up' a number of screws and bolts, perhaps one bolt to every three or four holes. It occurs from time to time that some holes are 'unfair' and the rivet would be thus placed at a slant. In such event the proper practice was to 'rimer' the holes with a long taper bar with cutting edges. Sometimes 'drifts' were used—conical pins driven to distort the hole by force, causing damage to the iron plate. 'Drifting' was not liked and, if there was much of it, was deemed to show lack of skill in shaping the work. The rivets had a 'pan-head' on the side where put in place and a neck formed by slight coning, more or less to fit the countersink. The rest of the shank was parallel. The lengths were cut so that the hole was filled and enough left to form a head flush with the surface when closed with the hammers. In some cases heads were slightly convex, being made complete by a 'snap' tool with a hollow end. Riveting was paid for as piecework. The foreman tested the complete rivets with a hammer, judging 'soundness' by the 'ring'.

The 'caulkers', a further trade, close the seams with steel chisel tools. With a 'lap' joint, a 'splitter' makes a groove to set down a burred edge in contact with the plate. By the same tool used the other way round the split part is forced in neatly against the lap. Flush butt-joints with a strap at the back need other treatment. Here a cut is made on either side of the line of butt and the burred part driven towards the butt edge. The double burr so curved is rounded off by the use of a 'fullering' tool, leaving a neat pattern. This caulking had to be done lightly or the effect of the staving up of the iron might force the joint open or the plate set away from the 'faying' surface.

§6. MERCHANT SHIPS OF IRON

APART from the big ships of Brunel most of the merchant vessels were of small size for many years. The simple form of structure served their needs because their chief demand was for local strength, for which there was more than enough material. Cost and ease of building were the main concerns and the use of transverse frames did not require deep thought nor extra care in fitting. From these aspects the early iron ships were mainly sides and bottom kept in shape by the support of transverse frames, which also carried the deck beams. The rib was made of a single angle running from keel to gunwale and to support the flat bottom a plate with a flange at its top ran across the ship from bilge to bilge. The extra strength thus supplied was seen to be useful to improve the frames, which being built up from small pieces needed a length of bar to cover the joints. Thus it was an easy step to combine the frame bar with an inner angle with its flange facing the other way, making a built-up Z shape, known as a Z-bar. This form of section bar was later rolled in one piece and found much favour for many uses. Later again the inner flange of the Z was squeezed into a bulb, just as for the beam section for which the L-bulb came to be used.

The frame and 'reverse' bar had other claims, since they could be run at the bottom and top of the plate floor in a simple manner. Lengthwise strength was given by the skin plating, the decks, the bottom and the keel. As yet iron decks were rare. There was a stringer plate at the side of the ship at the beam-ends. The lower deck was of beams only with some lengthwise ties. The upper deck was planked with wood below which cross-strips of plating were used to tie the tops of the beams.

Later, as the vessels became larger (see figure on p. 125), extra lengthwise members were fitted to the bottom of the ship. First, a built-up keelson in the shape of a box was run above the keel on top of the floors. Then a second girder of plates between the floors, which were fixed thereto and to the bottom plating, had double angles run lengthwise over the inside of the floor. A third support, where the floor plates end at the bilge, was made up of two bars and at times a bulb-plate again forming a lengthwise girder. Lastly, a fourth member of the same kind, made up of two angles, ran about midway of the depth to the lower deck. It will be seen that these details are very like the extra strength worked into wooden ships. This simple structure served for many types of small vessels, although it is clearly wanting in lengthwise strength.

A costly system used in the colliers taking coals from the Tyne to the Thames led to a great change in the bottom structure of such ships. (In 1876 more than 3,250,000 tons of coal were brought to London by sea.) These colliers had to return to their ports with empty holds and being so light in the water were at the mercy of wind and waves. Like the wooden ships they needed ballast to keep them under control, since to be seaworthy a vessel should never draw less water than about half her load draught.

A sailing collier from the Tyne to the Thames took three weeks to carry say 250 to 400 tons of coal. When she got there the custom of the river forbade her to discharge more than 49 tons a day, which meant that the larger ships had to stay at their berths some 10 days. The vessel then had to take on board river gravel, known as Thames ballast, for which the Trinity lighters charged 1s. a ton, with 6d. extra for putting it on board. That was not all the trouble, for on return to the Tyne the River Commissioners claimed 1s. a ton for dues for bringing a cargo into port and 10d. a ton extra for its discharge on to the bank-side. Huge mounds of ballast heaps were built up on the riverside which stayed well into this century and took up much space which was of great value to trade.

The steam collier was able to do the sea trip in 36 hours and, what is more, had pumps which could clear water from the bilges of the ship. It was soon seen that water could be let into tanks as the coal was taken out and when the ship got to the Tyne these could be emptied into and pumped out of the bottom of a ship.

As early as 1852 the *John Bowes* was built at Newcastle and fitted with iron tanks, and in 1854 the *Samuel Laing* had fixed iron tanks placed on top of the floors. The success of these plans made the time of a round trip for such colliers only about a week. It was noted that without much trouble the iron used for the tanks could be made to form a part of the structure, and somewhere about 1860 the McIntyre tank design came into service. An inner bottom was carried by lengthwise girders placed on top of the floors and on a 'margin-plate' running fore and aft just about the turn of the bilge.

The whole of the closed space between the inner and outer bottoms and the margin-plate could be used to take water ballast. The structure was still not made use of to the best purpose and many other designs were tried. In the year 1876 Messrs Hunter and Austin built the *Fenton* at Sunderland. This design, while keeping the margin-plate device of McIntyre, made use of both lengthwise members and

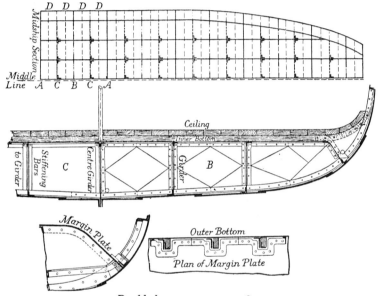

Double bottom structure, 1877

transverse members in the form of bracket-plates, to set the pattern for the structure of double bottoms for the future.

The 'room and space' of the frames was 22 in., and the ribs ran in one piece through all the other members and through the margin-plate. At every eight frame spaces, that is, at every 14 ft. 8 in., solid plate frames were fitted, filling the whole space across the ship. Between the keel and the margin-plate there were two lengthwise members, some 4 ft. apart, worked in one piece between the solid plate frames. Midway were fitted transverse bracket-plate frames, four triangular pieces at each corner of the cell formed by the lengthwise members, the frame bar and the reverse bar under the inner bottom. Between these bracket-frames and the solid plate frames the

nner bottom was carried by reverse bars running over the lengthwise
girders, and every second of these had a pair of vertical angles fixed
to the longitudinal frame and running from the rib frame to the
reverse bar. This account seems complex, but the figure on p. 140
explains simply how from keel to margin-plate the shape of the
structure is fixed by the solid plate frames, the bracket-frames and the
lengthwise girders.

One merit of this design is that when the double bottom is built,
which is the first part to be done, the margin-plate forms a base to
connect the frame ribs at their lower end. A small floor is built up of
a three-sided shaped plate, one edge of which takes the frame bar,
the upper edge the reverse bar, and the third is fixed by an angle to
the margin-plate. A stronger joint is made by taking the reverse bar
right on to the inner bottom or 'tank top' and fixing this to the
reverse bar within the tank. This joint is subject to perhaps the
greatest strain of any in a ship, and in large vessels has been a cause
of trouble. Still, this form of building the double bottom first and
then erecting the transverse framing thereon to this solid base, has
brought about a simple and yet complete type of structure.

Although such changes came about because of the needs of colliers,
it was some time before double bottoms came into use for deep-sea
ships. Slowly the gain of being able to immerse the ship at will to
proper draught and trim became clear. There was a further claim
for passenger vessels in the safeguard after damage which the
presence of an inner bottom affords.

§7. THE COMPOSITE CLIPPER-SHIPS

IT would have been thought that in the early days of iron someone
would have had the idea of a wooden ship with iron frames. But so
much work was needed for timber ribs that to replace these with bars
seemed against nature. Perhaps, too, the shipwright was out to keep
his job as long as ever he could.

It is said that a design on these lines was made as early as 1839 by
Watson of Dublin. The system was used for the *Excelsior* in 1850 and
the *Tubal Cain* in 1851, built by Jordan of Liverpool.

Then the clipper-ships began to loom large in the public mind. The
Americans started to build these vessels about 1830 for the opium
trade—smuggling from India to China. They built fine-lined fast

ships in the New England States and began to enter the China tea trade to London. British builders took up the challenge about 1852 with the *Cairngorm*, made stronger with deck beams of iron. To follow this, the *Lord of the Isles* was built solely of iron at Greenock in 1853.

The year 1863 saw a partial return of the wooden vessel with iron frames, wooden skin and deck planks. A. B. Lubbock, in *The China Clippers*, says that this type was in great favour for the tea trade 'where great strength was wanted and in which iron ships were never popular for two reasons; first, that iron was considered bad for the tea, and secondly, that they—iron vessels—could never equal wooden ships in light winds'.

They had high speeds for vessels of only 200 ft. long. The *Cutty Sark* had the credit of $17\frac{1}{2}$ knots—just over 20 land miles an hour. It is on record also that she made 362 and 363 sea-miles on each of two day's running, a mean speed of just over 15 knots. (It has been stated that she would need engines of 4000 h.p. to drive her 16 knots.)

The composite clippers proved themselves to be strong and able to stand the strains of hard driving without losing their shape, which often took place with the soft wood vessels built in the States. The *Cutty Sark*, which made a first voyage from London to Shanghai in 1870, was subject to a thorough survey in 1937, and although she had been used for much of her life for rough trade, was found to be sound. Little expense was needed to repair the main structure and the ship now lies in the Thames off Greenhithe as a tender to the training ship *Worcester*. The clipper-ship era lasted but a short time, being ended by the opening of the Suez Canal, which gave steamers a shorter journey to add further to their other vantage.

Except for racing yachts this method of building has passed, and it seems fitting to give an account of the *Cutty Sark* built at Dumbarton in 1869 by Scott and Linton and completed by William Denny and Co. The vessel, 212 ft. long and 36 ft. broad overall, had a depth of hold of 21 ft. Her weight at 20 ft. draught was 2100 tons on which she carried a load of cargo of some 1100 tons. Most of the goods she took were 'bulky', such as tea and wool, and would not bring her down to her 'marks'. In common with the practice of those days she carried ballast in the bottom of the holds which, with a wood cargo of 900 tons, weighed 200 tons. The 'form' of her 'lines' was as near ideal as any ship and, like most of these clippers, was based on the shape of yachts.

The structure started from a flat keel plate 31 in. wide and $\frac{7}{8}$ in. thick. This ran the whole length and up the stem-post and the stern-post. The butts were joined by inside straps between the frames. On

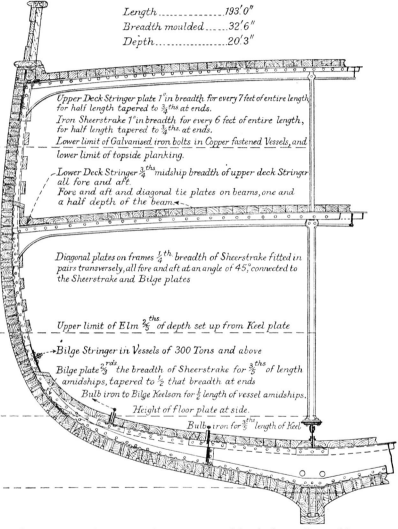

Length................193'.0"
Breadth moulded......32'.6"
Depth..................20'.3"

Upper Deck Stringer plate 1" in breadth for every 7 feet of entire length, for half length tapered to $\frac{3}{4}$ths at ends.
Iron Sheerstrake 1" in breadth for every 6 feet of entire length, for half length tapered to $\frac{3}{4}$ths. at ends.
Lower limit of Galvanised iron bolts in Copper fastened Vessels, and lower limit of topside planking.

Lower Deck Stringer $\frac{3}{4}$ths midship breadth of upper deck Stringer all fore and aft.
Fore and aft and diagonal tie plates on beams, one and a half depth of the beam.

Diagonal plates on frames $\frac{1}{4}$th breadth of Sheerstrake fitted in pairs transversely, all fore and aft at an angle of 45°, connected to the Sheerstrake and Bilge plates

Upper limit of Elm $\frac{2}{5}$ths. of depth set up from Keel plate

Bilge Stringer in Vessels of 300 Tons and above
Bilge plate $\frac{2}{3}$rds the breadth of Sheerstrake for $\frac{3}{5}$ths of length amidships, tapered to $\frac{1}{2}$ that breadth at ends
Bulb iron to Bilge Keelson for $\frac{1}{2}$ length of vessel amidships.
Height of floor plate at side.
Bulb iron for $\frac{3}{5}$ths length of Keel

Composite vessel, c. 1870. Structure as used by the later clipper ships.

his rested the floors 18 in. apart throughout the ship. They were in one piece from bilge to bilge of a length of 30 ft. amidship, that is about 80 per cent of the breadth. They were 24 in. deep at the centre line and 9 in. at the bilge stringer, being made of $\frac{9}{16}$ in. plate. The frame bars, $4\frac{1}{4}$ in. by $3\frac{3}{4}$ in. and $\frac{9}{16}$ in. thick, ran from keel to upper deck in one piece, the two sides being joined at the centre line by a 4 ft. length of angle bar. A reverse bar, 3×3 in. angle, was fitted at the top of the floors, butted at the centre line and running to the upper deck on every second frame and to the lower deck on other frames.

Beams were fitted at every *third* frame on both decks and made of bulb-plate with angles on both sides at the top. For the lower deck the plate was 10 in. deep and $\frac{11}{16}$ in. thick; for the upper deck the plate was 9 in. deep and $\frac{10}{16}$ in. thick. The beam arms were welded to the bulb-plate and made some 24 in. deep at the frame. A side stringer plate, $22\frac{1}{2}$ in. wide and $\frac{11}{16}$ in. thick, ran above the lower deck beam arms and was joined to the frames by a 5×4 in. angle. At the upper deck the width of the stringer plate was $30\frac{1}{2}$ in. and was fixed with the same size of angle. At the tops of the frames a sheer strake of iron $\frac{10}{16}$ in. thick was run, which was joined by the same size of angle to the stringer plate and reached above the deck angle to lap to the lower edge of the bulwark plating, which was of iron.

Lengthwise support was given by keelsons and stringers. At the centre line a built-up box girder, some 12 in. wide and 18 in. deep, made of $\frac{10}{16}$ in. plating, was run lengthwise on top of the floors. This took the heels of the pillars which were fitted to every beam and which were made of solid iron bar, $3\frac{3}{4}$ in. diameter below the lower deck and $2\frac{5}{8}$ in. diameter from lower to upper deck.

Then came the side keelsons, some 7 ft. away on each side of the middle line. These were formed of plates in short pieces fitted between the floors and fixed thereto and to the reverse bars by short angles. These plates were also joined to a bulb-plate 10 in. deep and $\frac{11}{16}$ in thick, which with a pair of angles 5×4 in. ran lengthwise above the floors.

A keelson of the same pattern, but without the lower plates, was fitted near the ends of the floors, and higher up, midway to the lower deck, was a side stringer made of a pair of angles of the same size as before.

One further tie was an iron bilge strake, 24 in. wide and $\frac{10}{16}$ in. thick which was placed on the outside of the frame at the heads of the floors.

Beyond this, a double system of diagonal tie-plates, sloped at 45 each way, ran from the bilge strake to the sheer strake. The ends of these were joined by butt straps to the sheer and bilge strakes and they were fixed by rivets to the frames where they crossed. These trusses formed the strong framework to resist the 'racking'—change of transverse shape—of the structure. Plates were run on top of the deck beams at the sides of the hatchways and these were joined to the side stringers by diagonal ties in the same fashion as at the sides of the ship.

In all details every care seems to have been taken to build simple structure of great merit in the way of strength and stiffness to resist change of form. The best iron was used, which could stand a pull of 20 tons per sq.in. and the highest grade of iron rivets, since in such a work good rivets were more needed than for a complete vessel of iron.

The same comment on high grade applies fully to the choice of the timber. Green wood was ruled out; seasoned stuff had to be used. There had to be freedom from 'sap' and from 'wane' (twist) and other defects. Ironwork was coated with good paint on the 'faying surface' and the planks were worked with the 'heart' side bearing on the frames.

'Rock elm' was used for the woodwork up to about the 10 ft. draught line. The keel was $17\frac{1}{2}$ in. deep and $15\frac{1}{2}$ in. wide, and fitted with a 'false keel' below of the same width but 6 in. thick. The purpose of a false keel was to take the damage away from the main keel—a keystone of the structure—should the vessel run aground.

The garboards, 11 in. thick at the keel rabbets, were some 12 in. wide and the next two strakes were made to taper down to a thickness of 6 in., which stayed up to the limit of the 'rock elm' planking. From hence East India teak was used and the plank thickness slowly changed until at the sheer strake the planks were $4\frac{3}{4}$ in. thick. As far as could be done, the width of the planking was made 12 in.

The planks were fixed with screw-bolts, two being used at each frame. Since metal bolts tend to injure the butts, iron plates of the width of the plank were fitted and fixed to the two frames on each side of the plank ends. These bolts were made of yellow metal which contained about 60 per cent of copper, 40 per cent of zinc and a little tin. The size of the screw-bolts was $\frac{15}{16}$ in. for the bottom and $\frac{13}{16}$ in. for the top sides. The heads of the bolts were sunk and the holes closed by dowels driven in with white lead; the nuts were hove up on the inside of the frames.

The wood keel and the false keel were fixed to the keel-plate by galvanized iron through bolts with dumps driven in the spaces between the floors. The keel butts were scarphed and fixed by bolts of yellow metal. The garboards were crossed-bolted from side to side with galvanized iron bolts, which were also used for the stem-piece and the stern-post.

The planks were laid 'carvel' fashion and the seams were caulked with an inner thread of tarred spun yarn and filled with brown oakum. The seams were stopped with a mixture of white lead and tallow. This was also used to cover the whole of the outer bottom under the paper which was laid below the yellow metal sheathing of thin plate, held in place by copper nails.

The upper deck planks were of East India teak $3\frac{1}{2}$ in. thick and those for the lower deck were of 3 in. pine. The planking was fixed with iron screw-bolts with sunk heads fitted with dowels as for the outer bottom planking.

Close portable ceiling of pine $2\frac{3}{4}$ in. thick was fitted on top of the floors. Pine 'cargo battens' were run 'room and space' inside the frames in the hold and 'tween decks to keep the cargo clear of the sides of the ship.

Cement was used in the bottom to cover the bilges and to form water courses. Those parts of the peaks which were hard of access were filled with cement concrete. The water-ways or side-gutters on the upper deck were flushed and rounded off with cement.

(The figure on p. 143 of the structure of a composite ship is not that of the *Cutty Sark*, but of a slightly smaller vessel. It has been chosen because it shows most of the details in clear fashion. It is to be noted in this case that the bulwarks are made of wood.)

§8. THE ADVENT OF STEEL

BY the year 1877 the pattern of building modern ships had become more or less settled. Apart from the *Great Eastern*, one of the large ships of that time was the *Britannic* of the White Star Line. Her length was 455 ft., the extreme breadth over 45 ft. and at a draught of 23 ft. 6 in. she weighed 8500 tons. She made eleven round voyages in a year between Liverpool and New York. Her mean speed was 15 knots with a horse power just under 5000, burning 100 tons of coal a day.

The structure of ironclads was proving itself, the merchant steamer double-bottom system was finding favour, the Suez Canal was at work and the day of the clipper-ships was passing. One further factor came nto the picture in 1877—'mild steel'—which was soon to replace ron for the building of ships.

The grade of iron that had been used was known as 'wrought'. As a first step in its making, pig-iron was smelted from iron ore, using first charcoal then coal and later coke. The pig was then heated and forged by smiths to become wrought iron, which could be rolled by machines into small plates and bars. The pig-iron was worked in heated furnaces by 'puddling'—stirring with wooden poles to reduce or 'burn-out' much of the carbon. As this mixture cannot be melted, casting was out of the question, but at a 'red heat' it becomes pasty in which state it can be rolled and welded. This results in a metal which has a silvery look, is strong and tough and fairly hard. It was found to be stronger lengthwise than cross-wise and its strength was found to depend on the amount of work that had been done on it by rolling and forging.

The Royal Navy laid down as tests that the iron should stand a tensile stress of 22 tons per sq.in. lengthwise and 18 tons crosswise. To see if it was 'ductile' forged tests were made by bending when hot to at least a right angle, and by a cold bending test to a smaller angle—35° for plates $\frac{1}{2}$ in. thick.

A curious point was that this wrought iron was not prone to corrode, whereas the mild steel which took its place soon rusted. It is thought that ships built of wrought iron might still be found on service although built some 100 years ago. The life of a steel ship with care is some 25 years, quite old enough for the rapid changes of modern times when types of vessels quickly lapse through change of trade.

The output of wrought iron was not large; it needed much hand labour and could only be made in small pieces. The world output of pig-iron in 1855 was about 6,000,000 tons, of which more than half was made in the United Kingdom. The share of this total taken for wrought iron was a much lower figure. It does not surprise that research was made to try to produce iron with greater ease. The first process, due to Bessemer in 1856, was to blow hot air through molten pig-iron, drawn direct from the blast furnace in a ladle. This nearly freed the iron from carbon, since only 6 parts in 10,000 were left. The iron was thus nearly pure, but the ores used to make the pig-iron had both sulphur and phosphorous which had the harmful effect of making the iron brittle. These defects were got over in time by lining the ladle with fire bricks of what was called a 'basic' nature, as distinct from clay which had an 'acid' content.

The strength of mild steel depends on the amount of carbon it contains, the least amount being $1\frac{1}{2}$ parts in 1000—so by the use of alloys of a known grade the extra carbon was put back into the molten charge. The Bessemer process, which gave a brilliant firework display, was a rapid one, taking less than half an hour. For this reason it was not easy to control the products and so the steel varied more than was thought proper.

A few years later Siemens brought out the 'open-hearth' process in which the molten pig-iron is run on to a hearth or bed over which gas flames play to maintain the heat and to burn out the carbon and other defects. This process took some eight hours and in the result was able to produce an even nature throughout. Shortly after came the Siemens-Martin process which with the use of a basic lining for the hearths had by 1877 got rid of most of the sulphur and phosphorus

The usual grade of mild steel contains $1\frac{1}{2}$ parts of carbon in 1000. If the amount is doubled up to 3 parts, the steel becomes stronger and harder, and if heated and quenched in water can get a 'temper'. It is like wrought iron in many ways, but is better because it can be cast into an ingot direct from the furnace. The liquid metal is run into a cast-iron mould of box-shaped form which makes an 'ingot'. This ingot when heated to the right degree can be passed through the roll to emerge as plates or section bars. By proper rolling it can be made of the same strength in any direction, and in this respect is better than iron.

In 1877 the process of making this steel was so well under control that Lloyds Register of Shipping were able to make rules for the testing of 'mild steel'. Strips cut lengthwise *or* crosswise would have to stand a breaking tensile strength between 27 and 31 tons per square inch, and to show whether the metal was ductile a test-piece, 8 in long, must stretch 20 per cent of its length before breaking. After heating and quenching in water it had to stand bending double over a round bar the diameter of which was three times the thickness of the plate. These stringent tests were met and before long the new steel was made in greater tonnage than could have been done with iron. To induce its greater use Lloyds agreed to accept 20 per cent less thickness for plates and angles than was needed for iron; except for the rivets, which were easier to work in iron than in steel.

Mild steel soon took the place of iron for the building of ships and remains to the present day as the best material for the structure of ships. It can be made with ease and in large amounts; it will stand he hard treatment needed in punching and shearing in the shipyard. True, some small changes have been made to improve tensile strength, but as yet mild steel holds its sway for most uses. Some few years ago, to avoid corrosion, a keel of iron was wanted for a river steamer working in tropical waters, and having to cross sandy bars in the rivers. The material could hardly be found; the next best thing was to use mild steel with a very low amount of carbon.

§9. THE SORROWS OF SCIENCE

N early days, long before knowledge and science had come to the front, ships were built to accord with the fashion of the times. Progress was made by trial and error on a full-size scale, a costly method which had some success for special types such as the frigate and the two-decker. These ventures did not wait for a basis of science to guide them; the art pushed forward as the need arose or as wishful thinking drove.

From the days of Charles II, here and there appear remarks as to the better sailing of French ships. As a set off it is also stated that the best vessels were those which were copied from the French design but built by the English shipwrights. It would seem that the choice of dimensions was better than the English practice laid down in the tables of Anthony Deane.

John Fincham, master shipwright at Portsmouth, in his *History of Naval Architecture* printed in 1851, gives an account of the growth of the study of science. He says that in several States of Europe the science of shipbuilding was held in higher esteem than in England. This want of respect had brought the craft low, whereas Spain, France, Russia and Sweden have to their credit one work or more of great merit dealing with the subject. The names of Don George Juan, Bouguer, Daniel Bernouilli, Euler, Romme and Chapman are known to the world, '... while England, though greater in maritime power, and far more deeply interested in the subject than either of those nations, has hitherto produced nothing comparable to the works of these authors'.

Such study made marked progress under Louis XIV, who had a great desire to be master of the seas. His wishes were given effect to by his Minister Colbert, who in 1681 brought out the famous *Ordonnances de la Marine*—the first modern rules to deal with ships. Far more than that was the holding in that year of conferences in Paris at which many of the leading men of science met to exchange views. Their concern was mainly with the outward shape of ships; the subjects of their talks were not so much the making use of the laws of science Renaud formed the curves by the use of sections of a cone. On this question Bouguer later, in 1746, made the comment that such curves were chosen because they were better known and more easy to describe. They were the first to hand and were not used because they had any special virtues. Famous mathematicians took up the study of the geometry of the ship's form, which provides many features of great interest. They also made attempts to learn the manner in which water opposed the motion of a vessel.

Later, in 1697, Hoste of Toulon brought out his study of the form of ships. He says:

It cannot be denied that the art of constructing ships, which is so necessary to the state, is the least perfect of all the arts. The best constructors build the two principal parts of the ship, viz., the bow and the stern, almost entirely by the eye; whence it happens that the same constructor, building at the same time two ships after the same model most frequently makes them so unequal, that they have quite opposite qualities

Chance has so much to do with construction, that the ships that are built with the greater care are commonly the worst; and those which are built carelessly, are sometimes the best. Thus the largest ships are often the most defective; and more good ships are seen amongst the merchantmen than in the royal navy.

It is true that French builders had made efforts to improve their art. Some made plans of all the frames throughout the ship, but their labour was vain because it lacked knowledge. Their ships were no better than those of men who could neither read nor write. They did not sail better, often they did not carry sail as well, they rather tended to 'hog' and were less lasting. Hoste wrote: ' . . . In a word the constructors of the present day agree with the ancients that *it is not yet known what the sea requires*. . . . A ship is too complex a machine and too many things are required to concur to make her perfect, to be able to meet perfection by chance.'

Hoste comments on the lack of stiffness of the French ships saying that almost all of them had to be 'doubled' to make them carry their sail. It ought to have been easy to give them the right form when the ship was being built, but there again the lack of knowledge was a hindrance to progress.

Chapman, the Swedish naval architect, laid down in the latter part of the eighteenth century the chief objects which ought to be studied, which read as follows:

1. That a ship with a certain draught of water shall be able to contain and carry a determinate burthen.
2. That she shall have a stability sufficient and also determinate.
3. That she shall behave well at sea so that the motions of rolling and pitching shall not be too quick.
4. That she shall sail well, before the wind as well as close-hauled, and that she shall be weatherly.
5. That she shall not be too ardent and nevertheless shall come about easily.

Just about the same time the study of resistance to motion by experiments with models was begun by Borda in 1767 and carried on by the Abbé Bossut in 1775. In a large basin, 100 ft. long, 53 ft. broad and 6 ft. deep, models made to scale were drawn by a line through a pulley at the end of the run, the force being applied by a falling weight. Romme, in 1776 and later, also towed models at Rochelle using a canal 40 ft. broad and 7–8 ft. deep. Under the action of a falling weight the time taken to run 75 ft. was used as a measure of resistance. An exact model of a 74-gun ship was made, 14 ft. long and 3 ft. 8 in. wide, which was one-twelfth of the full size. A second model with the same stem, stern-posts and midship section was formed by straight lines drawn from midships to bow and to stern— straight cones with the greatest 'bend' as the base. Romme judged from his work that the form of the bows of ships can vary widely without much increase in the force needed so long as the midship section was kept the same both in area and outline. This idea lasted until this century, that the area of the midship section should afford proper basis to compare the horse-powers of ships.

Studies were also made of the manner in which the shape of the ship led to stiffness, rolling and pitching, so that by 1800 the main outline of the problem was known. Attwood in England also studied these questions and brought them to a stage where they could be applied by arithmetic to actual ships. In 1791 Colonel Beaufoy founded in London a private society for the 'advancement of Naval Architecture' which made experiments with towed models. The State was not willing to help and the finance ran out before these trials were ended. He then carried on at his own expense and later his son printed the results of the tests at his own cost. It would appear that the naval service still thought that all that was needed for shipwrights was to be skilled craftsmen, and that for their guidance the work of Anthony Deane served the purpose.

It has been told how the early master shipwrights chose 'prentice lads of promise to train for dockyard service. The Commission of Naval Revision of 1806 stated that those who had the duty to design and build vessels of the Royal Navy 'were as a body sadly ignorant of the theory of naval architecture and lacking in general education' Their report led to the founding in 1811 at Portsmouth of the first School of Naval Architecture, for the training of a higher class of 'prentice lads, so as to fit them to become officers of the dockyard.

The Admiralty and the Navy Boards were, it was said, without any knowledge of science themselves and looked askance at these new students, who were kept without much work and were given little if any chance to employ their knowledge. The school trained some 40 students in the 20 years of its life, the greater part of whom left the naval service. It was closed in 1832 by Sir James Graham, First Lord of the Admiralty.

There was a lapse of 16 years before a further attempt was made to better affairs. There was set up at Portsmouth in 1848 the 'Central School of Mathematics and Naval Construction' for the higher training of dockyard apprentices. This school had a much shorter life being closed after five years' work by the same Sir James Graham 'whose conduct had the same merit of consistency' in putting a stop to the growth of knowledge. Only a score of students had been trained in that time, but these few were able to guide the Royal Navy in the drastic change from the wooden fighting ship to the ironclad.

Eleven years later a third school started at South Kensington by the joint action of the Admiralty and the Science and Art Department It was known as 'The Royal School of Naval Architecture and Marine Engineering', and lectures were given, as the title implies, both for shipbuilders and engineers who were being needed for the naval service with the growth of the steam engine. The founding of the Institution of Naval Achitects in 1860 was largely brought about by the efforts of Scott Russell who had the support of E. J. Reed, late Sir Edward and Chief Constructor of the Navy, who acted as it secretary.

This society has held meetings from that time onwards to discuss in public the problems of the shipwright and of the builders of marine

ꞃgines. It was through this forum that joint action to provide proper
ꞏaining in science and technical subjects was taken, brought about
ꞏy a paper read by Scott Russell, which led to the founding of the
ꞏouth Kensington School, which lasted until 1874. Its work was taken
ꞏver in that year by shifting the school to the Royal Naval College at
ꞏreenwich, where it still exists for the highest training of both naval
ꞏd private students.

The Institution brought to public notice many special problems,
ꞏom which came the chance given to William Froude, who more than
ꞏny man brought science within the grasp of the shipwright. Through
ꞏe support of Edward Reed he was able at long last to pierce the lack
ꞏ concern shown by the Navy Board in the use of knowledge.

§10. WILLIAM FROUDE

ꞮLLIAM FROUDE, the sixth child of a family of eight, was born
Dartington, on the River Dart in Devon, in 1810. The youngest,
ꞏmes Anthony, became famous as a historian, while the eldest,
ꞏurrell, was the driving force of the Tractarian movement. William
ꞏent to Oriel College, Oxford and took a First Class in Mathematics
ꞏd a Third in Classics in 1832. He stayed at Oxford until 1836 giving
ꞏuch time to studies of the motion of ships.

He then became a civil engineer, helping Brunel in the building of
ꞏe Great Western Railway, first from Bristol to Exeter and later to
ꞏewton Abbot. In the latter section he worked on the so-called
ꞏtmospheric system' under Brunel. In this project air was pumped
ꞏt of a pipe laid between the rails and the suction on a piston fixed
ꞏ the carriage drew the train along. The mechanical problems were
ꞏo complex and the scheme proved to be a costly failure.

He worked with Brunel on special subjects, among which were
ꞏdies of the rolling of the *Great Eastern*. Froude went on the first
ꞏp of that ship to the United States and because of his report she was
ꞏted with bilge keels. He lived at Dartington in 1846, giving up his
ꞏher work to devote his time to the question of the towing of models.
ꞏn the death of his father in 1859 he moved to Paignton, where he
ꞏed a large storage tank at the top of the house to tow models by the
ꞏe of a falling weight, on which method he found he could not rely.
ꞏ then built a tank in his garden to study the form and the rolling of
ꞏips by the use of models.

His advice was sought to help the water-supply to Torquay, wher
the pipes became choked with deposit from the water. He made tria
of the effect of the rough surface inside the pipe which led him t
doubt previous ideas on the nature of the friction of a surface i
contact with moving water. As a result of these labours, and th
measures that he took, he was able to double the water-supp
without the laying of new pipes.

Sir Edward Reed paid him a visit in 1867 or 1868 to see his exper
ments and asked Froude to send a statement of his work to th
Admiralty Board, and to offer his services to make experiments c
naval vessels. Their Lordships gave a grudging assent to his schem
and made him a grant of £2000 to build the tank, some 278 ft. lor
and 30 ft. wide, with 10 ft. depth of water, and to run it for two year
It had hardly begun to work in 1871 before the whole of this grant ha
been spent.

Well before this, Froude had seen clearly that the problem had tw
main aspects. The first was the friction between the skin of the sh
and the water with which it was in contact. This friction force varie
with the amount and the nature of the surface, and the rate of increa
was nearly, but not quite as the square of the speed. He said that th
front portions of the surface were rubbing against water at rest wi
the full speed of the body. This water was set in motion in the forwar
sense so that the after-parts of the surface came in contact with flu
already moving in the same direction as itself. Thus, the force on
square foot of the skin was greater forward than aft, and so th
friction force, taking the surface as a whole, fell off as the length
surface became greater.

The second factor was the wave pattern formed on the surface of th
water by the passage of the moving body, and this pattern neede
energy to create and to maintain. He had seen that the picture of th
pattern was much the same for various lengths of model, and cou
be made the same to a scale of length by choosing proper speed
From another angle it seemed that with the same model the pattern w
much the same at various speeds, except that the waves became farth
apart as the speed grew. He found that the ratio of the length of th
model to the square of the speed was the correct rule by which
measure the plan of the wave pattern on the surface of the water.

In a boundless fluid the power needed to create the wave patte
must depend on the size of the moving object of which the length
a measure. The speed must also have regard to size and here it w

nown that the length of water waves themselves varied as the square f the speed. Thus the idea of a measure of speed in respect of size, or corresponding speed' as it is called, should be the ratio of the length) the square of the speed. This relative speed is known more in the orm of the ratio of speed to the square root of the length. Froude hecked these views of the wave pattern by towing models of two ugths, 12 ft. and 6 ft., from a steam launch in the River Dart.

From the studies of wave motion that had been made by Rankine nd himself, Froude was able to show that the force needed to create

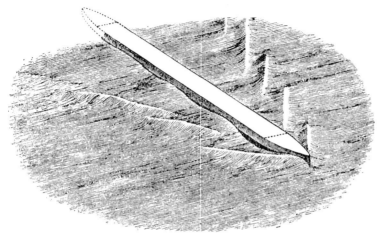

Wave-pattern of a ship

ie wave pattern varied as the cube of the length of the model or, in mpler terms, as the volume of the water displaced by the ship, which known as the 'displacement'.

Out of such views came Froude's simple Law of Comparison— hat for ship and model the resistance in pounds per ton of displace- ient was the same when the corresponding speeds were the same'. his only applied to that part of the total force needed for the surface- ave effect. There was still much to be done to measure the surface iction below water.

Froude thought, rightly, that the proper way to proceed was to easure the total force needed to drive a model at a given speed and en to work out the friction forces in terms of area and length of urface and speed. The 'excess', as he called it, due to surface-wave otion, was got by taking away the friction effect from the total given y the model test. It was the 'excess' which, by the use of the Law

of Comparison, was the same for ship and model at the proper speeds
The power to drive the full-size vessel was then got by adding th
'excess' to an estimate of the friction force needed for the full-siz
vessel.

Something must be said of Froude's skill as a mechanic in makin
automatic machines to record measurements, thus, as he put it, t
avoid the 'personal error'. He made most of his own gear for the tan
he built at Torquay and thus saved much money. Although this £200
had been spent by the time the tank was ready to use, Froude neve
took any money for his services. As he put it: 'I am thoroughly glad t
give my services, the matter is of such *extreme* interest to me.'

A full-size trial was needed to complete the proof and the *Greyhoun*
160 ft. long and 1150 tons weight, was towed behind a larger vesse
the *Active*. The speeds and towing forces were recorded by automati
machines. The results were found to agree with those of a model 10 f
long tested in the tank, and the Law of Comparison proved. Fro
that time onwards the Royal Navy has made such tests for all ne
designs.

In other aspects Froude laid the basis for the future in sure an
certain fashion. His studies on 'rolling' and the forces which can b
used to resist such motion have stood right up to the present. Her
again he made much use of automatic recording. As early as 1873 h
began to explore the working of the screw-propeller by the use c
models, and his work again showed the way to progress. As was h
custom, he built up in simple fashion a theory which in his own word
'brought to rule' the chief features of the working of the screw an
showed how the best results were to be got by changing the form, th
pattern and the dimensions.

Much of this work was done after he was sixty, and in the sho
period before his death in 1879 he had laid down the manner by whic
to find the form of a ship and drive it by screw-propellers on a basi
of science and knowledge. He said that many beliefs were 'distinctl
erroneous' and 'if scientific advancement is made dependent on th
present haphazard method, it will be very slow and incoherent
Writing of Froude's work some 60 years later, Admiral D. W. Taylo
who had been the greatest worker after Froude in this field of research
and who also had been the chief constructor of the United State
Navy, wrote:

It has always seemed to me that he was far ahead of his time, not only a
a pioneer in the rolling of ships and resistance and propulsion, but as

enius who, with a model tank which was very crude compared with those of o-day, established methods and quantitative coefficients which served the aval architect for more than fifty years. We know now that Froude's oefficients can be improved upon, but for practical purposes improvement as been astonishingly small.

After his death, his son, R. E. Froude, carried on the work at the admiralty Experiment Works at Haslar and brought to fruition many f the problems that his father had foreseen. In this place can still be een at work the towing truck and gear that William Froude had built argely by his own hands for the first tank at Torquay. This simple neans of testing has been copied by most countries, and his methods or the use of models have been applied to many other problems that rise from the motion of ships.

For his early work Froude used pairs of models 12 ft., 6 ft. and ft. long, of two shapes. One of each pair was made to what is now alled a 'stream-line' form, and the second had rounded ends like the hapes of the swimming water fowl. Of these tests Froude found very learly that strange forms may possess merits that are entirely unknown nd unexpected before experiment, since above certain speeds the ird-form gave better results than the streamline shape. To obtain the est results, therefore, a wide variety of shapes needed to be tried.

The figure on p. 155, drawn by Froude, shows the main features of he wave-pattern which is formed on the surface of calm water. There re two sets of waves. Those caused at the bow of the ship—the iverging waves—after the first crest move away from the ship in lines vhich slope at an angle to the middle line of the vessel. The second set f waves runs lengthwise in contact with the side of the ship, the crests nd hollows being clearly shown. Other like patterns occur towards he stern, and the whole wave resistance is due to all these factors nd to the manner in which one or other set aids or hampers the creation f the other waves.

§11. SHIPS AND ENGINES

ARLY steamers were for the most part sailing vessels fitted with ngines: the form of the ship and its type were changed but little. It ook some time to learn that the motion of the ship when forced hrough waves by power was not the same as when driven by sail. t was not easy to over-drive the clipper-ship even though life on board was driven hard, for if pressed too much masts and rigging carried away, often with the loss of the ship. These vessels were subject to a further serious danger, that of being 'pooped' by seas coming from astern moving faster than the ship; the term for this is 'following' seas. When engines came to have greater power steamers were more and more forced through heavy weather; the clippers had to be coaxed and nursed, rather than driven.

The sailing ships in the middle of the nineteenth century looked to have a flush deck from bow to stern: the sheer-line at the top side ran smoothly without a break. They had a 'sunk' forecastle forward and a 'raised' quarter deck aft, forming the poop, the tops of these being flush with the high bulwark rail. For some two-thirds of the length between the forecastle and the poop there was a long well within the shelter of the high bulwarks which was kept clear for the working of the sail and the rigging. In this well, at the middle line between the masts, were two deck-houses for the crew and for the apprentices. The officers lived in the poop from the top of which the ship was conned and steered.

The engines were fitted about midships to some such pattern of forecastle, long-well and poop. Seas broke into the engine room, put out the fires under the boilers and caused the ship to be out of control. To protect these openings, deck-houses were built over the entrance to the engine room. Then the control of the ship was shifted to an open bridge forward of midships. With increase of speed a forecastle, some 10 per cent of the ship's length, was added with a head-room height above the upper deck. This stopped water from breaking over the ship, but it still came over the side before the bridge and was liable to sweep aft in a mass, causing serious damage. To improve this bridge-house was built reaching to the side of the ship and closed at the front and the sides to divert a rush of water. Lastly, the poop was kept standing head high above the upper deck to protect the vessel against seas coming over the stern.

The bridge grew longer and lastly the three parts, the poop, the bridge and the forecastle, came to cover half the length of the deck. Thus was brought about the 'three island' ship, which was found to be more seaworthy than other types and from which most of the other changes of outline were made to accord with the varied nature of the service of the vessel.

It thus appears that to meet the needs of safety, there must be a certain amount of buoyant volume above water, and that above the upper deck the height of the bow and the stern and in way of the bridge-house should be added to by some 7 ft. or so. To ensure that this height is kept on service a 'load line', or Plimsoll mark, is scribed on the side of the ship amidship—a circle with a level line drawn at and below its centre. The fixing of this line is a part of the shipwright's trade, which would need a text-book to describe.

The effect of putting the engines amidships, which is nearly always the case in cargo ships, is to reduce the volume of the after-holds. Shafts have to be led to the screws at the stern, and since these have to be watched, a tunnel is built large enough to take the shaft and a passage-way for men. When the vessel is loaded the ship may be 'down by the head' or drawing more water forward than aft, which leads to less control when under way. To get over this failing, which has more effect in the smaller vessels such as colliers, the upper deck in the after part is partly raised between the bridge and the poop, thus forming the 'raised quarter deck' type. Sometimes the rise of the deck is such as to join the bridge to the poop, when there is only left a 'well' forward between forecastle and bridge, to which type is given the name 'well-decker'.

The oil tanker, for a very good reason, has the engines placed at the stern. Such vessels carry oil in bulk right to the skin of the ship. To put tunnels through the oil tanks would invite explosions of gas, should leakage take place through the 'working' of the ship. In this class when the vessel is 'light' or empty, water ballast can be carried in the oil tanks to bring the ship to an 'even keel' or to a proper 'trim by the stern'.

It does not do to let vessels be too light at sea. They should be sunk to a draught somewhat more than half that when fully loaded or else they are hard to handle in heavy weather. An oil tanker can arrange for this with ease, but in small cargo ships, such as colliers, special large tanks are built into the ship to secure the deeper loading.

It was not only in the form above water that changes had to be made. Ships driven by screw-propellers had to have the after parts shaped with great care to ensure that the flow of water to the screw is as 'smooth' as it can be made. If this be not done, heavy losses of power may take place when the flow breaks down. The eddies which arise will prevent the blades of the screw from 'thrusting' against the water. Just as with the form of the ship where every care is taken to ensure a smooth shape to prevent eddies being formed, so is it a matter of concern that the front face of the blade which first meets the water should have a pattern which tends to produce steady flow.

The water in which the screw works has a very mixed motion. The 'wake' in which it revolves is of a complex nature. First, there is the 'friction' wake, a body of water moving the same way as the ship, set in motion by the dragging effect of the friction between the skin of the vessel and the water. This friction wake moves faster the nearer it is to the surface of the water and the nearer it is to the outer skin. Thus the screw has to work in water which has various speeds at various parts of a revolution, and this lack of constant motion in the flow of water to the screw has to be taken into account.

Apart from this the surface waves, brought about by the passage of the vessel, themselves disturb the motion of the water and cause changes of speed in the wake in which the screw works. The power needed for a screw of given pattern can be found by tests with fair ease when the screw is pushed forward into 'open water'. But it is hard to predict from this knowledge what happens when it has to work in the mixed wake that follows a ship. If only a fair idea of the mean value of the speed of the wake could be found, many of the screw problems could be solved.

One further effect of the screw is the suction which it exerts well ahead of its place in the ship. This suction extends to the skin of the ship and thus gives rise to a further force tending to oppose the motion. Here it is that the methods of testing models, brought about by William Froude, afford the greatest help. For by towing the model the measure of the wave and friction forces is found. Likewise, by running the model screw in open or still water its power and thrust can be found. The model ship is then fitted with a screw, which can be driven by its own motors at various speeds, while the ship with the screw is towed along the tank. In this way the increase of force needed to provide for the suction of the screw can be found. At the same time by running the propeller at various speeds the revolutions at which the model propels itself can be got fairly simply. From these tests, by making the proper changes for size as between ship and model, the results for the full-size vessel can be forecast.

The thrust of the screw which pushes or 'thrusts' the ship has to be taken from the propeller shaft and passed on to the hull of the vessel by means of a 'thrust block'. If this were not done, the thrust would come on the engines and prevent them from working. In a large ship such as the *Queen Mary*, having four screws, each of which can make use of 50,000 h.p., the thrust on each shaft runs into many tons, and in early days the design of a bearing to take such heavy forces was not easy, although it is done with safety to-day. This thrust is taken from the shaft somewhere towards amidships, and special care has to be used to spread the heavy forces well over the bottom structure of the ship.

The driving of ships by machines has thus led to changes of form both below and above water to promote ease of speed and to make vessels seaworthy. Beyond that the need became clear to study the manner in which the form and the speed affect the working of the propeller and the way in which, in its turn, the screw affects the forces which oppose the motion.

§12. STEAM AND COAL

BRUNEL, a century ago, took the view that the *Great Eastern* should be able to carry enough coal to take her at a useful speed for the whole voyage to India without having to refill her bunkers. This outlook was a wise one in all ways, the more so as the coal burnt to provide one horse-power was a large amount in those days.

The manner in which the weight of steam engines was cut down and in which, by better use of coal, the weight of fuel needed per horse-power became less and less, is best shown from the Records of the Royal Navy in the 50 years or so before 1914. There is every reason for the fighting ships to reduce the sum total of the weights of the engines and of fuel needed for a given power. For, since such vessels are classed mainly by size, the less weight needed for the machines and fuel the greater can be the 'offence'—the number and size of the guns—and the more armour can be carried for 'defence'.

The progress in the use of steam and coal is best shown from the details of two vessels; the *Warrior* of 1860, almost the first ironclad, and the *Dreadnought* of 1906, the first modern battleship.

The table which compares the two vessels shows that the size has doubled and the speed gone up 50 per cent. To bring this about the power is $4\frac{1}{2}$ times greater, though the engines are only twice the weight. The total coal used per day is only $1\frac{1}{2}$ times the early figure. In other words the same amount of coal, 800 tons, would drive both ships at full speed for 1000 knots. The *Dreadnought* took two days on the voyage whereas the time for the *Warrior* was three days, or half as long again.

Progress of Power and Weight and Saving of Coal

	1860 *Warrior*	Ratio Increase or Decrease	1906 *Dreadnought*
Length (ft.)	380		490
Displacement (tons)	8850	2·0	17900
Speed (knots)	14·4	1·5	21·5
Horse-power	5500	4·5	24700
Engine weight (tons)	900	2·1	1900
Coal per day (tons: full speed)	265	1·5	400
For 1000 knots' trip:			
Coal, tons	800	1·0	800
Time, days	3	2/3	2
Horse-power, per ton (engines)	6·1	2·0	13·0
Coal per 1000 h.p. per hr. (tons)	2·0	1/3	0·6
Boiler pressure (lb. per sq. in.)	22·0	12·0	250

These gains were got through better ways of making the engines and the boilers in which the steam was raised; twice as much power came from a given weight. Then greater care was taken in the burning of coal and in the use of steam in the engine, so that more than three times as much power was got from a pound of coal.

With the coming of steel, starting from about 1888, better boilers could be made and the pressure of the steam raised. Towards the end of the century there came into use the 'water tube' boiler where the fire plays on the outside of the tubes holding the water, instead of inside the furnace leading to a number of small tubes, passing through the water, which take the hot gases to the funnel. This led to a saving of boiler weight of something like 50 per cent, since the amount of water in the boiler was cut down to a small figure. Higher steam pressures were able to be used, 250 lb. per sq. in. as against the early practice of 20 lb., and this increase brought about more saving.

Perhaps the coming of the Parsons' steam turbine did more than any other factor to increase the power for weight of engine by some 100 per cent. There was one drawback for the shipwright's trade, since the revolutions of the screw were raised many times, to well over 300 per minute (328 for the *Dreadnought*). This trouble was soon met. It came about because, to get the power out of the steam when acting on the blades of the turbine wheels, the speed of the blades had to be high. On the other hand, the revolutions of the propeller had to be kept low to avoid breakdown at the screw. This trouble led Parsons later to adopt gear-wheels between the turbine and screw-shafts so that the turbines run say twenty times faster than the propellers, and thus approach the speeds at which the losses for both turbine and screw could be kept at a low level.

It should be said also that there was as much saving of floor space as of weight, a vital point in warships whose engine-rooms are often cramped. A further gain was the low height of engines which could thus be placed below the armour decks well under water.

In the Merchant Marine the quest for saving of fuel was perhaps stronger than in the fighting ships. Rightly, the search was for cheap and safe transport for the cargo steamer. In regard to speed, a struggle took place to attain the quickest passage from England to New York. First, only English shipping companies took part, then the Americans joined in, and towards the end of last century the Germans also became rivals. There arose a fierce struggle for what was called the Blue Ribbon of the Atlantic, which really began in the days of Brunel and which ended with the building of the mammoth British ships the *Queen Mary* and the *Queen Elizabeth* of modern times. These vessels are 1018 ft. long, 118 ft. broad, 135 ft. high from keel to top deck and weigh more than 75,000 tons. They are driven by four sets of steam turbines which can make use of some 180,000 h.p. giving a greatest speed of some 33 knots. At a speed of 30 knots the Atlantic crossing to New York can be made in four days.

This progress has taken place mainly in this century. The last phase began with the German challenge with the *Deutschland* in 1900. This ship had twin screws, driven by reciprocating engines of 18,000 h.p. each, giving a speed of 24 knots from New York to Plymouth. The Cunard Line took up the challenge and with the aid of the British Admiralty began to explore the problem. It seemed that the limit of power from engines and boilers as then built had been reached, and that with such machines a speed of only $24\frac{1}{2}$ knots was likely. Some drastic change was needed to obtain a direct gain of a half a day in the crossing which meant a speed on service of 26 knots. In those days between 1900 and 1905 both the Royal Navy and the Merchant Marine were faced with the same problem, how to get greater power for weight. The use of Parsons' Turbines was the answer both for the Dreadnoughts, the modern ironclads of 1906, and the crack Cunarders, the *Mauretania* and *Lusitania* of 1907. The merchant vessels still kept to the round drum' type boiler, the fighting ships had the further saving due to the use of water-tube boilers; all these vessels still had to burn coal, the *Mauretania* and her consort using 1000 tons a day, stoked by hand.

§13. CHARLES PARSONS

THE Hon. Charles A. Parsons, sixth son of the fourth Earl of Rosse was born in 1854 and died in 1931. He was educated at home by tutors and had the run of the workshops at Birr Castle, Parsonstown where his father built the famous Rosse Telescope. He went to Trinity College, Dublin, and in 1873 to St John's College, Cambridge passing out as eleventh wrangler in the Mathematical Tripos of 1877

He became an apprentice at the Elswick Works at Newcastle to Sir William Armstrong, whom he thought 'the cleverest mechanical engineer I have ever known'. He became a partner with Clarke Chapman of Gateshead in 1884, and here he took up the problem of the steam turbine driving a high-speed dynamo. His machines were working well by 1886 and had begun to be a success by 1894. Parsons always strove to save fuel.

The time had come to tackle the use of turbines at sea. It was a major problem to know how to condense the steam so as to preserve fresh water for the boilers. The turbine was able to make use of a higher vacuum in the condenser than the usual steam engine, and on this account alone could give greater power for a given weight of steam. Parsons foresaw that because of the large number of revolutions needed for a steam turbine, its use could best be shown in a vessel of high speed.

There were three main problems that he had to face—the boiler, the turbine and condenser, and the screws running at high revolutions in regard to the speed of the ship. To avoid any likely sources of trouble, the Yarrow water-tube boiler was chosen because of its simple nature and because Parsons thought that straight tubes were the best. As to the condenser, there was nothing very novel to cause worry.

Parsons made tests with a model boat some 6 ft. long, from which, using a motor driven by twisted rubber cords, he made an estimate of the power needed to drive the ship and to work the propeller. It was said that when tests were made later in the Froude tank at Haslar his figures agreed within 2 to 3 per cent. This was a striking tribute to Parsons' skill with machines and their testing by simple means, a gift in which he, like Froude, was beyond compare.

From these tests, after three years' work, grew the *Turbinia*, a vessel 100 ft. long and 9 ft. broad with a total weight of 45 tons. It was fired with coal, and running at 2000 r.p.m. gave out some 1600 h.p., driving the vessel at nearly 33 knots and using under 15 lbs of steam for 1 h.p. hour.

Parsons tried using a number of screws on one shaft, but was unable to get a speed of more than 20 knots. He then made a spring coupling between the turbine and the screw-shaft, from which he was able to prove that the great loss of power was due to the breakdown of the screws. Just at this time, 1895, the naval vessels had been finding trouble of the same kind, cavities or hollows in the water being formed on the blades which caused the screws to lose their thrust. By March 1897 Parsons had found a way to deal with the screw problem; his final design had three turbines driving three shafts, on each of which were three screws of 18 in. diameter.

Parsons pursued for many years this question of the breakdown of the flow caused by the screw. He made model tests with a propeller working in boiling water. Later, in a closed circuit he used a partial vacuum to reduce the pressure and found that the 'cavitation' took place at lower thrusts. It was also seen later that serious pitting of a curious nature took place on the surface of the screw-blades, which Parsons was able to show was due to the collapse of the cavities or water bubbles formed under heavy thrust.

To further this work, he built a testing plant on a much larger scale in 1910, which was called a 'cavitation' tunnel. This closed circuit, some 60 ft. long, was formed of a round tube 3 ft. in diameter. Water was driven through the system by a screw and the pressure was made lower with a vacuum pump. In this way both pressure and speed could be found at various stages of the breakdown. The model screw, driven by its own motor, was placed in a part of the circuit which had glass windows. A strong light was thrown on to the propeller through a shutter such as is used for cinematography, with the result that the screw and the cavity seemed to the eye and to the camera to be at rest. In this simple manner the flow breakdown could be studied at every stage. This method of model test is in common use to-day to explore many questions of trouble that arise with the flow of fluids.

It was a stroke of genius to make the first public view of the *Turbinia* take place at the great Naval Review of 1897 which was held for the Diamond Jubilee of Queen Victoria. In defiance of orders this tiny craft cruised at will along the lines of the fighting vessels. A picket boat sent after her was left miles astern and hardly got away without damage. The idea that the Navy had been left behind moved that august body in a way that any amount of reason would not have done.

From that time the turbines had come to stay and when in 1905 and 1906 the engines were being built for the *Dreadnought* and the Cunarders, something like 1,000,000 h.p. of marine engines was in hand. By 1910 a total of 5,000,000 h.p. was being built or used on board ship. Whenever steam is used at sea to-day in large vessels there will be found turbines built on the lines first laid down by Charles Parsons.

§14. OIL AND OIL ENGINES

IT is a saying among sailors that troubles never occur singly. When something happens to disturb the way at sea, there is more than likely some other change lurking in the offing. Such a factor was the coming of oil to replace coal as the fuel for boilers, and later to be burnt in Diesel engines giving enough power for marine use.

For use in ships, oil has many points in its favour. The problem of digging out 1000 tons of coal a day from the bunkers and then placing it in the furnaces by manual labour was one aspect. The bunkers had to be built within the useful part of the cargo space, whereas oil can be carried in tanks, even in double bottoms of ships. In short, oil can be pumped to its place of burning, whereas coal has to be taken by hand.

The next point was that heavy oil for burning took up no more room and gave out 50 per cent more heat than coal. The figures are broadly, for normal grades of oil, over 18,000 thermal units per pound, and 12,000 for coal.

The burning in the furnaces of boilers was easier to control and this gave rise to further increase of power for weight. The question of cost of fuel was complex, and broadly the price was fixed above that for bunker coal in the ratio of the heat values.

This question caused the Royal Navy great concern round the years soon after the *Dreadnought* was built. The snag was that oil had to be brought by sea, whereas coal was here to hand. Still, from the fighting view, the risk was worth while, so in 1912 the battleship *Queen Elizabeth* was begun with the boilers fitted to burn oil fuel only, of which she could carry 3400 tons: she was ready for service in 1915.

From 1919 onwards the crack liners began to be fitted for burning fuel oil. Some six hours are all that is needed to put enough fuel for a round voyage to England and back on board the *Queen Mary* while lying at berth in New York.

The saving of time alone thus helped to bring about a weekly service each way by the use of two ships. Coal for such high power and speed is out of the question.

The second factor, the use of the Diesel engine for marine work came into notice with the *Vulcanus* in 1910 and the *Selandia* in 1912, the twin-screw engines of which gave 2500 h.p. That type of engine had been used for submarines in this country by this time, and in 1914 an experimental engine of one cylinder had reached 750 h.p. at 145 r.p.m. With this type a further saving of fuel arose, and in modern days well over $2\frac{1}{2}$ h.p. is got for an hour by the use of 1 lb. of Diesel oil.

In 1935 a vessel of 1800 h.p. with 9200 tons of cargo at a speed of 11 knots used only 6 tons of oil fuel per day for the whole voyage. The weight and floor-space needed is much the same as for a steam plant.

From 1919 the motor-ship grew in numbers until 20 years later, 1939, they were used for about one-fourth of the 8500 ships of the deep-sea fleet of the world, ships of 3000 tons gross and above. Some 1300 ships had steam turbines, of which over 75 per cent were fitted to burn oil fuel. There were still some 5000 steamers working with better types of reciprocating steam engine.

The motor engine had found a place in the Merchant Marine owing to the better use of oil fuel. The steam turbine using a lower grade, and therefore cheaper oil, held its own for ships of large power, but failed to achieve such saving of fuel as was got by the Diesel engine. The turbine weights were some 20 per cent lighter.

Progress in Saving of Engine and Fuel Weights, 1920–46

Tons weight for 10,000 h.p.

	Steam engines	Steam turbine	Diesel engines	Gas turbines
1920	2400	1430	1920	—
1930	2220	1330	1610	—
1946	2170	1160	1430	1070

Tons oil per day for 10,000 h.p.

	Steam engines	Steam turbine	Diesel engines	Gas turbines
1920	116	96	48	—
1930	104	75	44	—
1946	93	58	40	52

Note. Diesel oil costs more than boiler oil; the gas turbine uses heavy oil, at present midway in grade between Diesel and boiler oils.

A ship of such power could steam some 16½ knots or 400 nautical miles in a day, and carry 10,000 tons of cargo. She would take about 15 days to reach South America and 30 days to Sydney. The real test of service is the sum of the weight of engines and of the fuel needed by various types for such journeys; this table shows the figures:

	Weight of engine and fuel (tons)		
	Diesel	Steam turbine	Gas turbine
For 15 days	2030	2030	1850
For 30 days	2630	2900	2630

If, as is likely, fuel is only carried for 15 days, then from the weight aspect the Diesel and the steam turbine are equal, while the gas turbine saves some 200 tons.

The needs of war brought into being the gas turbine for high-speed fighters, the engines for which had only a short life of some 250 flying hours. This engine is now being developed for use in air transport and in ships. Rapid progress has been made and it is hoped that the engine life for merchant vessels may be as much as 100,000 hours or 11 years constant running. Since, roughly, cargo ships are only at sea for one-half of the time, such an engine should last as long as the hull, which needs heavy repairs after 24 years' service. It will take time before the fuel needed per horse-power will reach the low levels of the Diesel. The simpler form of machine as seen in the aerial pattern can be taken as a distinct gain and the gas turbine can use a cheaper kind of fuel than the Diesel engine.

The time will come when the scientist has learnt how to control the rate of output of heat given out by the break-up of the atom. When that is done the gas turbine is quite ready to convert that heat energy to rotate a propeller to drive a ship.

The shipwright's dream of a fuel that weighs little and requires little space on board ship is slowly coming nearer; if to that gain the fuel costs but little, the ease of ship transport should add largely to the welfare of man. It might quite well happen that a demand would be set up for higher speed at sea, leading to further problems in the shape and form of ships and screws. For there is not, as yet, any sign of a limit to the power that can be used for marine transport.

THE story of the way in which the structure of ships of iron and steel

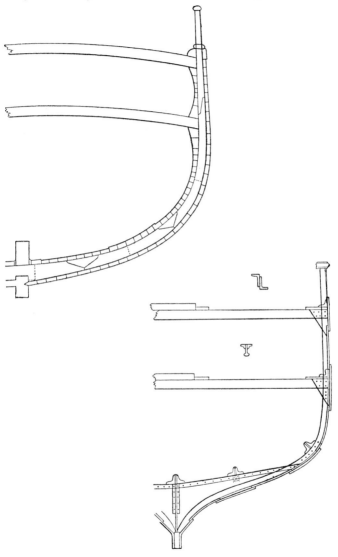

Transverse framed ships in wood (above) and iron (below), 1858

grew from the middle of last century, shows time and again how human advance goes round in circles. In the words of a motto which

Edison put up in his workshop: 'Man will adopt any expedient to avoid the real labour of thinking.' The figure on p. 143 of the composite ship shows a clearness of purpose in simple form which was not reached for the steel vessel until perhaps 1920 or later.

In 1858 Mr S. Pretious, surveyor for Holland for Lloyds Register of Shipping, had the first rules for iron vessels printed in French. In order that the meaning of the terms might be clear he made sketches of the sections of a wood ship and of an iron vessel. These show the simple ideas of the time and, what is more, confirm the view that attempts were made to copy in iron the chief features of wooden structures.

There is a stout keel of wood and also its equal in iron—there is a keelson above the floors—there are inside stringers in the iron ship where 'thick stuff' found a place in the wooden vessel. The iron beam arms are simpler, but in purpose show much the same plan.

The pattern set by Brunel and the teaching of Scott Russell became the practice for special ships, but hardly made much change for the simple merchant types. This was due to the dislike of change felt by the craftsmen, to a lack of knowledge of the purpose of the structure, and more perhaps to the wish to have a pattern which was simple to erect.

Steel began to be used somewhere about 1880, from which time progress began to be made. The feature of a double bottom for merchant ships started in a practical form just before this date and set the design for the future. The frames fixed by a small floor plate to the 'margin plate' were formed by an outer angle to support the skin plating, and an inner angle with its flange placed the reverse way to give stiffness to the inner edge. These two bars were lapped and joined by rivets to make a built-up Z-bar. The technique of the rolling mills which had learnt much from the making of steel rails, was soon able to produce a Z-bar in one piece. This was a distinct step forward and later, since the inner flange was found prone to corrode, a section was made in which the inside part of the 'Z' was squeezed into a bulb. This angle-bulb, or angle bar with a round nosing on its inside edge, became the choice for the main framing of the ship as well as for the deck beams.

The rolling of bars is a complex process and the number of patterns and sizes in use has become a burden. To increase output in the War of 1914–18, many ships were built with only some dozen patterns for the whole structure, without adding to the total weight.

The practice was to support the frames by beams at every deck height, say at some 7 ft. apart. This was done in the cargo holds where tiers of beams were fitted, although a deck of wood or plating was not laid. It was hard to stow cargo with such inside hamper. Then again in the engine and boiler rooms a greater height was needed in the hold spaces, and there to replace the support of the deck beams which had to be left out, a system of deep frames was worked. These web frames

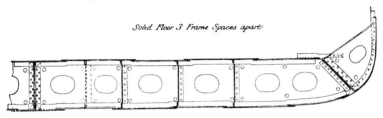

Solid Floor 3 Frame Spaces apart

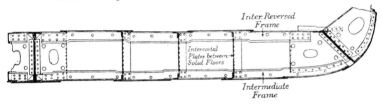

Intermediate arrangement of Frames and Reversed Frames and Bracket Plates

Inter. Reversed Frame

Intercostal Plates between Solid Floors

Intermediate Frame

Elevation between Centre Girder and Side Girder shewing spacing of Solid Floors and Intermediate Frame and Reversed Frames.

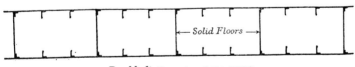

← Solid Floors →

Double bottom structure, 1910

were fitted at every four to six frame spaces and the usual ribs were worked in between. The webs were of plate some three times the depth of the ribs, with double angles to stiffen the inner edges. These in turn were kept in place by deep plate stringers worked lengthwise and some 6 ft. apart. They were of the same depth as the web and joined thereto by double angles and by diamond plates worked flush on the inside of both stringer and web. This complex cage-work at the sides of the holds took up much space and besides being costly was prone to corrode on service.

Slowly this part of the structure became simpler, although the web and stringer system was still in favour in 1914. From that time,

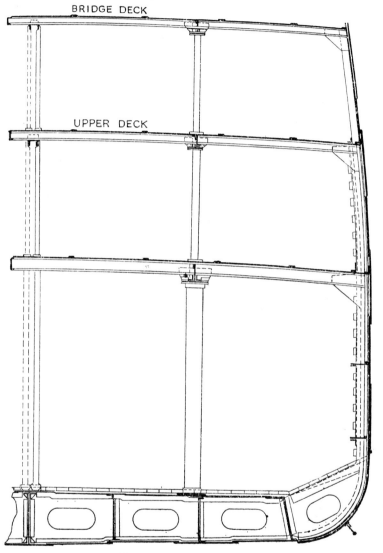

Cargo vessel structure, 1909

progress was made to rely once more on single frames of even depth, a step that became easier when deeper and stronger bulb-angles and other bars were able to be rolled by the steel works.

The web frame and stringer system was kept for the forward part of the ship for a much longer time. Here, owing to the forces caused by heavy weather, the more so when ships were only partly laden, much damage could occur by the 'pounding' on the bottom of the ship which came about as a result of heavy pitching. There was a further reason which was due to the form of the ship at the bow, where large areas tend to be almost flat or but slightly curved. Under heavy strain, such parts of the structure tend to 'pant', to move 'in and out' in a manner which causes much working of the structure and great strain on the rivets. With hard driven ships it might happen that because of such action the forward holds could be filled with water after a rough passage. The cure was to stiffen the side plating strongly, and webs and stringers were needed to bring this about.

Pillars below the beams were used at the centre line both to tie the ship and to transmit the deck loads to the bottom structure. Then, to make loading easier, the cargo hatches were made larger and longer, taking up perhaps one-third of the breadth of the deck and some half of the length of the hold. These large holes caused weakness at the sides and in way of them the centre line pillars could not be used. The structure had to be shaped to provide support by heavy transverse beams near the hatch ends and by strong lengthwise girders near the hatch side which ran between the main bulkheads. These heavy members themselves needed pillars of large size, which at first were made up by joining section bars to form one piece. The way to achieve this more simply came about with the making of hollow tubes of large size which could take heavy loads. Somewhere before 1910 the deck was carried by four round pillars only—one near the middle of the hatch side, and one near the hatch-end beams at the middle line. In this respect also, clearer holds and simpler structure were brought about.

The whole of the lengthwise strains have to be withstood by the main structure, which at the same time has also to take into account local need. To meet the stresses the ship tends to bend about a transverse axis near middle depth but somewhat lower owing to the greater local strength which is needed below water. When the vessel is 'sagging' there is a pull or a tension on the bottom part and a push or compression on the upper deck plating. If there is 'hogging' the stresses change about to a push on the bottom with a pull at the top. The thin deck plating can withstand a pull with ease, but when compressed may fail by 'buckling' or 'crumpling', leading to cracking or shearing. The double bottom with its strong support is much better able to resist such 'crumpling' action. It may be said that many of the failures of structures of ships occur from buckling strains taking place in the thin plating of the topmost decks.

The axis about which bending occurs must be nearer the stronger part of the structure, and thus, if extra stuff is added to meet local needs a greater strain may be brought on a weaker part of the structure because the axis of bending is shifted. The paradox that the adding of more structure may cause greater weakness elsewhere is well shown in the case of the double bottom. The inner bottom plating or 'tank top' in a cargo vessel of normal size forms perhaps 15 per cent of the weight of the whole lengthwise structure. If this plating is left out, the stress on the upper deck is changed very little—not two per cent— and nearly all the weight is saved except for a small increase of thickness of the outer bottom. Here is a direct instance where a large amount of lengthwise plating is little more than a mere deadweight, giving little or no help to the structure as a whole.

This problem raises the question as to the reason for making the double bottom so strong as to upset the balance of the structure. The outer skin of the double bottom has to withstand a water-pressure due to the full draught of water, and this when the tanks inside are empty. In the same fashion, the inner bottom may be subject to such a strain when water ballast is let in direct from the sea. Again, this inner bottom has to take the load of the cargo and spread it over the structure in even fashion whether the tank below is empty of water or not. As the holds may be 20 ft. deep or so and as cargoes may be heavy, such as iron-ore in bulk, it is clear that the structure of this part cannot afford to be too light. There is another question which comes from the docking of ships on a single line of blocks at the centre line under the keel, when the framing of the double bottom has to withstand the straining action of the structure above.

Ever since the first design of the double bottom, brought out in 1877, many efforts have been made to lighten the structure, but with only small success. As a rule there are solid transverse floors at every frame space or some 30 in. apart, joining the two bottoms and reaching from the keel to the margin plate. These have manholes punched for lightness and access; there are angles top and bottom to connect and upright angles some 6 ft. apart to stiffen the plating of the floor. Between the frames, girders of full depth are worked lengthwise in short pieces between the bottoms, not more than 10 ft. apart. The outer bottom plates, of say one $\frac{1}{2}$ in. thickness or more, have supports

some 30 in. apart lengthwise and 10 ft. apart sideways, forming a panel
of plating without support of some 25 sq.ft. in area.

The result of long service shows that the thin plating can stand up
to its duty with such support. This result could be got by putting the
frames and girders some 5 ft. apart both lengthwise and sideways or
10 ft. apart lengthwise and 2½ ft. across the ship.

This design with a solid transverse floor on every frame is liked for
the building of cargo ships because it is simple and easy to erect. It

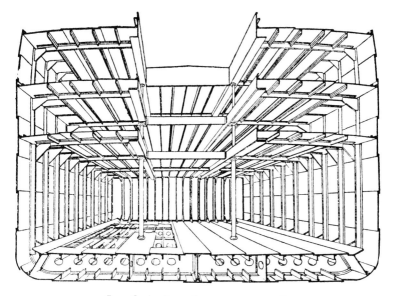

Lengthwise framed structure, c. 1918

has also been found to be cheaper than any built-up floor and in effect
is little if any heavier when the duties of these members are taken into
account. In a modern design which came into use about 1910, it can
be seen that solid floors were only used for every third frame, and that
lengthwise girders running for three spaces were used to join floors
and bottoms. Between the solid floors at the usual frame space,
support is given by top and bottom ribs ending at bracket-plates at the
vertical keel and at the margin plate and having upright bars at each
lengthwise girder. It can be shown that this design does not save
enough weight to be worth while in view of the extra cost and the
labour in making and fitting. Once again it may be noted that in the
long run simple means give the best results.

In 1908 J. W. Isherwood, later to become Sir Joseph, brought out a modern design to make use of lengthwise framing. Deep transverse webs were spaced some 10 ft. apart to support lengthwise frames of simple bulb-angle section at every 30 in. The frames ran through slots cut in the webs and were fixed to these by short angles. This system formed a transverse ring round the ship, through the double bottom, at the sides and under the deck.

Isherwood saw that the failure of previous plans of this kind was the trouble of erection, and in his scheme, after the keel was put up, the bottom transverse webs were set in place as far as the margin plate to form the framework of the lower part of the ship. The lengthwise frames were then placed in the slots and when fixed the skin could be laid in the usual manner. The inner bottom, carried in the same way, was laid on the top of the transverses, and the margin plate put into place to finish this part of the structure.

The upper webs, to include also the deck supports, were set up in one piece and fixed for the time with ribbands and cross-spalls. Main bulkheads were put in place as far as could be done and then the lengthwise frames were run through the slots left for them in one piece between bulkheads, to which their ends were fixed by brackets. This seemed a better design than any previous one and had the further merit that both the webs and the frames passed over and through each other without break, a distinct gain for any form of structure.

A ship of 400 ft. long framed on the common transverse pattern would have about 64 per cent of the steel placed lengthwise, whereas for the Isherwood design this figure ran to nearly 84 per cent. The deeper transverses gave equal strength in the crosswise sense. Thus the new plan saved some 8–10 per cent of weight while being perhaps as much as 20 per cent stronger to withstand the main stresses on the hull.

As usual, dislike was shown to any novel change in the system of building merchant ships. There was also an outcry from owners who had been asking for clearer and more clear holds in which to stow package cargo. The webs in the holds were some 24 in. deep, being less in the 'tween decks where the depth was only 12 in. These pockets, 10 ft. long at the sides of the vessel, were thought a nuisance of such a nature as to offset the greater weight of cargo which could be carried because of the saving on the structure.

This rather drastic change would have had a long uphill struggle had it not been for the growing demand for oil tankers to carry both crude oil as well as finer products, in bulk, in tanks forming the structure of the ship and in which the oil extends to the outer plating. In the large vessels, some of which carry 15,000 tons of fine oils in as

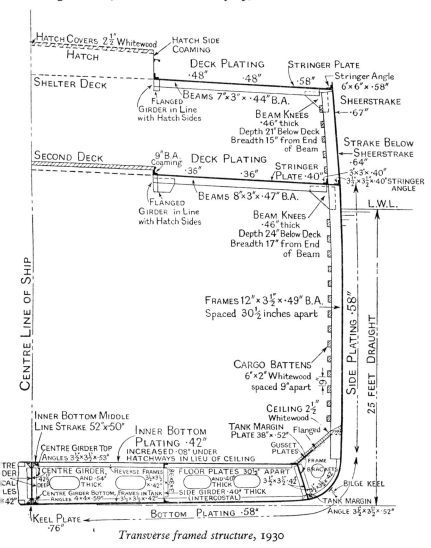

Transverse framed structure, 1930

many as 24 tanks, each say 30 ft. long, reaching from the middle line bulkheads to the side of the ship, and some 30 ft. deep, the highest skill of the shipwright is needed. It is something much more than the phrase used by an American who said: 'Your ship is only a can to carry my oil.' The structure had to withstand all the heavy main strains and to remain oil-tight, which is a harder task than water-tight, because a water leak can rust and close itself. For the carriage of fine oil every care has to be taken that water does not have access to

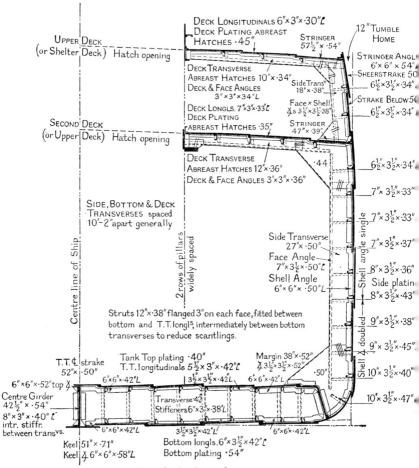

Lengthwise framed structure, 1930

the cargo and spoil its value—there may be perhaps as many grades of oil as there are tanks in the ship, and these grades must not come into contact with each other.

The greater lengthwise strength that such vessels need was given by the Isherwood design without undue increase of weight. The depth of the webs did not matter with a cargo of oil, and the lack of a double bottom in these ships made the structure more easy to erect.

The War of 1914–18 brought about a large growth in the sea transport of oil, and the demand for such ships helped to provide work for

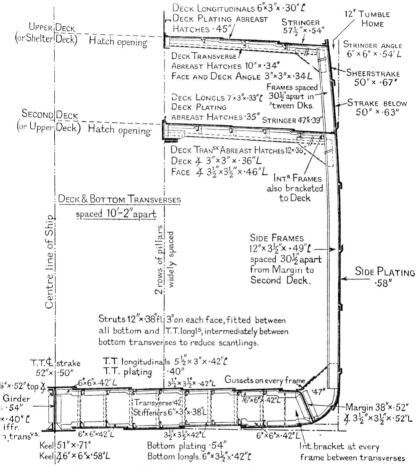

Structure with 'combined system' of framing, 1930

the shipyards in the years between the wars when trade had to suffer many setbacks, of which the painful memory remains in the shipwright's trade to this day.

For the cargo ship design did not make much progress, but about 1918 a further change for the better in such vessels came about with what was called the 'combination system'. This design took parts of both the lengthwise and the transverse methods of framing and brought about something which suited the manner in which the main stresses on the structure had to be met. Briefly, it amounts to this, that since thin plating requires frames to support it, 'vertical plating should have vertical framing and horizontal plating needed lengthwise frames'. This system is also better suited to the problems of erection. The structure weighed much the same as for the Isherwood ship, but the amount of material placed lengthwise was only 10 per cent more than for the transverse framed ships as against the figure of 20 per cent in Isherwood's design.

The War of 1914–18 saw the start of changes for which the full use was not found until the War of 1939–45. The first was the greater use of machine tools, worked by compressed air, to close the rivets. The hand labour needed to set up these large rivets such as were used for the bigger ships was a heavy task. Much was said at that time that the riveters were prone to 'absenteeism', which was judged by the number of hours out of a week of 48 hours when the men were absent from work. It was more than human to expect a full week from the strongest of men day after day, and this coming of the power-tool, which works on the same idea as that used in the rock-drill for breaking up the roads, was a distinct step towards a better state of welfare.

The second change was the start of the use of electric welding to join both plates and frames. In this process a rod of mild steel was wrapped with a flux of asbestos or some such stuff and then an electric current was passed through the rod forming an arc with the steel plate. The rod was melted and the melted iron stuck to the plate, the flux stopping the access of air to the molten metal. The scoffers termed it 'sealing-wax', but there was much more than a sealing process at work. For the joint had to withstand all the strains on the structure, which with care it could be made to do, so that the welded results were better than with rivets. The old idea that the ship had to find herself by the slip of the riveted joints was passing, though it cannot be said that welding alone can solve all the problems of a large steel structure.

Once again Laird's, now Cammell Laird, showed the way, and in 1920 built the first all-welded ship, the *Fullagar*, in which there was not a single rivet. She was a coasting vessel with a raised quarter-deck, some 150 ft. long, to carry 500 tons of cargo, and was driven by a Fullagar Diesel engine which the same firm also built. It was thought, with reason, that the trying coastwise trade, where at times vessels lie on the ground at low water when fully laden, would form a severe test of the welding. A case of this kind took place not long after she went on service, when, fully loaded with coal for Belfast, she ran on a steep sand-bank at Garston, Liverpool. It was clear that the hull was strained, but since the soundings did not show any leakage, the vessel went on to Belfast where, when the cargo was taken out, the bottom was found to be set up some 12 in. over a length of 70 ft. She came back to dry dock at Birkenhead and although there were no failures in the welding nor the structure, apart from the buckling of the bottom, the surveyors for the underwriters stated that the vessel was a 'constructive total loss'. This term implies that it would cost more to repair the ship than the insured value, and thus she was sold as salvage. After being bought at the price of scrap she was taken to Scotland and by methods known to those who repair ships, the bottom was pushed down, made straight and fitted with a few extra webs for stiffness. The vessel was put back into service, which she carried out for some 17 years before being sunk by collision in 1937. A full survey held in 1931, and after the vessel had been subject to much rough service, found that the welding had never failed, although other parts of the structure showed signs of much damage. It was thought at the time, and held to be proven, that the process then begun could be used for building much larger ships; the view then being that structures up to some 400 ft. long might within reason be welded, a view that was more than upheld by the work that was done in the War of 1939–45. It ought to have been said above that at the time of the survey in question there were no signs of any rusting of the welding nor of the structure which it joined.

In those early days while welding on the level plate working downwards from above could be done with fair ease, this was not the case for vertical joints or for those to which the weld must be applied from below. These troubles have been met in modern practice, although the best work is still done with the plates and angles laid on the flat or nearly so. There is a further question to be taken into account, which is to prevent the heat that comes from the welding process from buckling the edges to be joined and from causing stresses to be tied-up within the plates thus fixed. It would not be good practice to carry out welding on all the edges of a plate at one and the same time. One side should first be joined to its neighbour, while both plates are free to adjust themselves in other ways. The manner of making a closing weld or a final weld calls for great care, if it is not to result in leaving behind sources of failure.

These limits cause special care to be taken in the design of the detail of the steelwork, which has to be somewhat changed although the main pattern of the structure is kept. The knowledge gained with the building of the *Fullagar*, in which welding was used throughout, showed that it would be well to make use of both rivets and of welding in order to make erection more easy and the better to spread the strains over the structure. Thus, the skin plating might be fixed to the side frame by rivets rather than by welds. For large pieces, such as complete bulkheads, and the main floors of the double bottom, welding could be used. In the War of 1939–45 the United States made use of electric welding to build great numbers of large cargo ships. There were certain failures, due to slavish methods chosen to suit output of welding rather than the needs of a large structure. There were cases in which the butt ends of the strength deck were welded in one line right across the ship. This made a hard line which had a bad effect on the mean stress which the deck had to bear, for, as a rule, any hard lines or points are sources of weakness, and may cause the structure to fail through minor cracks that start from small defects.

The shipwright from early times learnt to avoid weakness by 'stepping' joints, and to-day even with steel and welding the same kind of safeguards are needed. All joints ought to be stepped both lengthwise and sidewise to produce a more even strain.

With the modern love for high-flown terms, often with vain meaning, the blessed word 'prefabrication' came to be linked up with the building of ships. In the United States it meant that by the use of cranes large pieces could be built on the ground and lifted into place on the slipway. With the coming of iron and steel a shipyard has become largely a place to assemble plates and angles which are made elsewhere. True, the final fitting and shaping have to be done on the spot, but even now plates can be made with rolled edges, only needing to be bent and to be cut at the butt-end, to slip into place on the ship. Further, owing to troubles of transport, there is a distinct limit to the size and weight of parts which can be made outside the shipyard. This practice carried to extremes helped the American yards to claim the building of a ship in four days; no mention was made of the lapse of time which took place between the order for the plates and the launching of the vessel.

In the use of welding for structures there is a need to study closely the question of erection, and a short account of one of such methods would seem to be useful. In this case the keel structure was built up in units of one 'plate length' welded in the shape of an I-section. The keel-plate is the lower flange of the I, the vertical keel the upright part, and the centre strake of the inner bottom or tank top running lengthwise forms the top flange. These three plates are joined by double welds of triangular section, one at each side of the top and the bottom of the vertical keel. A short upright bracket is placed at every frame space to which the plate floors are welded when they are put into their proper place. Lengths of such units are set up on the keel blocks perhaps for the whole of the straight length of the keel. They are sighted fore and aft, squared and shored into place before the butts are welded. The keel-plate and the tank top-plate are made to break joint so that their butts do not occur in the same frame space.

The flat of the bottom is laid, the first two plates next to the keel being welded together at the edges to form panels of 'plate length'. They are put in place and supported by shores and other means, after which more outer plates are made to cover the flat of the bottom. Then 'special' floors are set up some six frame spaces apart so that the rivet holes through which the bottom plating is fixed to the floors can be proved and the whole then checked and faired and shored. If the seams and butts of the shell plating are to be welded, this is done before the other floors are put into place. If the seams and butts are joined with rivets, then all the floors are put up so that the workmen can have a clear run for riveting.

Some three 'plate lengths' around amidships are put in place before welding takes place and during this work checks are made both on the 'square' and on the 'flat' of the bottom. The floors are then riveted and the margin plates shipped. In one design the margin plate itself is built up in 'plate lengths', say some ten frame spaces long, to which are welded brackets to attach to the plate frame by rivets. Floor plates are also welded above the margin plate to take the heels of the side frames. The margin is flanged over the floors to take the flat of the inner bottom and has also a welded flange plate to support the heel brackets of the side frames.

The inner bottom, or tank top plating, is laid in a transverse manner between the centre plate and the margin plate. These seams and butts are welded, but the top angles of the plate frames in the double bottom are fixed with rivets.

Strakes of shell plating are now worked to above the turn of the bilge and the first side strake to be put up is checked for shape and height. Careful watch is kept on this strake throughout the whole erection as it forms a key to the upper structure. This strake can be fixed to the bracket for the side frames above the margin plate, either by welding or by riveting.

Erection of the upper structure starts by setting up the main or partial bulkheads as well as special frames to support the side shell which are placed some six spaces apart. On this framework three or four more of the side strakes are laid and checked by height and shape and shored to prevent movement. At this stage the rest of the side framing is dropped into place and fixed with bolts. When enough

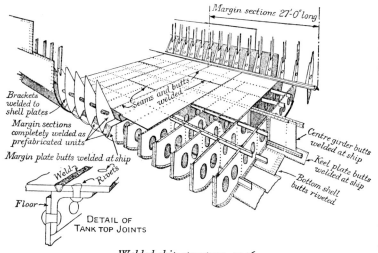

Welded ship structure, 1946

plating is in place the shell butts are welded and their edges are joined by rivets which are also used to fix the plates to the frames.

It will be seen that great care has to be taken to check the structure for shape and to ensure that it is in proper line fore and aft. To help this process some six square lines are set out on the berth itself and the lines are made sure by the use of copper nails on which, with the use of a plumb-line, the proper places for framing shell and deck can be checked. A special steel tape is made for each ship to measure any lengthwise movement which may occur to a small extent and which must be taken into account when the checks are applied.

The deck plating is worked in welded panels of plate length or more and is fixed to the beam by rivets. Before being put into place the wide spaced pillars and the deck girders are set up and carried at their ends by the bulkhead brackets.

There is broadly a proper mixture of welds and rivets, and with due regard to a proper stepping of joints, such a structure should stand up to its work. The process of welding after some 25 years practice or more has been brought under simple control. The erection problems are still hard, but the saving in steel and labour is thought to be worth while.

The reason for the old shipwrights' liking for a transverse system of framing can be seen clearly, and it has a further gain that the form can be checked at any stage with ease, if not by sight. The coming of welding seems to favour the idea of plating the ship first and placing the frames later—a return to that very old practice which, as far as is known, was first brought into use for the building of the Viking ships.

The figure on page 184 gives in a broad fashion some of the points in question, but it must be made clear that many changes of detail are likely to take place in the years to come.

§16. THE SHAPE OF MODERN SHIPS

THE change from wood to iron led to the actual building of the ship passing into the hands of special grades of tradesmen who may be called ironworkers. The dockyard shipwrights have kept most of this work in their hands, and thus may be the last of the skilled craftsmen.

The form of the vessel is still the concern of the shipwright whose duty is to lay off the proper shapes of the frame and to supply the moulds and templates needed. He has to see that the blocks are laid in proper fashion, and to check the erection of the structure. He has to line off the plating and any special features, and to see that the shape is proper and is kept in place by ribbands and shores. It is his duty to carry out all the work of launching the ship; the laying of the ways, the building of the cradle and so forth. In a sense too the loftsmen who work in the mould loft and also at the ship, are also shipwrights; while the ship draughtsmen should come from that source, since a part of their work has to deal with the details of the structure. In the higher grades, the question of the propulsion, and the form of the screws, their size and shape, have to be settled. It is the duty of the engineer to deliver to the screw the power which is needed, and the part of the shipwright or the naval architect to ensure that this power is used to the best purpose.

The early shipwrights took much care to obtain a proper and smooth shape for the body of the ship, so it is well to set out broadly the effect of the advance in knowledge which has largely come about since William Froude built his first model testing plant over 70 years ago. Since his time the number of tests that have been made is beyond count; the United States Model Basin had by 1933 tested more than 3000 ships. There are thus good reasons for giving in broad fashion an account of the main factors upon which depend the power needed to drive a ship of given size and length at a certain speed.

Account has to be taken of two chief groups of knowledge—the friction and the wave-making forces. When the speed and purpose of a ship is known, a first idea of its weight—displacement—and its length can be got. Weight and length are the two major factors, the third being the draught of water when loaded. The force needed to deal with friction depends on the area of the surface below the water and the mean amount per square foot is less, the longer the ship. Broadly, the extent of the surface is given by taking the product of the weight and the length, and then taking the square root of that product. It thus follows that for a fixed displacement the longer the ship the greater the surface and thus the greater the force of friction. It is also clear that if the length be kept the same there will be very little change in the area of the surface for a constant weight. Thus, other things being the same, the forces of friction will alter very little with changes in the outward shape.

On the other hand, the wave-force becomes less with increase of length. For example, for a fast naval craft of 5000 tons weight, the wave-force needed for 22 knots is 50,000 lb., or 10 lb. a ton for a length of 400 ft. If the length be made 470 ft. in place of the 400, still keeping the same displacement, the wave-forces are halved, or only 5 lb. per ton.

There is thus some 'best' length for the ship since, while the friction force goes up with the length, the wave-force becomes less. The choice of the right length for a given weight and speed is a matter of great concern. A further factor that effects the choice is the strain on the structure, which also depends on the products of weight and length. The amount of steel needed to meet the strain must increase, not only as the length but as the square of the length. It thus appears that, except for fighting ships, vessels need to be kept on the short side so long as the power needed for the speed is not too costly.

The length, weight, speed and draughts of water being known, the problem is to settle the manner in which the under-water volume is to be set out. The breadth is chosen to give the stiffness of ship needed for the draught. From this the shape of the 'midship bend' can be drawn. The usual plan is to give a small 'rise of floor' from the keel outwards to allow the vessel to take a slight list or heel without adding to the draught. Then follows the 'round of the bilge' and above this the section is more or less upright to the water-line and above. It ends at the upper deck with a small 'tumble home' again to allow for a slight list to the ship.

One of the main factors in setting out the form is the area of the midship bend, taken as a fraction of the rectangle of the breadth and the draught. This is called the 'mid-ship section coefficient', which for a merchant ship is about 95 per cent. The product of this area and the length gives the volume of a prism within which lies the whole of the form, and its ratio to

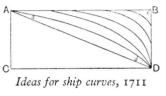

Ideas for ship curves, 1711

the under-water volume proper to the displacement is called the 'prismatic' coefficient. This measure of the lengthwise 'fineness' of the form, forms a good guide to the value of the wave-making forces.

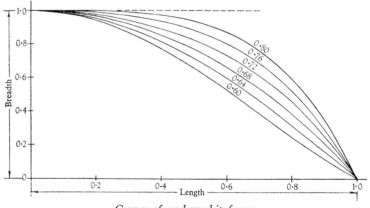

Curves of modern ship forms
(Figures against curves give area below curve,
as a fraction of length × breadth)

Clearly also the shape of the water-line has much to do with causing waves, and in its turn needs a measure of 'fineness'. This is known as the 'water-line area coefficient' which is the ratio of the actual area to the rectangle formed by the length and the breadth. The value of this fraction is always greater than that of the 'prismatic' figure by some 10 per cent since the form falls away downwards.

The next step is to draw out chosen curves on a base of length taken on a proper scale such that the length is unity. At right angles to this base-line, curves are drawn in which both the area of the midship section and the greatest breadth of the water-line are also unity. Such a set of curves as shown for various fractions apply to the two main factors, which are the shape of the water-line and the curve of areas of transverse sections. One of these curves, when the fraction value is about 66, is a 'true' parabola—a section of a cone, and the other curves are based on this by certain changes. They all, except the lowest ones, are 'smooth' or free from sudden changes of shape, a result which the old shipwrights always sought to obtain.

To set about drawing the 'lines' the place for the greatest midship section is chosen, which for fast ships is taken at mid-length. Length is no longer taken at the keel or at the lower gun-deck; it is the length of the form itself at the load water-line, or the line at which the ship floats on service. For ships of 'medium' speed, such as are most merchant types, there is merit in placing the greatest cross-section nearer the bow than the stern. The form is thus 'fuller' forward than aft, which conforms with the old idea of 'cod's head and mackerel tail'.

The measure of the 'relative' or corresponding speed is the ratio of the speed in knots to the square root of the length in feet. Thus, for a length of ship of 400 ft., the square root is 20 and at 20 knots the value of the 'speed-length ratio' is 20/20 or unity. Vessels of the value of unity or below may be termed of medium speed, and over that value are called high speed because of the rapid increase of the wave-forces. This simple rule forms a good measure of the nature of the form.

The second factor to be taken into account is the lengthwise or 'prismatic' form. At low speed the wave-forces in pounds per ton weight remain nearly constant for similar ships. At high speed the wave-forces depend mainly on the actual weight that has to be driven and change very little with changes in the lengthwise 'fineness'.

The length being drawn out to scale, the place for the midship bend is chosen and there is set up the area of the midship section and the greatest half-breadth. From these as starting points are drawn two lengthwise curves, the curve of areas of cross-section and the curve of the water-line. The first, which gives the area of cross-section at any place in the length, is drawn for the lengthwise fraction chosen, say for example 0·70. The second curve will have a higher fraction, say o·80 or so, and this in turn when drawn out will give the breadth of the water-line at any place in the length.

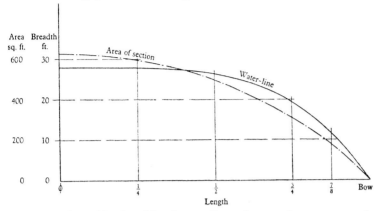

Modern merchant ship: breadths of water-line and areas of transverse sections

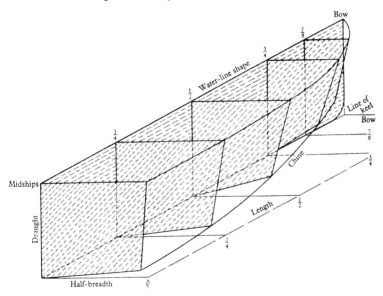

Lines of modern merchant ship (perspective)

The shape of a section curve can now be drawn. At the place chosen the area A is read from its curve and the half-breadth of the water-line B from the second curve. To get the 'chine' point C at this section divide the area A by the breadth B which gives the depth of the chine below water. To obtain the level distance from the middle line divide the area A by the draught of water 'd' at that section. Join C by straight lines to the keel and to the extreme breadth that is K, C and C, B. The figure K, L, B, C gives the correct area. The figure on p. 189 of the under-water form of a modern ship shows the 'chine line' at

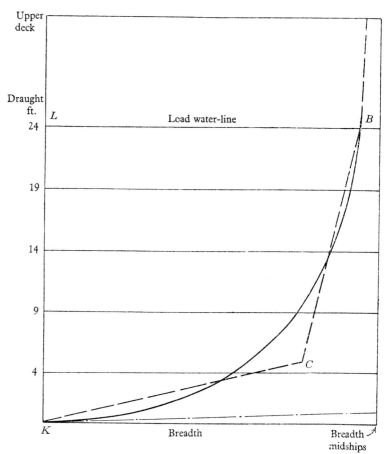

Modern merchant ship: section half-way to bow
(Area outside chine = area inside. Above-water shape
suits type and speed of ship)

various sections. Such a line is used for high-speed craft, but for ship use at medium speeds suffers from the making of eddies causing more resistance. It is curious to see that the 'chine' is somewhat like the old shipwright's 'rising line' and serves the same purpose to raise the form towards the ends of the ship.

The next step is for the skilled draughtsman to 'smooth out' the chine into a ship form. This is not so hard to do as might seem, and for that purpose use is made of 'sets of moulds' or curves of thin wood with edges shaped to conform to parts of parabolas, much the same as the standards used for the area and water-line curves.

The process is shown in the drawing of the section at the quarter length from midships which is half-way to the bow (see figure on p. 190). The curve must lie outside the 'chine' figure near the top and towards the keel. As the area must be the same it passes inside the 'chine' itself. It 'touches' the 'rise of floor' line towards the keel and at the water-line takes up a slope to suit the form 'above water'.

After each section is shaped in this way the lines as a whole are 'faired' by drawing the various water-lines and sections, and by diagonal planes which are all made 'smooth' by slight changes.

This is the progress of a century or so, though now by the choice of proper patterns the form as a whole is almost fair from the start. When this stage is reached the lines are in the first instance often drawn on a scale of $\frac{1}{4}$ in. to 1 ft.

Much more can now be done, since Froude built his first tank, from the growth of data which can be used to obtain with fair ease a measure of the power needed to drive a ship within a small percentage. Better still by tests in a model basin; a check on the results can be made in about a week in normal cases.

The 'lines' of the picture refer to a normal cargo ship 400 ft. long, 58 ft. beam and of 10,000 tons weight at 24 ft. draught of water. The square root of the length is 20 and to get the 'relative speed' divide the knots by 20.

The Price of Speed

(These figures are for a merchant ship, 400 ft. long and 10,000 tons weight.)

Speed, knots	12	14	16	18	20
Speed, relative	0·6	0·7	0·8	0·9	1·0
Force (lb. per ton): Friction	2·7	3·5	4·4	5·5	6·8
Wave	0·8	1·3	2·5	5·5	18·0
Total	3·5	4·8	6·9	11·0	24·8
Power factor (force × speed)	42	67	110	198	496
Engine h.p.	2580	4120	6750	12200	30600
Oil fuel per day (tons)	17·5	27·5	45·0	81·0	205
Knots per ton (oil)	16·5	12·2	8·5	6·3	2·3

This table sets out for the lines as drawn the power needed to drive at speeds from 12 to 20 knots. It should be borne in mind that the 'economic' speed for cargo ships of this size is under 12 knots. It will be seen that the friction force grows at a fairly steady rate. The wave-force rises quickly after 16 knots and is seven times greater at 20 than at 16 knots, and over twenty times more than at 12 knots.

The horse-power of the engines, which is some 2500 at 12 knots, has grown twelve times to 30,000 for a speed of 20 knots. The worst feature is the rise in oil fuel needed. Thus 600 tons would suffice for a voyage of 12,000 knots at 12 knots speed, a fair amount for a vessel which might carry 7000 tons of cargo. To reach 20 knots over that distance would need some 4500 tons of oil and would leave perhaps 2000 tons for cargo.

In settling the form and shape of the screw-propeller, model tests have been of the greatest value. It would seem simple to drive a cork-screw with sharp edges into water and thus to push the ship along. From this idea the form of screw has grown up by taking parts of three or four corkscrew edges, shaped as blades, like ellipses or even circles, around a lengthwise axis to which they are set askew.

This skew is called the 'pitch', which is the distance moved forward with one turn of the shaft, if water were solid. In fact, the screw 'slips' relative to the ship and it is this 'slip' which causes the 'thrust' to drive the vessel. The 'leading face' which meets the water is made to a fixed pitch. In a solid medium the distance moved forward is the product of the pitch and the revolutions, which is greater than the speed of the ship.

Since the blades of the screw take a heavy thrust they must be thick enough to transmit the strain to the axis. This 'thickness' effect alters the measure of the pitch by an amount which only model tests can show. The 'pitch' on service is got by pushing a screw ahead of a carriage in the model basin into still water at various revolutions and finding at what speed the propeller gives zero thrust.

The 'thrust' needed to drive the vessel can be got from the forces found by the model tests or otherwise. To get this thrust the blades must have enough area, and if the pressure exceeds a certain amount there is a breakdown of the flow. This is known as 'cavitation' because hollows or cavities are formed on the surface and back of the blade, and in those regions there cannot be a thrust because the water is no longer in contact. It has been found that if the pressure per square inch of the blade reaches 12 lb. breakdown is highly likely. This in turn depends on the even running of the engines, and there is one known case where the pressure rose to 15 lb. using a steam-turbine drive. The area needed is spread over the three or four blades used which, when made as ellipses or circles, have a known area and hence the chief factor is to fix the 'diameter' to the blade tips.

Since it is proper to know the measures of the linear sizes of a screw, the ratio of 'pitch' to 'diameter' or the 'pitch-ratio' gives a useful figure to compare various propellers. Its value lies between say 1·6 and 0·6, changing with engine revolutions. As a mean value it can be said that the 'pitch' is somewhat more than the diameter.

Much thought has been given to the way in which the area of the blade is set out. In the usual fashion the shape is an ellipse, the long axis being the radius of the screw and the short axis, midway to the tip, being the 'blade width'. The lower part of the area, some sixth part, is taken up by the shaft and the boss which carries the blades. The 'leading edge' of the blade which first meets the water has by this fashion the bounding curve of an ellipse. There is at times a need to bend back or to give a special shape to this leading edge. Even if this is done, the blade width at a certain radius is taken from the ellipse.

The design of the screw is in itself a special problem. Froude said that to plan a bad screw was nearly as hard as to get a good propeller, which would make proper use of the horse-power supplied by the engines. It is a wasteful method judging by the standards of machines, for at its best some 30 per cent of the power supplied is wasted.

There is the problem of the shape below water which will ensure a proper flow to the propeller, as stated in detail before. The question of the speed of the wake to be taken, the place for the screw in respect of the skin surface, and the hull as a whole, are all matters that call for close concern at the stern of a ship. For the thrust of the screw depends on the speed of the water which surrounds it and that is bound to suffer unless great care is taken to produce an even flow.

Once again it should be said that Froude's ideas of the testing of model ships have proved of the greatest value in solving the problems which arise from such complex movements.

§17. THE GREAT WARS

THIS story of the shipwright's trade would seem to be drawing to a close about 1914, for after that came the two world wars, with the years of stress between. In the 25 years or so before the War of 1914–18 this country led the world in the building of merchant ships. In 1914 it owned half the tonnage of the world and had built some three-quarters of the deep-sea ships of other nations. The lead was the envy of many countries and of these, starting from say 1890, the Germans were the most jealous. The Emperor Willhelm II had not been long on the throne when he said, about 1895, that 'our future lies on the water'...'I will not rest, until I have brought my Navy to the same height at which my Army stands.' He preached that Germany was fated to be the world power, must expand and impose itself upon the nations, and for that to happen must be strong enough to challenge the command of the sea as well as of the land.

From 1895 there came about a great building of ships because of the rapid growth of world trade, the value of which had doubled by 1910, and by 1913 had become two-and-half times that of 1895. The normal annual world output of ships during the 15 years before the War of 1914–18 was some $2\frac{1}{4}$ million tons, of which the United Kingdom turned out nearly two-thirds, broadly $1\frac{1}{2}$ million tons of merchant vessels. It was judged that the shipyard plant in this country could produce a further half million tons of warships, making a total output of some two million tons of vessels of all kinds each year.

World fleets grew apace between 1895 and 1914 until they had risen from nearly 17 to over 43 million tons. The British Empire had doubled its merchant marine in that period and owned 20 million tons in 1914. Germany, intent on war, started the War of 1914–18 with some five million tons of merchant ships. This figure of five million was thought by some to be the size of the supply fleet needed to support a fighting navy when used for ocean duties. It is curious to note that Japan had built up her merchant tonnage to about the same figure before she began to take part in the War of 1939–45. Japan's mistake was to ignore the length of her supply lines, and her widespread actions could not have come about had the allied fighting navies been able to spare more ships. Once those supply lines were tackled, by supreme effort, her defeat was sure.

When the period between the wars started, most of the countries who traded in the world began to build ships for themselves. They seem to have thought that the British had won the war by their command of the sea and that they must follow her practice if they wished to make themselves a power in the world. Alone, or almost so, the British Fleet stayed at about the same size as it was in 1914, the total tonnage being little greater in 1938, some 24 years later. In that same period the tonnage of the world merchant marine had grown by some 50 per cent to attain 64 million tons. So it was that in those years the shipyards of this country passed through hard times. The building for this country was small and there was little done for export to other nations. Only once was the building plant in full swing, in 1929, and the United Kingdom's share of the annual world output dropped to under 50 per cent, turning out under one million tons of ships a year for all that period.

This lack of work led to a great decline in the numbers of shipyard workers from 1932 onwards, many of whom had to leave their trade. Efforts were made to prevent the slump, but it was not until March 1939, that, thanks to State aid, enough work came forward to keep in work those who were left. Six months later, when the War of 1939–45 started, most of the old hands came back to the yards. Some, who were almost beyond the heavy task, made their return to perhaps the greatest demand ever made on the shipwright's trade.

In both the great wars the United States made heroic efforts to secure that surplus of ships without which action at sea is futile. The War of 1914–18 showed that if success at sea is to be obtained, there would be more merchant ships afloat than ever before when fighting ceased. In 1924 the Americans found themselves with many more ships under their flag than the world needed. After the War of 1939–45 the amount of tonnage left afloat, which had had to be built to deal with the huge beach landings, must be enormous. This great output of ships came about by the use of mass-output methods, applied to the same sort of vessels which people were in the habit of building. There was little change of form or detail, but there was a great increase in the use of electric welding and, by and large, there was much success in these giant efforts, without which the war could not have been won.

There were heavy losses of ships during the War of 1914–18, brought about by the 'sink at sight' tactics of the Germans. Such losses, rising to a danger level in the spring of 1917, stressed the need to build ships, and yet more ships, to maintain the life-line across the North Atlantic. Shortage of men and of steel led to the use of other kinds of materials, and of workers drawn from sources which were not being used for the war effort.

One such venture was the building of concrete ships, using the same methods of working cement and steel rods in support, such as had grown up for large structures and bridges. 'Reinforced' concrete formed the skin and deck and many other details of ships with a fair amount of success. N. K. Fougner of Christiania, the builder of some

30 vessels of concrete in the five years from 1917 onwards said they should be cast in one piece and the concrete poured at one time without break. The outer form of wood was fixed to suit the normal shape of ships and the steel rods used for the extra strength were set up in their proper places. The inner 'shutters' of wood were put up and into the troughs thus formed concrete is poured in the usual manner. Fougner held that there was nothing to be gained by building concrete vessels in other shapes, or in other ratios of length, depth and breadth from the practice used for steel ships. In short, the need did not arise for any other methods than those 'which hundreds of years have shown to be best for ships of wood and steel'.

Concrete vessels were built for many uses, and one of the largest of these was an oil-tanker 420 ft. long which carried 6400 tons of cargo. The concrete used was a high grade cement mixed with equal volumes of sand and of small pieces of stone or gravel. Tightness was got by spraying the surface with coatings of liquid cement in dilute form, with further linings of the usual nature applied to parts which were likely to be subject to acid attacks, such as in oil tankers. In the short time such craft were on active service there was little sign of the failure of the concrete or of the steel used to give extra strength.

Coasting steamers often had to lie on uneven ground abreast a quay —a 'foul berth'—and such craft needed frequent repair of damage to the bottoms on this account. Steel double-bottoms could not be built strong enough to resist such treatment, and it was thought that the concrete ships with their thicker skins—the slabs being 4 in. thick— would fare better. Such was not the case, for within a short while two mishaps took place in an English Channel port where the concrete barges failed, and what is more the slabs cracked under this rough usage.

It may be helpful, as showing the skill used by the concrete engineers in building these craft, to give some idea of the 'scantling' or thickness of the various parts of the structure. In this case the vessel was 170 ft. long and built to carry 1000 tons of cargo. The thickness of steel used for such a ship for the sides and bottom would be say $\frac{3}{8}$ in. The keel and keelson in the concrete ship were made in one piece 32 in. deep and 11 in. wide. The floors at every 4 ft. had depths up to 28 in. with a breadth of 10 in. The side frames came out at depths up to 17 in. and were $6\frac{1}{2}$ in. wide. The inner bottom was not fitted in this vessel although larger types were built with a double bottom. The bottom slabs were 4 in. thick, the side slabs ran from 4 to 6 in. and the deck slabs from $3\frac{1}{2}$ to $4\frac{1}{2}$ in.

Such thickness was needed to enclose from within and without the steel rods used to strengthen the structure. The steel is needed to provide for tension or pull stresses, since concrete can only withstand compression or push strains. Care was taken to ensure that the concrete and steel were closely in contact—the two had to work in unison.

The shortage of steel and of workers also gave a spur to the building of large wooden ships in the United States where, on the Pacific slopes, the Columbia river which divides the States of Washington and Oregon has within easy access the forests of Oregon pine, a famous timber for the building of ships. The purpose behind this project was to use wooden vessels to replace steel steamers on coastwise trade in the Pacific, and to release these ships for service to Europe across the North Atlantic.

Here, near Portland, Oregon, were built some fine samples of the shipwright's trade. Plate XVIII shows the inside looking aft of one such craft, built with very little steel. The length over all was 307 ft., the breadth 44½ ft., the depth 26 ft. and on a draught of just over 23 ft., some 4500 tons of cargo were carried. The vessel had the usual deckhouses, poop, bridge and forecastle, and was driven by a steam engine with water tube-boilers, the horse-power being some 1500.

These vessels served their purpose, but those who direct sea transport often regard a ship as just a ship and nothing more—they sent these vessels later to serve in the North Atlantic, where weather and seas caused the structure to strain and the owners to complain about the leakage due to working. It was a wise thing to build them, but it was more than foolish to put these vessels into service in regions which tried even the best of steel-built ships.

The War of 1939–45 brought about in these islands a great demand for the building of small wooden vessels. The fisher-folk liked their boats to be built of timber except perhaps for the deep-sea trawlers, and there were a number of shipwrights spread over the country who were used to such work.

Further, in time of war, fishermen were wanted in numbers for duties of great danger; the laying of mines and the sweeping of channels through enemy mine-fields, a task which they could tackle better than most. Quite apart from this, the beach-landings in North Africa, Sicily and Normandy called for many such craft of special types to help the Navy to deal with the fighting units. Then again there was a naval base, and there were quite a few around the country, each base needed perhaps a hundred or so of such craft for ferry and transport routine uses of the ships afloat.

But before all this, the retreat by sea from Dunkirk, in which by the use of some 1000 small vessels over 335,000 men were brought to England in a little under a week, had taken heavy toll of such craft. There was a crazy armada, massed almost in a night, of cross-Channel

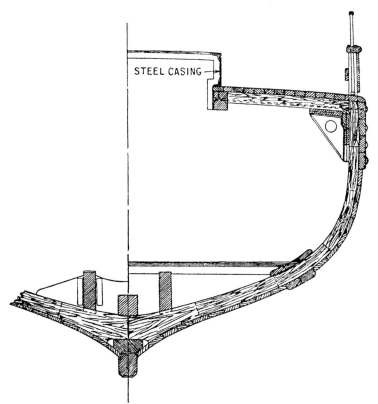

Midship section of wooden motor fishing vessel

steamers, pleasure craft, trawlers and drifters, motor-boats and sailing barges. Every tug of the River Thames went as well as twenty of the lifeboats from the ports between Lowestoft and Poole. Admiral Sir Bertram Ramsay on 9 June 1940 said that these craft came without charts, without fuel, and without food, and after a short briefing all set out for the beaches at Dunkirk more or less on their own. He added that on 8 June, he got an inquiry from the Port of London Authority which controlled the Thames River. They had sent away over 900 ships' lifeboats: six had come back and they wanted to know where were the rest? The Admiral made the comment: 'If they get back another dozen they will be lucky. The beach over there must be strewn with wrecked boats.' As witness of this unique feat, in one day some 66,000 men were taken off the beaches in spite of heavy German attacks.

The Admiralty had built a number of large wooden mine-sweepers to deal with the magnetic mines to which they were immune. The builders of such vessels acted as parents to groups of smaller firms in order to construct numbers of motor fishing boats of wood to meet the shortage of sorely needed craft. It was thought that such a type suited well the needs of service, and since the fishing fleet had been taken away in large numbers, some might survive for use in peace time. Steel was out of the question—there were neither the steel nor the ironworkers. So men and women of all kinds in out-of-the-way places came from the country for the building of this fleet. Perhaps a farmer worked the saw mill and a house-joiner did much of the timber-shaping, although he would admit that such 'curvy' work was not in his line. The whole process had to be planned mainly by the use of moulds and patterns so that the layman could be guided. There might be, and often was, only one shipwright with two or three hundred laymen to help.

The countryside was scoured to find oak for most of the parts, and green oak at that. The stem- and stern-posts and the keel, the floors and 'grown' frames, the beams, and knees and shelves were all of oak, as was the 'thick stuff' for the wales at the bilge and for the sheer strakes. Planking was mainly of larch or Oregon pine, the garboard strake being of English elm. Most of the builders of East Anglia built their vessels of oak throughout.

The largest of these motor fishing vessels was 97 ft. long overall and the outside breadth was 22 ft. 3 in., and the depth moulded at the side of the ship was 10 ft. 9 in. The draught of water was 5 ft. 6 in. forward and 11 ft. aft, giving a displacement of 200 tons on which a cargo weight of 70 tons could be carried. A Diesel engine of 240 h.p. gave a speed of just over 9 knots.

The type was based on a Lowestoft steel trawler drifter, but built in wood. The cruiser stern, a noted feature, is not at all easy to build in wood, but one which the East Coast fishermen prefer. The section drawing shows the pattern of the main features as built on those lines which the old shipwrights had found to be good for service. The keel of oak was 14 in. deep and 10 in. wide, the lengths being scarphed; the keelson was the same width, but 10 in. deep. The two side keelsons, one on each side, were also of the same width, but as deep as the keel. The frames were double, that is frame and futtock. They were $4\frac{1}{2}$ in. on the siding and some 9 in. deep at the floor; the 'room and space' was 20 in. The bilge wales were built up of four strakes, 8 in. wide and 4 in. thick; the bilge stringers inside the frames were of four planks, each 7 in. wide and $3\frac{1}{2}$ in. thick. The outer skin planks were $2\frac{1}{2}$ in. thick. Deck planks, $2\frac{1}{2}$ in. thick, were carried by 6 in. beams, with a heavy shelf and with iron clamps to form knees. The sheer-strakes were four in number and 4 in. thick, bolted through to the shelf planks.

The wooden shipyards also turned out larger vessels and the famous motor torpedo boats and the steam gun-boats, some of which were said to be able to reach a speed of 50 knots, that is nearly 60 miles an hour. Such types needed all the skill of the expert builder of yachts, a class by themselves, and every known device of their craft was studied, proved, and worked into a structure some 125 ft. long and 25 ft. broad.

§18. SHIPWRIGHTS OF THE ROYAL DOCKYARDS

AS it seemed that the only shipyards in which the shipwright had been able to maintain his status as craftsman were those of the Royal Navy, visits were made to Portsmouth Dockyard through the kindness of the present Director of Naval Construction, Sir Charles Lillicrap, K.C.B.

Here, unlike the merchant yards, there are few trades used in the building of the ship: other than shipwrights, these are smiths, drillers, riveters, welders and caulkers. All ironwork is dealt with by the shipwright with labour helpers, except for the bending of the frames and the plating which needs to be heated, which work is done by the smith. Modern practice has learnt how to bend frames and angles cold, that is, without heat, and design has changed to dispose the details in such a manner as to make use of 'cold bending'.

Skilled labour, 'machinists', has charge of the various machines used to shape the steel. These include the bending rolls, the shearing and planing machines which cut and shape the edges and butts, and the punches, drills and countersinks to make and to finish the holes for the rivets.

The shipwright receives moulds and patterns direct from the mould loft; the scrieve-board is not used at Portsmouth. He fetches the plate or angle needed from the stock-pile, marks it off and sees to the shearing, planing and punching. After this, the plate is rolled to shape

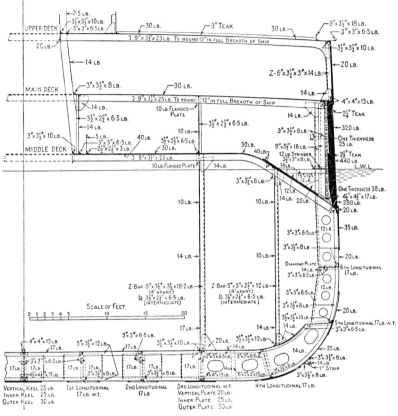

Structure of H.M.S. Dreadnought, 1906

under his guidance. The frames are handed to the smith to bend and to bevel the flanges, which work the shipwright checks.

While the steel is being made ready, the shipwright has laid the keel blocks and set them to a proper line and slope. The two keel plates—warships still have an outer and inner keel plate—are now laid and sighted both lengthwise and crosswise. The vertical keel and the centre plate of the inner bottom are set up and checked. The double angles at the top and the bottom are put up and when, say, three 'plate-lengths' are ready, riveting or welding takes place.

The 'bracket system' is still in use. The brackets running crosswise are spaced 4 ft. apart and extend in one piece some 6 ft. long between the lengthwise members. The main framing lengthwise is run in long pieces between watertight frames, which are solid plate brackets perhaps some 24 ft. apart. Both the bracket and lengthwise members are made on the ground before placing in the ship. It is to be added that these lengthwise frames are worked so as to be normal to the outer skin as far as that can be done; seen from the end they are twisted, and therefore care is needed to make their shape correct.

The structure is begun by putting in place the brackets joining the keel to the first 'longitudinal' (as the lengthwise members are called) which is then put up, fixed to ribbands, checked and shored. This process goes on until the first watertight lengthwise member is reached, say the third or fourth longitudinal. At this stage a thorough check of shape and correct place and stand of the framing is made; ribbands and shores are set up to support the form. After this rivets are placed and welds are made.

Skin plating now begins, the plates being worked on the 'in and out' fashion. To save the weight of liners the angles at the top and bottom of the brackets are 'joggled' or shaped to fit the inside of the plates quite closely. This can be done with the short length of the bars used in this system, the ends being set up sharply by presses so as to lie flat both on inner and outer strakes. This 'joggling' is also used for merchant ships and for the same reason. Since the frames in this case are run in long pieces, the process calls for much skill to ensure the proper bedding of the plates.

The garboard strake is laid first, its inner edge resting on the outer keel-plate and then follows the next strake, which is below the first longitudinal. Perhaps only outer strakes are put in place in the first instance, these as a rule being below a lengthwise member. One of the inner strakes is left off for some time, until the inner bottom is fitted and ready for closing in; this provides for easy access during the building of the double-bottom.

At this stage the erection of the side-framing below the lower edge of armour which extends some distance below water is taken in hand. Here the transverse frames are of solid plates with central holes for lightness. The lengthwise bulkheads used to protect and to provide water-tight cells to restrict damage below water are set up as well as any of the transverse bulkheads which are used for a like purpose. A thorough check is now made to ensure that the shelf on which the lower edge of armour rests is as correct as it can be made. For thick armour has to be bent into shape at the steelworks so as to drop direct into place. Its form cannot be changed in the shipyard; the only slight treatment there for lack of fit has to be done by grinding. The upper structure can now proceed with the side frames behind the armour and elsewhere, the beams and decks and so forth.

The shipwright lays the wooden deck and deals with any part of the main structure where wood is used. At the proper time he prepares the launchways; he lays the groundways which are fixed to the slipway and over which glide the heavy slidingways which form the base of the wooden cradle built to fit the shape of the ship and running for more than half its length. There are two such frameworks, one on each side of the ship, which have to be cross-tied. The groundways are fitted with strong side-shores to confine the movement of the sliding cradle.

The cradle is kept in place by a 'dog shore', a heavy square timber one on each side of the ship. The lower end beds against heavy timbers fixed to the groundways and the upper end rests against a spur forming part of the slidingways, the face of which is set at a slight angle and faced with iron plates. These two dog-shores or triggers have to take the weight of the ship and the cradle and are knocked downwards by heavy falling weights set free by cutting a single rope with a mallet and chisel. Great care is needed to ensure that both the upper ends of the dog-shores are hit by the weights at the same moment.

To transfer the weight from the blocks to the launching cradle is a lengthy process taking perhaps three days. The framework, which has been closely fitted to the ship, is 'set up' tightly by a series of wedges, a process carried out in stages by gangs working in concert on both sides of the ship at the same time. Setting up needs careful judgement; starting from aft the building blocks are knocked out by splitting away the soft cap-pieces and then taking away the other parts. Shores are put up in place, some of which are left to be tripped by the ship as she passes on her way seaward. Slowly, more and more blocks are withdrawn, any movement of the cradle being noted by marks from the slidingways on to the groundways. If, as may happen, the amount of 'creep' appears to be too great, no more blocks are taken away until a few hours before launching.

It would seem that as in Tudor and Stuart days the shipwright of the Royal dockyards carries out in the truest sense the building of a ship. Like those craftsmen he also repairs the ship after damage and may take part in salvage work. In fact the main purpose of the dock-yard is to maintain and repair the fighting fleets, although the ships themselves are largely built by contract in outside merchant yards. The practice has been to allow the dockyards to build some warships in order that the shipwright can have knowledge of changes in methods and details. This seems wise because thereby questions of repair become more easy for the craftsman.

It is said, perhaps with some amount of truth, that warships can be built more cheaply in private yards, where the work is split up into a number of partial trades. Such sharing may reduce costs, but against this should be set the troubles that arise because of the rigid limits as to work which are laid down by a number of rival trade unions. This much is true, that repairs to His Majesty's ships are carried out more cheaply in the Royal dockyards than by outside firms. The cost of building merchant ships in private repair yards would be much too great, and is never done.

Right up to the present the training of shipwright apprentices has been a strong feature of policy. As of old, the best of the young talent within the dockyard areas is drawn upon to find the future shipwrights, engineers and electric tradesmen. Many of the leaders in the naval world have been apprentices or have come from Keyham College where the engineer officers of the fleet were trained.

There grew up from more than a century ago the dockyard schools for the apprentices. These became, and still are, high grade technical schools, dealing largely with mathematics and physics, somewhat at the expense of the humanities and other branches of knowledge. Apprentices are chosen from an entrance examination open to all. Every student attends school for the first year at the end of which, after tests, some three-quarters go on for further study. The weeding process goes on until for the fourth and last year at school the numbers fall to some 20 per cent of the first entry.

At the end of the fourth year the best students compete for entrance to the Royal Naval College at Greenwich. They rank as Naval Con-struction Cadets and after taking with success a three-year course of study they become members of the Royal Corps of Naval Constructors, the body which has charge of all matters dealing with the design and building of warships. They do not enter Greenwich until the end of their fifth year as apprentices, the gap of one year being filled with special courses tending to broaden the training.

Those who fall out earlier become craftsmen, draughtsmen, and charge hands and the best can rise to be foreman of the yard, still a post of honour. Some may become constructors and a very few have been chief constructors, the modern title of the old master shipwright.

There is nothing to compare with this system of training in the outside world, where apprentices, in the craft sense, are dropping out of favour, being only taken for special branches of trade without regard to a broad outlook. Yet this modern version of the tradition of Tudor and Stuart times as pursued in the Royal dockyards has trained most of the leaders of thought in the shipwright's trade for a century past.

★   ★   ★

Here this errant tale of the shipwright's trade must stop. Better than many things that man makes, the shipwright's work can withstand with credit the forces of nature. There is as yet no sign of the limit of power that may one day be found in a ship, nor are there as yet any bounds to the size of ship that man can build and man can control. Size and speed without safety are of little worth, and ease and cheapness of transport avail more for the peace of the world than to travel with the speed of sound. As the Chinese saying puts it: 'It is better to be five minutes late on earth than to be twenty-five years too soon in Eternity.'

NOTES ON AUTHORITIES

PHINEAS PETT. *The Autobiography*, edited by W. G. Perrin. The Navy Records Society, 1918.

The manuscript records the story of the life of Phineas Pett in his own handwriting from his birth in 1570 to the end of 1638. Pepys copied the whole of the manuscript into the first volume of his 'Miscellany'.

The Introduction contains an essay by Perrin under the title 'The Shipwrights', which tells of the rise of the Master Shipwrights and their standing with the Shipwrights Company or Guild. There are two further essays, one dealing with the family of Pett. The second contains notes of various State papers bearing on the work of Phineas Pett. Appendices mention other papers which include the two Charters of the Shipwrights Company of 1605 and 1612.

WILLIAM SUTHERLAND. *The Shipbuilders Assistant, or some Essays towards compleating the Art of Marine Architecture.* London, 1711.

Further editions were printed in 1755 and 1794 which contain changes by other hands whose names are not stated. The same author wrote a larger book, *Britain's Glory, or Shipbuilding Unveiled*, London, 1717, with a second issue in 1729 which contains in much detail accounts of materials with weights and costs.

The *Assistant* was the first text-book of its kind, and Sutherland seems to have drawn on Anthony Deane's work for his data, although he ascribes the main credit to Phineas Pett, the third of that name. The chief points he brought forward are given in the chapter of that title. These books seem to have been in great demand and led to a spate of books of this kind by David Steel about 1805. (See later.)

JOHN CHARNOCK, F.S.A. *History of Marine Architecture.* 3 vols. Quarto. London, 1800–2.

These volumes of nearly 1,400 pages and 85 plates include as the title-page says: 'an enlarged and progressive view of the Nautical Regulations and Naval History, both civil and military, of all nations, especially of Great Britain; derived chiefly from Original Manuscripts, as well in private collections as in the great public repositories; and deduced from the earliest period to the present time.'

The second volume is rich in plates dealing with Stuart ships and contains official accounts of the state of the Navy in those days and Tudor times. The third volume deals with the progress of the eighteenth century, but in less detail.

The language of the author attracts by its phrase and tune, of which the last words give a good sample:

'The science of Marine Architecture has for many ages been subservient to the impulses of ambition, avarice, luxury or curiosity; it remained for Britain, in the eighteenth century, to direct it to purposes more truly noble and patriotic, of general benefit and of universal extent—to the prevention of domestic misery; to the maintenance of national population; and to the preservation of the human species.'

DAVID STEEL. *The Elements and Practice of Naval Architecture.* Quarto. London, 1805.

425 pp. text with some 100 tables of data giving the forms and scantlings of war-vessels and merchant ships. A series of some 38 large folio draughts in a second volume gives drawings of the vessels and details of 'laying off' an 80-gun ship.

The book was printed 'For P. Steel at the Navigation Warehouse, Little Tower Hill' and the preface refers to a previous work, *Elements and Practice of Rigging and Seamanship,* which came out in two quarto volumes ten years before. The success of this work and the lack of printed accounts of the shipwright's trade led his father and David Steel to produce *The Elements, etc.*

JOHN FINCHAM. *A History of Naval Architecture.* London, 1851.

The author, Master Shipwright of Portsmouth Dockyard, had written a treatise on Masting of Ships in 1829 and a book on Laying-off Ships in 1840. This history was meant as a preface to his *Outline of Shipbuilding,* the third edition of which came out in 1852. Fincham thought that the amount of data he had at hand could best be dealt with in a book by itself, which in its early part is based to a great extent on John Charnock's *History.* The introduction of some 80 pages contains a brief survey of the science of shipbuilding from the seventeenth century up to 1850 and deplores the lack of such knowledge in England.

There are some 58 plates, a few of which are helpful so long as care is used to check the sources. The book contains many tables of data and of sizes. It also gives accounts of certain naval actions and the numbers of the ships in the Royal Navy and the Merchant Marine, which the author explains is needed since 'most of the improvements in the British navy have been made only after experience had demonstrated their necessity'.

JOHN SCOTT RUSSELL. *The Modern System of Naval Architecture.* London, 1864. Imperial Folio. Vol. I, Text. Vols. II and III, Plates.

This very large book, too large to handle, contains much of the knowledge of the time in regard to both ships and engines and this in great detail. It is written in clear and simple language, for which Scott Russell was famous. It is a pity that its mere size tends to prevent easy access to the mass of data it contains.

SIR EDWARD J. REED. *Shipbuilding in Iron and Steel.* London, 1868.

The aim of the author was to put on record the details of the knowledge gained in the building of ships of iron and steel at that time. It contains accounts of the various systems of work which had grown up in the Mersey, the Clyde, the Tyne, the Thames as well as the Royal Dockyards. It describes the first useful steps to bring about the 'bracket frame' system for the building of warships which set the pattern for the future. It deals with the tests found useful for iron and the changes needed when steel became good enough for structures, and this at a time when there was much mistrust of its use.

It became the text-book for shipbuilding of the Royal Dockyards, partly because of its good plates and the many wood-engravings of the details of the structure.

ISAMBARD BRUNEL. *The Life of Isambard Kingdom Brunel, Civil Engineer.* London, 1870.

This book contains a first-hand account of the building of three 'Great' ships. The *Great Western*, a large wooden paddle-steamer, which made her first Atlantic voyage from Bristol to New York in 1838. The second, the *Great Britain*, a screw-steamer of iron, sailed from Liverpool in 1845, making the passage to New York in under 15 days: her stranding on the coast of Ireland in 1846 and her later salvage proved the value of iron structures for ships. The design of the *Great Eastern*, begun in 1854, was made with the help of Scott Russell who later built the ship on the River Thames. This vessel, nearly 700 ft. long and over 30,000 tons weight, made her first voyage in 1858 and was the largest ship to be built until the end of the century. The book contains a good account of the many troubles of her building. Both paddles and screw were used to drive her at 14 knots. There is an account of Brunel's work on the use of screw-propellers and on bridges and railways.

Transactions of the Institution of Naval Architects. 1860 onwards.

The Mariner's Mirror. The Quarterly Journal of the Society for Nautical Research. 1914 onwards.

INDEX

INDEX